A Curious Invitation

THE FORTY GREATEST PARTIES
IN LITERATURE

Suzette Field was born in 1978 in Los Angeles. In 1996 she moved to London where she set up a cinema in a converted warehouse and renovated a five-storey Georgian building in Shoreditch. Since 2000 she has produced parties under the auspices of The Modern Times Club, The Last Tuesday Society and latterly A Curious Invitation. Her legendary masked balls now regularly attract up to 3,000 revellers. She also curates literary salons with the National Trust and organizes taxidermy workshops. She lives in Muswell Hill, North London, and has two children.

www.acuriousinvitation.com

SUZETTE FIELD

A Curious Invitation

THE FORTY GREATEST PARTIES
IN LITERATURE

PICADOR

First published 2012 by Picador

First published in paperback 2014 by Picador
an imprint of Pan Macmillan, a division of Macmillan Publishers Limited
Pan Macmillan, 20 New Wharf Road, London N1 9RR
Basingstoke and Oxford
Associated companies throughout the world
www.panmacmillan.com

ISBN 978-1-4472-2896-7

1 3 5 7 9 8 6 4 2

A CIP catalogue record for this book is available from the British Library.

Designed and typeset by Andrew Barker Information Design
Printed and bound by CPI Group (UK) Ltd, Croydon CR0 4YY

Visit **www.picador.com** to read more about all our books
and to buy them. You will also find features, author interviews and
news of any author events, and you can sign up for e-newsletters
so that you're always first to hear about our new releases.

To my daughters, Tilly and Una

Contents

Contents

Contents

Contents

Introduction

It was Ptah-Hotep, an Egyptian official of the 24th century BC, who first expressed the sentiment 'All work and no play makes Jack a dull boy' and it has been used as an excuse for throwing a party ever since. From ancient times human beings have come together for social purposes. Men and women, hunters and gatherers, shared food and lodgings as a natural consequence of tribal living. All major events in the life of a community and its members — births, marriages, deaths, victories, harvests — were marked with a ritual or festivity. These would have included eating, drinking, dancing, singing, perhaps the odd virgin sacrifice — most of the elements we recognize of a successful party today.

It was only towards the mid-eighteenth century that the word 'party', meaning a group of people gathered together for a common purpose (e.g. a political party, a hunting party etc.), began to acquire its modern sense of a group of people gathered together for the common purpose of drinking, talking, flirting and networking. As the Industrial Revolution took hold and human beings started to move away from small communities and became increasingly urbanized and isolated in their lives the traditional structures began to change, yet the psychological need for festive gatherings remained. As public festivals declined private parties began to grow in importance.

Unfortunately, there are very few records of these events. The food consumed at parties occasionally survives via menus or tradesmen's invoices and guest lists sometimes appeared in the society pages of newspapers, but for the most part we have little knowledge of what these gatherings were like. We can find accounts in the diaries of individuals of the time, but Samuel Pepys, for example, only went to a handful of parties in the whole nine years he kept his journal. Maybe the problem is that the sort of people who would have time to sit down in the evening and write up a diary were those who by definition didn't have much of a social life.

This is where literature comes in. As Aristotle said, 'art takes nature as its model', and the creative works of an age can offer a valuable insight into what form contemporary celebrations would have taken.

Some of the parties that feature in literature are drawn directly from reality: the Duchess of Richmond's Ball, which appears in works by Byron and Thackeray, was an actual party hosted on the eve of the Battle of Quatre Bras in the Napoleonic War. Agathon's dinner party, immortalized in Plato's *Symposium*, really took place with the philosopher Socrates and the playwright Aristophanes on the guest list.

Other literary parties are thinly disguised fictionalizations of occasions which the author attended: Satan's Rout in *The Master and Margarita* is based on a lavish Spring Ball given at the American Embassy in Moscow in 1935 and the Society of Artists' Fancy Dress Ball in *Steppenwolf* was inspired by a Dadaist party in Zurich.

That is not to say that writers don't sometimes just make the whole thing up. Douglas Adams clearly never went to a Flying Party hovering over the surface of an alien planet, and one wonders if the notoriously reclusive Thomas Pynchon ever actually attended an orgy like the one he so graphically describes in *Gravity's Rainbow*.

In writing about parties authors are doing more than just

giving us a glimpse of the mores of their time. A social gathering is a useful dramatic tool, providing a location where characters can interact. A party can be the scene for a meeting, a snub, a seduction, or a murder. It can be an opportunity for social advancement (Roxana, Oskar Matzerath, Alice) or failure (Charles Pooter, Sherman McCoy, Ross Conti). A character can experience triumph (Jim Dixon, Pooh Bear, Rafaël de Valentin) or humiliation (Mrs de Winter, Carrie White, Lord Simon Balcairn).

An encounter at a party can be the instant where characters' fates are determined: Augustin Meaulnes falls in love with Yvonne de Galais at the Strange Fête, Ivan Ivanovich and Ivan Nikiforovich fall out for ever at the Chief of Police's Reception; or the occasion can supply the backdrop for dramatic events: Dmitri Karamazov's arrest for murder, the destruction of Thomas Ewen High School.

People have always pointed out that 'there is nothing new under the sun' (the expression comes from the Book of Ecclesiastes) and this is never truer than when applied to parties. Dress codes and etiquette may have varied over the ages but social behaviour has remained remarkably consistent. The conversation at Trimalchio's dinner party (which is set during the reign of the Emperor Nero) revolves around sport, the cost of living, the weather and how young people have no respect for their elders.

It has been a common complaint over recent decades that our culture is in moral decline, but, as we can see from the above, this belief was equally prevalent in Roman days. Society today is no more decadent (and possibly even less so) than in previous centuries. Alan Hollinghurst writes about gay sex, but so did Plato and Petronius (the latter rather more raunchily). Perhaps decadence goes in waves and we, living in the supposedly permissive society that began in the 1960s, are just starting to get up to speed again after the extreme puritanism of the Victorian age. Or maybe our definition of what constitutes decadence varies. *The Satyricon* and *The Bonfire of the Vanities* show the contrasting forms that excess can take. Roman banquets were all about how much you could eat and 1980s Manhattan dinner parties about how little. Both were essentially ways of bragging about how much money you had.

Parties, being occasions where people are at their most ostentatious, provide writers with the perfect vehicle for a spot of social satire: the pretentiousness and vulgarity of nouveau riche hosts (Trimalchio, Mrs Leo Hunter, the Bavardages); the boorishness of guests (the bankers at the Wonderland Banquet, the hobbits at Bilbo Baggins's birthday, the 'hoolivans' at Finnegan's Wake); the faux sophistication of food (lobster mayonnaise comes in for a lot of stick) and truly terrible musical entertainment (Dickens's 'something-ean' folk ensemble, Mrs Ape's Angels in *Vile Bodies*, Ric and Phil's disco show in *Hollywood Wives*).

In addition to these historical and satirical functions parties are a good embodiment of another precept from the Bible: 'Eat, drink and be merry, for tomorrow we die.' For some party hosts and guests the bit about dying can come true rather too literally: Belshazzar, Lord Simon Balcairn, most of the seniors at the prom at Thomas Ewen High and absolutely everyone at the Masque of the Red Death fail to make it through to the hangover stage the next morning.

Merry-making and mortality are routinely linked in literature. Trimalchio stages his own funeral at his dinner party in a mawkish illustration of the biblical maxim. The warriors taking part in Valhalla's permanent bacchanalia frequently die, but are handily restored to life the next day to continue feasting. Tim Finnegan manages to come back from the dead during his wake. The guests at Satan's Rout are already long dead, but this doesn't seem to diminish their appetite for good living.

Luckily for the purposes of this book, literary heroes and heroines have a lot of spare time to go to parties. This is because very few of them have anything resembling a job. And on the odd occasion when the central protagonist of a book does hold down some form of proper employment it is usually just an excuse for the author to poke fun at them (Mr Hokosawa is a workaholic, Mr Pooter a drudge, Sherman McCoy a Yuppie, etc).

So art, as we have seen, imitates life, but it can also be the other way round. Oscar Wilde stated that 'the self-conscious aim of Life is to find expression, and that Art offers it certain beautiful forms through which it may realise that energy.' Following this principle, literary parties can serve as the inspiration for real life parties.

My career as an impresario began in 2000 as a co-founder of the Modern Times Club, an organization devoted to jazz age decadence which paid homage to the parties of F. Scott Fitzgerald and Evelyn Waugh. Dubbed 'the Rolls Royce of cabaret' by *Tatler*, we would throw tea dances, pyjama parties and midnight revels, featuring all-night burlesque acts and swing bands in suitably period venues around London: railway station hotels, art deco ballrooms and old Victorian libraries. Guests arrived with dance cards for an evening of 'sparkling conversation and the finest attire' and abandoned themselves to inter-war nostalgia.

From 2006 to 2013 I ran the Last Tuesday Society with Viktor Wynd. This purposely more eclectic organization didn't espouse a particular style or reference a specific era. Our parties (like the ones in this book) encompassed a wide range of periods, cultures and fashions. One of our most popular nights was a recreation of Gunter Grass' Onion Cellar in a party we called

Loss — An Evening of Exquisite Misery. London's fashionable crowd gathered to chop onions at midnight, weep together and wallow in collective melancholy. The dress code was 'decaying beauty'. Guests sobbed over portraits of deceased childhood pets and signed their divorce papers on stage, while bands strummed dirges on themes of spiritual gloom. A splendid time was had by all.

These days I run my own events business, also called A Curious Invitation, and I continue to draw on literary influences for my parties. I like to use venues that have multiple rooms (the Coronet, a disused 1930s picture palace in South London, is a particular favourite) so each space can be themed with its own unique decor, creating a labyrinth of escapism. I've recreated Satan's Rout at Halloween with a full symphony orchestra, accordion-playing polar bears and a cast of naked women; Plastunov's Inn with bear dances and gypsy bands; Genji's Palace with a swathe of cherry blossoms outside; and McMurphy's psychiatric ward, complete with hospital beds and sadistic nurses wielding racks of surgical instruments.

If you're looking for inspiration in staging your own parties perhaps this book will prove useful. Maybe you can even push the life–art dichotomy a stage further. Take Satan's Rout for example, which, as I mentioned above, was inspired by a party at the US Embassy in Moscow. If you decided to hold your own version, based on what you've read here about my re-enactments of literary parties, then it would be life imitating art, imitating life, imitating art, imitating life.

And for any non party-givers this book will hopefully serve as a crib, allowing those who haven't read Proust or Joyce (as, I must confess, I hadn't before I started my research) to talk knowledgeably about them. At parties, naturally.

Suzette Field, London, 2014.

Picking the Parties

When I was picking the literary parties to write about in this book I had to set myself a few rules. First, they had to be parties that are described in works of fiction, rather than parties given or attended by writers (Truman Capote's legendary bashes, for example). A couple of the parties I've included though are fictionalized versions of real historical events.

Secondly, I decided to exclude poetry and drama and only feature parties from works of prose. This was partly to limit the amount of reading I would have to do (already considerable) and partly because poems tend not to have much description of the conversation and plays usually lack details about the location. So no Montagues and Capulets' ball and no *Eugene Onegin*, I'm afraid.

Thirdly, I tried to select parties from works of fiction that were as varied as possible in terms of genre, country, period and style. It would be easy to compile a whole book featuring just nineteenth-century society balls, but I preferred to have Plato rubbing shoulders with Pooter and Proust with Pooh.

So if I've missed out your favourite fictional festivity it may be for one of the reasons above. Or it may be that I forgot about it or didn't know about it. Do please email me and point out any omissions. Maybe there'll be room for them in a future edition of the book.

I chose to feature forty parties for the reason that it's a nice classical number (forty days and forty nights, forty thieves, etc) and also because the appearance of the book coincides with my publisher Picador's fortieth birthday. So I'd like to take this opportunity to wish them many happy returns (but not, I hope, returns of this book . . .).

Suzette Field, London, 2012

suzette@acuriousinvitation.com

A Curious Invitation

I

Trimalchio's Dinner Party

LOCATION: CAMPANIA, SOUTH-WEST ITALY
HOST: GAIUS POMPEIUS TRIMALCHIO
DATE: MID-FIRST CENTURY AD

From *The Satyricon* (AD 63–5)
attributed to Gaius Petronius Arbiter

The Invitation

Only a fraction of the original text of *The Satyricon* has come down to us today, so it's unclear who its narrator, Encolpius, and his friend, Ascyltos, are. In the first surviving section of the book we find Encolpius arguing with a professor named Agamemnon at a school of rhetoric in the Campania province of southern Italy, so we can perhaps assume that they are scholars there. The case for them being students is made by the fact that they do no discernible studying for the rest of the book, spending most of their time in orgies, petty thefts, fights and squabbles over Giton, who is Encolpius's catamite (a sort of rent boy).

In the first century AD, to be schooled in rhetoric was something of a meal ticket. It ensured invitations to the tables of the wealthy to perform your party turn (like karaoke, but where the performers actually have some talent).

This appears to be how Encolpius, Ascyltos and Giton come to be invited to accompany Agamemnon to a dinner hosted by the wealthiest man in Campania: Gaius Pompeius Trimalchio.

The Host

Bald, fat, wearing a scarlet robe and weighed down with jewellery, Trimalchio is the perfect vulgarian host: he picks his teeth with a silver quill, makes public use of a piss-pot, treats his guests to a commentary on the state of his bowels and eulogizes the medicinal benefits of farting. A devout voluptuary, his dissolute lifestyle is believed to be based on that of Nero (the emperor at the time). However, Trimalchio is a self-made man, a former slave who earned his millions in the shipping trade and effortlessly lives up to the stereotype of nouveau-riche boorishness. He boasts about buying Sicily so he can sail to North Africa along his own coasts. He orders that a silver dish dropped during the banquet should be swept away with the rubbish. He keeps a water clock and a liveried trumpeter in his dining room to remind him of the passing of time, which serves as a way to justify his decadent and ostentatious lifestyle. As he puts it: 'Since we know that our death is in the offing, why don't we enjoy life?'

The hostess is Trimalchio's wife, Fortunata, an ex-lap dancer with a shrewd eye for personal advancement, who now runs Trimalchio's business affairs. She refinanced his business by selling her jewellery when his first shipment of wine sank. These days she is a respectable lady, though apparently she has lost none of her skills at performing the *cordax* (a sort of Roman pole-dance).*

---

* No one knows how the *cordax* was danced but it was considered lewd. Actually just to dance at all was deemed improper in Roman times. The Emperor Tiberius had all the dancing masters driven out of Rome and Cicero opined, 'One could do a man no graver injury than to call him a dancer. A man cannot dance unless he is drunk or insane.'

The Venue

Trimalchio's house shares his humble beginnings. He boasts about how, in a spate of home improvements, he transformed the former hovel into a palace with 'four dining-rooms, twenty bedrooms, two marble colonnades, a suite of small apartments upstairs, my own bedroom, the boudoir of this viper here (his wife), and a pleasant office for the doorman.' His personal touches to the decor include a wall-mounted golden casket containing the first shavings of his juvenile beard and a mural depicting the history of his rise to wealth and social standing.

The entrance to the dining room chosen for the evening's festivities is constructed from the bronze prow of a ship, overlaid with rods and axes (the insignia of a consul, to which Trimalchio has no entitlement, making it the Roman equivalent of a bogus coat of arms).

The Guest List

About sixteen people are invited. Most of them are drawn from the ranks of the local professional class and several, like their host, are ex-slaves made good. The rhetorician Agamemnon and his pupils are in attendance, plus Phileros, a lawyer (and ex-travelling salesman); Habinnas, a stonemason; Echion, who works in the rag trade; Proculus, an undertaker; and Diogenes, another self-made businessman. The gathering also includes Hermeros, Seleucus, Dama, Ganymedes, Niceros and Plocamus.

Roman etiquette did not permit unaccompanied women to attend dinner parties, so the only females present are Fortunata and Scintilla (the wife of Habinnas).

The superstitious Trimalchio insists that his guests enter the dining room with their right foot first (to bring good luck), after which their hands are washed in snow-chilled water (later in wine) and their toenails trimmed by attentive Alexandrian slave boys. To illustrate his superior status Trimalchio has his hands washed in perfume.

The Dress Code

Petronius tells us a lot about what the guests said and ate, but little about what they wore. We can assume that the dress code was togas, setting the precedent for a lot of modern-day campus parties.

The host and hostess share a fondness for ostentatious jewellery. Trimalchio boasts of his wife's bijoux, 'She must be wearing at least six and a half pounds' worth of the stuff', but to avoid being outdone in the bling stakes he orders a slave to bring scales to verify the superior weight of his own accessories.

The Food and Drink

Despite it being a relatively modest gathering (Trimalchio hints that he hosted a grander party the night before) the catering is sufficient to feed a small army. Twelve punishing courses are presented on a dinner service made out of silver and Corinthian bronze. The food is washed down with hundred-year-old Opimian Falernian, a sweet white wine regarded as the Château d'Yquem of Ancient Rome.

THE MENU:

First course — A bronze donkey bearing a double pannier of olives flanked by a gridiron of sausages, damsons and dormice coated with poppy seeds and honey.

Second course — A wooden hen sitting on a nest full of peahens' eggs, which in turn contain garden warblers cooked in spiced egg yolk.

Third course – A zodiacal arrangement of hors d'oeuvres concealing a surprise dish of winged hare surrounded by stuffed capons and sows' bellies.

Fourth course – Whole wild boar accompanied by pastry suckling piglets and filled with live thrushes.

Fifth course – A hog stuffed with sausages and meat puddings.

Sixth course – A boiled calf wearing a helmet, sliced up by a slave dressed as the hero Ajax who serves the meat on the point of his sword.

Seventh course – A statue of the fertility god Priapus whose paunch holds a medley of saffron-squirting cakes and fruits.

Eighth course – An array of boneless fattened chickens served with pastry-capped goose eggs.

Ninth course — Thrushes made out of pastry, stuffed with nuts and raisins, accompanied by quinces.

Tenth course — A dish of pork dressed up to look like a fattened goose garnished with birds and fish.

Eleventh course — Water jugs full of oysters and scallops accompanied by a gridiron of snails.

Twelfth course — An improvised early hours addition to the menu: a cock which had crowed early (regarded by the superstitious host as a bad omen) is captured, slaughtered, pot-roasted in wine and served to the guests, who somehow find the appetite to devour it.

At this point there is a lost section of the book's text, which admits the frightening possibility that the menu might have been longer.

As if serving dishes of this complexity was not demanding enough, the slaves waiting on tables are obliged to do so while singing, dancing, doing bird impressions or reciting Trimalchio's hack poetry. Even the carving of the meat is choreographed in strict time to music.

The Conversation

The rhetoricians never get to put their public-speaking skills to the test as there is far too much competition. When the bombastic Trimalchio finally vacates the room to pay a visit to the lavatory to relieve his constipation it merely provides an excuse for other, equally verbose guests to take over.

Dama complains about how bad the weather has been of late. Ganymede grumbles about the price of corn and rues how mercenary everyone in today's world has become (which he blames on a decline in religious faith). Echion gives vent to a long discourse on sport, in this case gladiatorial combat, bemoaning the decline in quality of the fights. He follows up with a lecture on the importance of getting your children a good education so they can enter a lucrative profession, like the law. Hermeros, one of the freedmen, unleashes a drunken rant concluding with how young people don't have any respect for their elders any more.

This is the earliest literary record we have of dinner party conversation and perhaps we should be slightly embarrassed to realize how little table talk has evolved in two thousand years.

The Entertainment

Actors and acrobats perform between courses, but no one can match the spectacle provided by the host himself, with his poems, homilies and philosophizing, all laced with pomposity, boastfulness and vulgarity and interspersed with outbreaks of cantankerousness, sentimentality and self-pity.

Just in case his guests are in any doubt as to how busy, important and wealthy Trimalchio is, his secretary arrives halfway through the dinner to read aloud the accounts of the estate.

The Outcome

After supper the slaves are permitted to join the diners, but this proves to be just another excuse for Trimalchio to show off. He sends for his will and reads it out in its entirety, announcing the slaves' imminent freedom and graciously accepting their humble expressions of gratitude.

Now thoroughly drunk, the host becomes maudlin and morbid. He issues Habbinas the stonemason with instructions for designing and building his mausoleum. 'It's quite wrong for a man to have an elegant house in life, and not to give thought to our longer place of residence', Trimalchio opines, managing to be profound and crass at the same time. He stipulates that the size of his fortune (30 million sesterces) should be engraved in his epitaph.

In a final act of glorious sentimentality (which the narrator says 'was enough to make you spew'), Trimalchio stages a dress rehearsal of his funeral, complete with musicians and weeping mourners. He sends for his shroud, lies back on a mound of pillows and instructs his trumpeters to 'Imagine I'm dead. Play something nice.'

Perhaps looking forward to the demise of their master more than he supposes, the slaves blare out a funeral march with such gusto that it wakens the whole neighbourhood. The city sentinels, assuming that the building is on fire, arrive and smash down the door with axes. The students grab the chance to slip gratefully away in the confusion.

The Legacy

Gaius Petronius Arbiter, generally held to be the author of *The Satyricon*, went one better than Trimalchio by genuinely combining his death with a party. He had been Nero's *elegantiae arbiter* (literally 'arbiter of taste' – an early version of a style consultant), but subsequently incurred the jealousy of the head of the Praetorian Guard and was arraigned on a charge of treason. Left with no option but to commit suicide he decided to make an occasion of it. He invited some friends over and opened his veins accompanied by wine, poetry and sparkling conversation. So good was the party that he temporarily bandaged up his veins again so he could enjoy a little more of it.

2

Gatsby's Saturday Night Parties

LOCATION: LONG ISLAND, NEW YORK

HOST: JAY GATSBY

DATE: 1922

From *The Great Gatsby* (1925) by F. Scott Fitzgerald

The Host

Jay Gatsby is the 'Trimalchio of West Egg',* West Egg being a dormitory town on Long Island, New York, which finds itself living forever in the shadow of its more fashionable neighbour, East Egg.

'An elegant young roughneck, a year or two over thirty,' Gatsby is the twentieth-century embodiment of the millionaire host of Ancient Rome. He claims to be a decorated war hero, a big-game hunter, a ruby collector and an Oxford scholar. He wears a pink suit, owns a hydroplane, drives a cream and nickel Rolls-Royce with a musical car horn and calls everyone 'old sport'. His true background appears to be rather more louche: he has a shady business associate (Meyer Wolfsheim, who is rumoured to have fixed the World Series in 1919) and is owed favours by the commissioner of police. In the age before mobile phones he is only able to show how busy and important he is by

---

* This was Scott Fitzgerald's preferred title for the novel, until his publisher pointed out that no one would be able to pronounce it, let alone understand the literary reference (see chapter 1).

being constantly summoned to his study by his butler telling him that Chicago or Philadelphia is on the phone.

The lavish parties he throws in his impressive mansion every weekend epitomize the spirit of Prohibition-era decadence where his guests conduct themselves 'according to the rules of behavior associated with amusement parks'.

The Invitation

'People were not invited – they went there' we are told. 'They got into automobiles which bore them out to Long Island, and somehow they ended up at Gatsby's door.' The only guest known to have received a formal invitation is the novel's narrator, Nick Carraway, a Wall Street bond salesman, who has just moved into 'a small eyesore' next door to Gatsby's mansion. Nick hasn't been introduced to his neighbour and naively assumes this is an impediment to going along to his parties, unaware that many of the guests at the bashes 'came and went without having met Gatsby at all, came for the party with a simplicity of heart that was its own ticket of admission'.

Nick is rescued from his social diffidence one Saturday morning when Gatsby's chauffeur, dressed in a robin's egg blue uniform, delivers a note from his employer requesting Nick's attendance at the next 'little party' and signed 'Jay Gatsby in a majestic hand.'

The Venue

Gatsby's waterfront mansion is 'a colossal affair by any standard', a 'factual imitation of some Hotel de Ville in Normandy' with an ivy-covered tower and a marble swimming pool, set in 'more than forty acres of lawn and garden.' Inside this opulent pile are

'Marie-Antoinette music-rooms and Restoration salons' and a copy of the library at Merton College, Oxford: a 'high Gothic library, panelled with carved English oak, and probably transported complete from some ruin overseas' in which, to the amazement of his guests, the books on the shelves are actually real.

However, as estate agents will tell you, the important thing in property deals is 'location, location, location'. Gatsby only bought the mansion because it is conveniently situated across the harbour from the house where Daisy Fay – the woman he loved and lost five years previously – now lives. When he went off to fight in the Great War she married Tom Buchanan, an ex-college football player and scion of a wealthy Chicago family. Tom and Daisy 'drifted here and there unrestfully wherever people played polo and were rich together' and have ended up in East Egg. On clear evenings Gatsby sits and gazes across the bay at the green light that shines at the end of Daisy's dock.

The Guest List

Despite working in a bond office by day and studying investments and securities in his spare time, Nick Carraway clearly has plenty of leisure to flick through the society papers, because he is able to drop the names of over a hundred celebrity guests who frequent Gatsby's parties. They include social luminaries such as Dr Webster Civet, the Leeches, Edgar Beaver, the Blackbucks, James B. Ferret, Cecil Roebuck and Francis Bull. And those are just the ones that happen to have the same names as animals.

Here and there Nick provides us with a few additional salacious details: 'Henry L. Palmetto who killed himself by jumping in front of a subway train in Times Square', 'Young Brewer who had his nose shot off in the war', 'G. Earl Muldoon, brother to that Muldoon who afterward strangled his wife' and Ripley Snell, who was there 'three days before he went to the penitentiary'.

The one person who Gatsby earnestly hopes will turn up at one of his parties, but so far has never done so, is Daisy Buchanan. Gatsby could of course just hop into his hydroplane and whizz over the bay to call on his lost love, but he knows this would make him look like too much of a needy loser in her materialistic eyes. His instinct tells him that the best way to win round this girl whose 'voice is full of money' is to first impress her with the magnificence of his home.

The Dress Code

The female attire is vibrant: 'The halls and salons and verandas are gaudy with primary colors and hair shorn in strange new ways and shawls beyond the dreams of Castile.' The male guests are more sedate, perhaps anxious not to upstage their host's pink suit, and seem to be attired mostly in white, including flannels and knickerbockers.

The Food and Drink

Gatsby falls a little short of his illustrious predecessor Trimalchio in the food he serves his guests. Skinniness was high fashion in the 1920s and flat-chested flapper girls had to fit into their beaded dresses. At the beginning of the evening, buffet tables are merely 'garnished with glistening hors-d'oeuvre' and spiced baked hams replace the whole wild boar, but the pastry piglets remain intact from the Roman banquet. Later in the evening, two suppers are served alfresco on the lawn, but no details of the menu are provided.

Gatsby's hospitality is more fulsome on the drinks front. Despite the prohibition laws in force in the 1920s, the host has certain business connections who are able to equip his bar 'with gins and liquors and with cordials so long forgotten that most of his female guests were too young to know one from another.' Champagne is served 'in glasses bigger than finger bowls'. In addition five crates of oranges and lemons have been freshly squeezed by the butler, perhaps to ensure an ample supply of soft drinks for guests to grab if the party is raided by the police.

Oddly enough the only two people in the book who enter into the spirit of the Eighteenth Amendment and don't drink alcohol are Daisy and Gatsby (though female revellers have a habit of rubbing champagne into Gatsby's hair).

The Entertainment

As well as swimming and taking rides in the host's motorboat there is music. Gatsby's parties feature a full orchestra, 'no thin five-piece affair, but a whole pitful of oboes and trombones and saxophones and viols and cornets and piccolos, and low and high drums.' As well as popular hits of the day, such as 'Three O'Clock in the Morning, a neat, sad little waltz of that year', the band also tackles the more heavyweight repertoire, including Vladimir Tostoff's 'Jazz History of the World' 'which attracted so much attention at Carnegie Hall last May', the name of the composer suggesting what we might be expected to make of the music.

The various Broadway stars and other entertainers who find themselves at the party also perform turns: a tenor sings in Italian, a contralto sings in jazz, a pair of stage 'twins' do their baby act in costume and a red-headed lady from a famous chorus who has 'drunk a quantity of champagne' blubs an impromptu ballad.

The Conversation

'The air is alive with chatter and laughter, and casual innuendo and introductions forgotten on the spot and enthusiastic meetings between women who never knew each other's names.' The hottest topic of gossip among the guests is speculation as to Gatsby's true identity and the possible source of his wealth. While they swill his champagne on his lawn, they exchange various theories, including that he is a cousin of Kaiser Wilhelm, a murderer, a German spy, a bootlegger and a 'nephew to von Hindenburg and second cousin to the devil'.

The Outcome

Gatsby's instinct about Daisy's mercenary bent is correct. Via the intermediary skills of Nick she is lured over to the mansion, where Gatsby gives her a guided tour, during which she bursts into tears on seeing the beauty of his shirts.

Finding his wealth to her satisfaction, Daisy finally attends one of Gatsby's parties, but afterwards he sinks into gloom, convinced that she didn't have a good time. So he abruptly fires his domestic staff and cancels all future hospitality: 'and, as obscurely as it had begun, his career as Trimalchio was over'.

Perhaps Gatsby has realized the truth of Nick Carraway's observation that 'You can't repeat the past.' As Nick tells us, Gatsby 'knew that when he kissed this girl, and forever wed his unutterable visions to her perishable breath, his mind would never romp again like the mind of God. So he waited, listening for a moment longer to the tuning-fork that had been struck upon a star. Then he kissed her.' Carraway is clearly the most eloquent trader who ever worked on Wall Street. He wouldn't have found it hard to sell you a few short-dated railway bonds while he was at it.

Soon afterwards Gatsby is unmasked by Tom Buchanan as a bootlegger (né Jimmy Gatz) who has reinvented himself as a gentleman squire. Daisy is predictably horrified to find out that her lover is 'new money' and promptly goes back to her properly patriarchal but philandering husband.

Gatsby washes up dead in his own pool. Unlike Trimalchio, who staged his own funeral while still alive so he could appreciate the sycophantic adoration of his mourners, Gatsby has a real funeral and only three people bother to show up. Just in case we hadn't picked up on earlier hints that 1920s New Yorkers were a pretty shallow, fickle bunch.

The Legacy

Francis Scott Fitzgerald knew a lot about parties. His house on Long Island, though more modest than Gatsby's, played host to an endless succession of weekend soirées. A notorious alcoholic, he wrote out a series of house rules for importunate guests including 'Visitors are requested not to break down doors in search of liquor, even when authorized to do so by the host and hostess.'

Sadly he never got to drink his way through much in the way of royalties from *The Great Gatsby*. Though it is now considered by many to be the greatest American novel ever written, it sold under 20,000 copies in the first year it was published. In 1939 its author collected just thirty-three dollars in royalties and by the time of his death a year later at the age of forty-four *The Great Gatsby* was out of print.

The securing of the book's posthumous reputation was due to the efforts of a small group of friends and admirers including Dorothy Parker (purportedly his lover) who published a collection as *The Portable F. Scott Fitzgerald* in 1945.

3

Queen Alice's Feast

LOCATION: LOOKING-GLASS LAND

HOSTESS: QUEEN ALICE

DATE: 4 NOVEMBER 1859

From *Through the Looking Glass and What
Alice Found There* (1871) by Lewis Carroll
(aka the Rev Charles Lutwidge Dodgson)

The Hostess

Bored one snowy November afternoon, Alice Pleasance Liddell,
the heroine of the previous novel, *Alice's Adventures in Wonderland*, climbs though her living-room mirror to see what is on
the other side and finds herself a pawn in an enormous game of
chess being played all over the world. After various adventures
she advances to the eighth square and (in accordance with the
rules of the game) is promoted to Queen.

Aged just seven and a half, Alice is perhaps a juvenile hostess but a relatively mature monarch in the course of British
history. When Mary, Queen of Scots came to the throne of Scotland in 1542, she was six days old. Unlike Mary, Alice has to pass
an examination administered by the Red and White Queens.
This consists of her being set, and found wanting in, a long
list of tasks, all of which are either impossible or pointless or
both.

The Invitation

Alice's elevation to royalty is to be marked with a feast. In accordance with the back-to-front way of doing things in Looking-Glass Land, the guests invite each other to the party and the hostess herself is the last to find out about it.

The Venue

The landscape of this backwards realm is divided into giant chess squares by a series of criss-crossing brooks and hedges. At the eighth square Alice finds herself standing before an arched doorway with 'Queen Alice' displayed in large letters on it.

Despite her newly acquired status Alice has problems getting in to her own party. 'No admittance till the week after next' a creature with a long beak tells her before slamming the door in her face. She is also unsure as to which of the two doorbells, marked 'Visitors' Bell' and 'Servants' Bell', she should press. 'There ought to be one marked "Queen" you know,' she muses, her new title having gone a little to her head.

Finally the door is flung open and Alice is greeted with a song. Silence falls as she enters the large hall.

The Guest List

'Are you animal – vegetable – or mineral?' the Lion asks Alice earlier in the story, during a time-out from his permanent scrap with the Unicorn. In Looking-Glass Land this is not a facetious question. Inanimate objects are capable of speaking, arguing and being generally disobliging.

At the feast we find representatives of all three categories. Flowers, the usual decor at a dinner party, are seated at the table (though what they eat is a moot point). Animals and birds are present, both as guests and as dishes. In this topsy-turvy world Alice is considered to be a 'fabulous monster'.

Looking round the table as she sits down the hostess is secretly a little relieved: 'I'm glad they've come without waiting to be asked,' she thinks: 'I should never have known who were the right people to invite!'

Their Red and White Majesties have invited each other and are in attendance. Having three queens present creates issues with protocol, not to mention seating arrangements.

The Food and Drink

As already noted, the menu and the guests appear to be inter-changeable. The animals at table find themselves 'being served' in both senses of the phrase.

On arriving Alice is told that she has missed the first two courses. Perhaps this is no bad thing. 'Sprinkle the table with buttons and bran, put cats in the coffee, and mice in the tea,' the guests sing to her as she enters. 'Then fill up the glasses with treacle and ink, ... Mix sand with the cider, and wool with the wine'.

Food in Looking-Glass Land tends to be unappetizing: from the dry biscuit the Red Queen gives Alice in the first square to the hay the White King is fed with in the sixth, and not forgetting the pudding recipe that the White Knight describes to Alice in the seventh, which is of his own invention and whose principal ingredients are blotting paper, gunpowder and sealing wax. Maybe the Reverend Dodgson was thinking of the college hall dinners he had to endure as an Oxford don.

In any case eating doesn't seem to be on the menu at this party. Alice is obliged to go through the formality of being introduced to each dish that is brought to table. Once she has exchanged small talk with a leg of mutton and a plum pudding she is forbidden from slicing them up and serving them to her guests. As the Red Queen points out, quoting no doubt from the Looking-Glass *Debrett's*, 'it isn't etiquette to cut any one you've been introduced to.'

Drinking however is permitted and the guests toast their new Queen's health, though in a rather dysfunctional manner: 'some of them put their glasses upon their heads like extinguishers, and drank all that trickled down their faces – others upset the decanters, and drank the wine as it ran off the edges of the table – and three of them (who looked like kangaroos) scrambled into the dish of roast mutton, and began eagerly lapping up the gravy'.

The Conversation

As ever, the strangest creatures that Alice comes across in her adventures are the grown-ups, who tend to be bossy, rude, cantankerous and pedantic. The shy, stammering Reverend Dodgson preferred children's company to that of adults and was probably writing from the heart.

At dinner Alice is seated between the Red and White Queens (on the chessboard their chess-piece avatars all occupy adjoining squares). These ladies are like two contrasting, but equally annoying aunts: the Red Queen stern, aloof and quarrelsome; the White Queen eccentric, blethering, and semi-senile. The only things they have in common are a short attention span and an annoying tendency to change the subject without warning. The Reverend Dodgson was staying at a house in Guildford inhabited by his six spinster sisters at the time he wrote the book and one wonders if they served as models.

So the conversation mainly consists of Alice being corrected and told off: the normal state of being of a Victorian child at the hands of parents, nannies, governesses and schoolmistresses.

The Entertainment

None to speak of. The closest thing to it is a riddle asked by the White Queen (just to spoil it for you the answer is: an oyster).

Perhaps the proper entertainment was scheduled for later in the evening. A ball has been promised for after the feast, but unfortunately we never get that far . . .

The Outcome

As Alice rises to make her speech of thanks to the assembled guests she begins to float upwards. 'And then . . . all sorts of things happened in a moment. The candles all grew up to the ceiling, looking something like a bed of rushes with fireworks at the top. As to the bottles, they each took a pair of plates, which they hastily fitted on as wings, and so, with forks for legs, went fluttering about in all directions'. The White Queen turns into a leg of mutton and the soup ladle strides towards Alice in alarming fashion. The Red Queen has shrunk to the size of a doll and is running round the table.

One begins to wonder if something more powerful than mice has been put in the tea.

As it turns out this is all just a rather surreal representation of the chess moves: 10. Qb6+ 11. Qxe8 1–0. Alice's Queen takes the Red Queen which puts the Red King (who has been sound asleep for the whole story) in checkmate and wins the game (though White appears to get two moves in a row which seems a bit unfair).

Of course the whole thing turns out to have been a dream. If we'd read the previous book we might have guessed that. However, the more profound question we are left with is whose dream was it? Alice's or the Red King's? Or maybe a dream within a dream?

The Legacy

Lewis Carroll's two Alice adventures have been translated into most world languages and are in almost as many homes as the Bible and Shakespeare. Carroll also churned out (under his real name) twenty-five less popular volumes devoted to mathematics, with titles like *The Enunciation of the Propositions and Corollaries in Euclid*.

Despite fame and wealth he didn't give up his day job teaching mathematics at Christ Church college, Oxford. In his spare time he wrote regulations for lawn tennis tournaments, devised a braking system for his tricycle, concocted a machine for writing in the dark, designed a new form of postal order and invented an early prototype of Scrabble. He campaigned against vivisection and for vaccination and proposed a scheme for transporting the famine-stricken population of Tristan da Cunha to the coast of South Africa.

4

Dmitri Karamazov's Revel at Mokroye

LOCATION: PLASTUNOV'S INN, MOKROYE, RUSSIA

HOST: DMITRI FYODOROVICH KARAMAZOV

DATE: 1870S

From *The Brothers Karamazov* (1880)
by Fyodor Dostoyevsky

The Invitation

When the inhabitants of the sleepy (literally, it's two in the morning) town of Mokroye are roused from their beds with news of the unexpected arrival of Dmitri Karamazov, they are in no doubt as to what this betokens. Just three weeks earlier he had pitched up there, his pockets bulging with 3,000 roubles, which he proceeded to lavish on a huge carousal to which all were invited.

The Host

Dmitri (also known as Mitya, Mitenka or Mitri) is the eldest and most notoriously hedonistic of the Karamazov brothers. He is an intemperate, recklessly extravagant sensualist with a passion for vice and little regard for money: all in all the natural party host. He inherited these character traits from his father, Fyodor Pavlovich, who married his mother, Adelaïda, a beautiful and intelligent heiress, for her fortune. She ran off with a destitute divinity student when Dmitri was three and subsequently died in penury. Old Karamazov's approach to single parenting was to forget he had a son, to turn 'his house into a regular harem' and to devote himself 'to the most dissolute drunkenness'. His second wife, Sophia 'the Shrieker', bore him two more sons: Ivan, a coldly intellectual atheist, and Alexei, now a trainee monk. He also fathered an illegitimate offspring – the Gollum-like Smerdyakov – by a local bag lady nicknamed Stinking Liza.

Dmitri, now twenty-eight, is suffering the Freudian aftermath of his turbulent childhood: 'He dropped out of school, ended up in a military academy, then found himself in the Caucasus, was promoted, fought a duel, was reduced to the ranks, was promoted again, led a wild life and burnt his way through rather a lot of money.'

One of his last acts before setting out for Mokroye was to redeem his duelling pistols, which he had earlier pawned, as he plans to blow his brains out at the first light of dawn.

The Venue

A four-bedroom inn in Mokroye ('the wet place' in Russian), a small provincial town of 2,000 residents, hardly sounds like the most promising venue for a debauched revel. Fortunately the innkeeper, Trifon Borisovich Plastunov, 'who was very fond of fleecing drunken guests', offers rather more than basic room service. Dmitri merely has to mention the word 'gypsies', for the landlord, despite the late hour, to promise to supply a Jewish band, an array of buxom village girls, a female chorus and even to throw in his own four daughters. He has not forgotten how Dmitri had blown 'over two hundred roubles, if not a whole three hundred' on his spree at the inn the previous month and the landlord 'scented his prey once more as soon as Mitya drove up to his door'.

The Guest List

The motive behind Dmitri's impulsive binge is the same now as it was on the previous occasion: to win the affection of Agrafena Alexandrovna Svetlova – a twenty-two-year-old 'rosy-cheeked full-figured Russian beauty', known to her friends as Grushenka ('little pear'). There are two standard female characters in Dostoyevsky's novels: the meek, noble, self-sacrificing woman who is browbeaten and ill treated; and the proud, domineering vixen who is passionate, cruel and vindictive. Dmitri has thrown over his fiancée Katerina Ivanovna (type one) for Grushenka (type two).

Having no family money, Grushenka 'had got involved in what is known as *geschäft*' ('business' – the use of the German word here shows what a profoundly unRussian activity Dostoyevsky considered this to be). Her particular line of work is buying up debts and she had come into possession of some of Dmitri's IOUs. They first met when he called on her with the intention of beating her up. Typically he decided to fall in love with her instead and she is now the 'tsarina' of his soul, despite the competition for her affection from his own father, who has left a bait of 3,000 roubles at his house should she decide to come to him.

However Grushenka has decided to spurn both these romantic offers and instead headed off to Mokroye for a tryst with her first love, a retired Polish customs official named Mussyalovitch, who had jilted her five years previously. He is accompanied by his lanky travelling companion and occasional bodyguard Vrublevsky.

Two Russians have joined them at the inn: Kalganov, a young handsome buck of twenty, and Maximov, a sixty-year-old landowner from Tula.

The remainder of the guest list is supplied by a willing stream of the local peasantry, lured from their beds 'By the prospect of another legendary night's entertainment, like the one the previous month' in which Dmitri had handed out cigars, Rhine wine and cash to all present.

The Dress Code

Dmitri's coat and trousers are soiled with large bloodstains, but no one, including Grushenka, appears to notice. Perhaps she's too distracted by her Polish former flame's change of appearance: his 'rather flabby, almost forty-year-old face' now sports 'fine, dyed and cocky little moustaches' and is topped by a 'shabby wig, made in Siberia, with love-locks combed absurdly forwards at the temples'. Both Poles are 'wearing rather soiled clothing'. Grushenka by contrast is dressed up in all her finery as a way of seeking revenge on the man who broke her heart: 'He left me as a seventeen-year-old, skinny, consumptive cry-baby . . . I'm going to sit by him, flirt with him and turn him on.'

The only full sartorial description we get is of the innkeeper, Trifon, who is dressed in the Russian style wearing 'a shirt with buttons down the side and a long-waisted coat'.

The Entertainment

The evening begins in fairly restrained fashion with a game of faro (the poker of its day). But the situation soon degenerates as the Poles are caught using a marked deck of cards. Further

ructions are caused by their refusal to drink a toast to Mother
Russia and Dmitri's unsubtle attempts to buy off Mussyalovitch's interest in Grushenka for 3,000 roubles.

Finally the Poles are booted out and 'a semi-orgy began,
a free-for-all feast'. The band arrives with fiddles, zithers and
cymbals and a chorus of local girls launches into a 'rollicking
dance song'. As 'the drinking went on the girls' songs became
correspondingly coarser and raunchier' (Dostoyevsky provides
lyrics in case the reader would like to sing along). The explicit
words of one song about a group of maidens choosing between
various potential lovers causes 'a furore in the listening public,'
while another traditional ditty tells the more prosaic tale of a
young girl's love for her porch: 'ah you, porch, my porch, my
new porch, new maple wood latticed porch'.*

Their performance culminates in a novelty dance as
two peasant girls dressed up as bears are led by Stepanida, 'a
boisterous girl with a stick in her hand', who starts to 'show'

* Modern Russians are more likely to sing about the glories of their Porsches.

them until they end up 'rolling on the floor in a distinctly unseemly fashion'. The assembled muzhiks find this hysterical, but Kalganov deems it 'peasant vulgarity'. After the girls sing another bawdy song, Maximov attempts to restore decorum to proceedings with a clog dance, which 'consisted of a sort of hopping in which he kicked out his legs to the side, with the soles up, and with each hop slapped his soles with his palms'. Only Dmitri is amused. Despite this lukewarm reception Maximov follows up with a comic song involving farmyard impressions.

The Food and Drink

Dmitri had brought a half-case of champagne with him, which the guests quickly get through (the Russian custom is to down alcohol in one, so no one cares that it's not chilled). Not long afterwards a wagon arrives bearing copious provisions which Dmitri had earlier ordered from Plotnikov's store in his home town of Skotoprigonyevsk. Here 'there was everything that could be found in any shop in the capital', and Dmitri has splashed out on four dozen bottles of champagne, cheeses, Strasbourg pies, smoked fish, ham, caviar, dessert, sweets, pears, watermelons, chocolate, candy, toffee and fondants.

Dmitri 'is in his natural element' and greets and embraces the peasants, jovially refilling their glasses. 'Only the peasant girls had a taste for the champagne. The men preferred rum, cognac, and especially the hot punch.' There is also hot chocolate and three samovars are 'kept boiling for tea and hot punch: anyone who dropped in could just help themselves'.

The Conversation

The second half of the party is dealt with in a chapter entitled 'Delirium', which quickly justifies its name as the guests descend into drunken rambling, Grushenka being the most overzealous contributor. Like Dmitri, she tends to alternate between bursting into laugher and into tears. She switches from pleas for more alcohol, to professions of repentance, to sobbing over having wasted five years of her life on the bewigged Pole, to profuse declarations of love for Dmitri, then announces her intention to become a nun and finally to run away to Siberia and till the land with her own hands. Dmitri 'dumb with ecstasy' kisses his tsarina who eggs him on: 'Kiss me, kiss me harder. That's right. If we're going to love then let's love! I'll be your slave now and for the rest of my life. It's sweet to be a slave! Kiss me, beat me, ill-treat me, do what you want to me … Oh, yes. I really need to be treated badly…' All this from the woman who, twenty-four hours previously, had claimed she 'loved him for only one short hour'. It's not hard to see why *The Brothers Karamazov* was Freud's favourite novel.*

The Outcome

In view of Grushenka's change of heart Dmitri shelves his plans to shoot himself and they retire to bed, as 'the noise from the feast in the hall grew louder and louder'. Just as Grushenka is dreaming of the two of them speeding over the snow to Siberia in a troika they are rudely awakened by the arrival of an inspector and captain of police, the deputy prosecutor and a forensic

---

* Freud described *The Brothers Karamazov* as 'the most magnificent novel ever written'. He wrote an article on it, which concluded that Dostoyevsky was a repressed homosexual and his gambling compulsion was a sublimation of his desire to masturbate.

investigator, who prove themselves to be a regular bunch of party-poopers by announcing that they have come to arrest the host for the murder of his father.

Dmitri stands trial, but was it he or one of his brothers who bumped off Old Man Karamazov? Of course it doesn't really matter in this novel whose spiritual message is that we are all responsible for each other and for each other's sins. In other words: they all did it. And, if Ivan Karamazov and Smerdyakov are right that in a godless world 'everything is permitted', then perhaps there wasn't even a crime in the first place. Agatha Christie would never have been so sloppy.

The Legacy

The Brothers Karamazov has pretty much everything one can ask for from a work of fiction: love, death, obsession, God, the Devil . . . with a murder mystery thrown in too. Despite its epic proportions Dostoyevsky originally intended the novel to be merely the first book in a series titled 'The Life of a Great Sinner'. The author himself knew quite a lot about the subject, being an inveterate gambler, adulterer and debauchee, who wrote many of his books just to keep himself out of debtors' prison. Sadly his death, four months after the publication of *The Brothers Karam-azov*, meant he was never able to share in full his insights into the condition.

5

A Little Ball at Roxana's House

LOCATION: PALL MALL, LONDON

HOSTESS: MADEMOISELLE DE BELEAU

DATE: 1680S

From *Roxana: The Fortunate Mistress* (1724)
by Daniel Defoe

The Hostess

Mademoiselle de Beleau is a beautiful, wealthy and single lady, recently moved into handsome apartments in Pall Mall in seventeenth-century London. Through the medium of her maid Amy ('a tattling Woman, and a true Gossip') rumour circulates in *haute société* that the mysterious new resident is 'the Widow of a Person of Quality in *France*' with a private fortune of 40,000 livres.

In Restoration England the nobility, as in any other age, tended to live beyond their means and were 'almost all of them, Borrowers, and all in necessitous Circumstances'. So the soi-disant wealthy widow's house is quickly 'throng'd with Admirers' including 'some Persons of very great Figure' and she finds herself 'harass'd with Lovers, *Beaus,* and *Fops* of Quality in abundance'.

What these fortune-hunters do not know is that the object of their attentions has no intention of marrying any of them, as she 'knew no State of Matrimony, but what was, at best, a State of Inferiority, if not of Bondage'. She declares herself 'a *Man-Woman*; for as I was born free, I wou'd die so'.

The Invitation

Nevertheless she is not averse to a bit of social advancement and so she announces that she will be holding a 'little Ball' for the benefit of her devotees. Unbeknown to the guests, the party's luxuries will not be provided at the expense of a husband deceased, but from their hostess's flourishing career as a professional mistress to a string of wealthy gentlemen.

The Venue

Mademoiselle de Beleau's apartments in 'a House, out of which was a private Door into the King's Garden' consist of a dining room and five drawing rooms. For the ball they are set out for eating, dancing and gaming; with one room exclusively reserved for the hostess herself, in which she can receive 'all the Company that came to pay their Compliments to me'.

The Guest List

The exact guest list is hard to ascertain as Defoe abides by the eighteenth-century literary convention of referring to members of the aristocracy obliquely as 'Lord — ' or 'my Duke of — '. Many of the gentlemen are also in masquerade. This convenience aided social mobility, allowing the gentry to mix with prostitutes and generally facilitating licentious behaviour.

However, even when a gentleman's face is concealed behind a mask there are still discreet ways for him to advertise his pedigree. Blue garters, for example, show their wearer to be a Knight of the Garter – the highest of the chivalric orders.

The Food and Drink

Our hostess supplies us with scant information about the fare she has laid on, apart from observing that three rooms are set out with tables 'cover'd with Wine and Sweet-Meats'.

The Dress Code

Mademoiselle de Beleau is 'dress'd, you may be sure, to all the Advantage possible' and has 'all the Jewels on, that I was Mistress of' but, hearing a rumour that the King may be attending her party, she effects a mid-evening costume change. She is soon 'dress'd in the Habit of a *Turkish Princess*' – a little number she picked up in Leghorn in Italy – consisting of a damask robe adorned with blue and gold flowers, topped with a turban. Her

girdle is set with diamonds (which in an aside to the reader, she reveals are fake 'but no-body knew that but myself'). She grants the ladies a private view of her outfit and receives their compliments before making a show-stopping re-entrance to the party.

The Entertainment

The house band are a 'Sett of fine Musick from the Play-House' kindly provided by 'My Lord —'. Despite her frock's five-yard train, the hostess somehow manages to execute a courante and two other French dances, with a 'tall, well-shap'd Person, but who had no Name, *being all Mask'd*'. She then performs a solo number ('a Figure which I learnt in *France*'), which her guests take to be a Turkish dance, leading a gentleman to christen her 'Roxana' (a generic name for Oriental queens in late-seventeenth-century dramas) 'upon which foolish Accident I had the Name of Roxana presently fix'd upon me all over the Court End of Town'.*

The gentleman who dances with the hostess is rumoured to be the King himself. However, Roxana is sceptical of the mystery guest's identity and makes the possibly treasonable observation that he danced like a young man, which contrasts with 'His Majesty being at that time in an Age'.

The party goes on till dawn: 'some of the Ladies were dancing at Six in the Morning' (by which time our hostess confides that she is 'sick of the Night') and the gentlemen continue playing cards until an unspecified hour, though they contribute a hundred guineas from their winnings to the servants' tip box.

---

* 'Roxana' was also a name given to prostitutes, as namechecked in the 1978 song 'Roxanne' by the Police.

The Outcome

The party is a huge success and Roxana informs us that 'my Ball, but especially my Dress, was the Chat of the Town for that Week'.

The next morning sees the arrival of a messenger with the sum of 500 guineas from an anonymous benefactor, who requests that Roxana should throw a party again the following Tuesday.

Servants show up on the Saturday bearing 'Bottles of all sorts of Wines, and Hampers of Sweet-Meats'. On the evening of the second party 'there came such an Appearance of Gentlemen and Ladies, that my Apartments were by no means able to receive them' and 'the Street was full of Coaches with Coronets, and fine Glass-Chairs'.

The glitzy occasion attracts 'a promiscuous Crowd, and some of them scandalous too', so a Party of the Guards is stationed on the door to deter gatecrashers, and admittance for guests is by password.

One gentleman at the party does not remove his hat (signalling his seniority over the other guests), causing tongues to wag that he is the King. It seems that Roxana has succeeded in catching the royal eye.*

The Legacy

Daniel Defoe had what would now be called a portfolio career: he was variously a merchant, a tax accountant and a ship insurer,

---

* King Charles II was famous for his love of keeping mistresses and for keeping them well. He would bestow generous gifts, plentiful allowances, titles and apartments in the palace. It is perhaps no coincidence that Roxana resides on Pall Mall, as did the King's most famous mistress, Nell Gwynne.

as well as a pamphleteer, propagandist and secret agent. He took part in a couple of rebellions, was captured by Barbary pirates, went bankrupt and was imprisoned several times: all of which gave him the perfect pedigree to write his last book: *The Compleat English Gentleman*. He also found time to invent the English novel.

Roxana was first published on 29 February 1724 under the exuberant title: *The Fortunate Mistress: Or: A History of the Life and Vast Variety of Fortunes of Mademoiselle de Beleau, Afterwards Call'd the Countess de Wintselsheim, in Germany. Being the Person known by the name of the Lady Roxana, in the Time of Charles II*.

In the early eighteenth century the novel was considered a downmarket art form and there was no convention of listing an author's name on the cover (perhaps there wasn't room with those long titles). Publishers would frequently rewrite a book's ending without its author's permission (there were three separate endings to *Roxana*) or compose unauthorized sequels. As a result there is no definitive evidence that Defoe wrote *Roxana* or even his most famous work, *Robinson Crusoe*.

6

The Strange Fête

LOCATION: SOLOGNE, FRANCE

HOST: FRANTZ DE GALAIS

DATE: DECEMBER 189–

From *Le Grand Meaulnes* (1913) by Alain-Fournier

The Invitation

Seventeen-year-old schoolboy Augustin Meaulnes, 'The Great Meaulnes' of the title, gets hopelessly lost on an impromptu expedition to fetch his friend's grandparents from the local railway station. On his second day stranded 'in the most remote place in the Sologne' in central France during the depths of December he spies a dilapidated turret rising above the fir trees. Wishing for nothing more than a bed for the night he heads for the building only to find himself suddenly overcome by an 'extraordinary sense of wellbeing, a perfect and almost intoxicating tranquility'. He overhears a group of children discussing a party they are going to at the estate. 'You know we're allowed to organise the fete just as we please' a little girl brazenly proclaims. Having lost his horse, injured his knee and slept rough the previous night in a sheepfold the wanderer needs no further encouragement to tag along and gatecrash their party.

The Venue

The Lost Estate, hemmed in by fir woods that make it invisible to the outside world, is a jumble of ramshackle and derelict outhouses clustered round a main building. 'Everything here seemed old and in ruins. The openings at the foot of the staircases gaped as their doors had long ago been removed. The panes hadn't been replaced in the windows either, which appeared as black holes in the walls', yet the paths had been swept and lanterns hung in the windows and 'all these buildings had a mysterious festive air'.

The courtyard turns out to be full of carriages, 'vehicles of every type and shape; slender little four-seaters, with their shafts in the air; charabancs; old-fashioned bourbonnaises with moulded racks and even old berlins with their window panes raised.'

Meaulnes climbs through a half-open window of the house and finds himself in a vast low-ceilinged bedroom where all of the furniture is 'laden with large vases, objects of value and old weaponry'. He lies down in a bed hidden in an alcove 'to rest and think over the strange adventure that he had fallen into'.

The Host

The 'strange fete' is being thrown by Frantz de Galais — 'a boy who must have been very young and very impulsive' and who is 'a student or a sailor or perhaps a midshipman cadet, no one knew for sure'. The one thing we know is that he is 'an eccentric lad who had some extraordinary ideas'.

Frantz is absent at the time of Meaulnes's arrival, having gone to fetch his hostess and bride-to-be. The slight drawback to this arrangement is that the lady in question doesn't know that she is to host a party or even that she is Frantz's fiancée. She is a weaver's daughter he had met once in a garden in Bourges. 'She was extremely pretty and Frantz had straight away decided to marry her.' Frantz is possibly putting the cart before the horse in scheduling the engagement festivities before having popped the question, but being something of a spoiled brat the possibility of her not accepting his proposal has never crossed his mind.

The Guest List

The party has an odd demographic in that the guests all seem to be either young children or old peasants, with the age bracket of twenty to sixty pretty much unrepresented as far as we can gather.

Perhaps this is what happens when you let children organize their own festivities. The juvenile ensemble, like Peter Pan's lost boys, are left to their own devices 'even to hurt ourselves if we want to'. The older folk are bland and amiable and don't seem like they'd be of much use in imposing any discipline on the younger generation. 'There wasn't one of his fellow guests who Meaulnes didn't trust and feel at ease with ... Indulgent grandparents who were sure in advance that everything you did was just right.'

Oddly, Meaulnes seems to have been expected, or has been mistaken for someone else, for a full set of clothes has been laid out for him in Wellington's room – his adopted bedroom. 'I shall just be a guest whose name everyone has forgotten,' he decides.

The Dress Code

The party takes place over two days, with a different dress code for each day. Period costume is the overarching theme with fancy dress on the first night and elegant classic attire on the following day. The boys don clothes from a bygone era: top hats and frock coats with high velvet collars, silk waistcoats, velvet jerkins, white tie and patent leather shoes from the 'start of the last century'. The girls wear knee-length dresses, flounced skirts, wide-brimmed bonnets, quaint knickers, feather boas, velvet bodices and decorative hats with ribbons and feathers.

Meaulnes has been given instructions to dress 'as a marquis' and his room has been stocked with all the necessary apparel to transform the itinerant ragamuffin into a 'dandy'.

The Entertainment

All fairly standard fare for a kids' party with both indoor and outdoor activities. There is a magic lantern show, boating on the lake, a gymkhana and, of course, clowns: a tall pale-faced Pierrot who the children chase through the house 'with shrill cries'.

Meaulnes wanders around the party, which has a dreamy Alice in Wonderland ethos. In one room he sits and listens as a beautiful girl in a large brown cloak plays the piano. Around her little boys and girls sit, quietly attentive or 'leafing through picture books on their laps'. Meaulnes drifts back to the dining room, picks up a book and finds himself 'immersed in the most tranquil happiness imaginable'. Perhaps not most parents' image of a party where 'children are in charge'.

The Food and Drink

'It was the sort of meal that is provided on the eve of a country wedding for relatives who have come from far away.' The author doesn't provide us with any further insight into the fare. Perhaps he expects us all to be instinctively familiar with the menu on such festive family occasions. In any case the whole ambience of the party is so unearthly that one wonders whether anyone present eats or drinks at all.

The Conversation

Amid all this etherealism a couple of old peasant ladies are discussing how long it will take Frantz and his fiancée to get there from Bourges: 'Let's work it out ... An hour and a half by train from Bourges to Vierzon, and seven leagues by coach from Vierzon to here ...' And you thought only the English had conversations about routes.

At the boating lake Meaulnes is drawn to a mysterious blonde and he looks to strike up a conversation with her. He almost blows things with his choice of opening line: 'you are beautiful', which causes her to run off. An apology secures a little more conversation with her. She introduces herself as Frantz's sister Yvonne. We are not privy to details of their discourse or the various 'suggestions' that Meaulnes apparently makes to her, but she suddenly reverts to her original attitude: 'We're two children. We've been foolish ... Farewell, don't follow me.'

The Outcome

Frantz's 'fiancée' does a no-show. He is utterly distraught at losing the woman he had organized the party in honour of (perhaps he should have checked her diary first). He dashes off an apology to his guests and then disappears into the forest with a pistol to blow his brains out. Somehow he manages to miss. It's just not his day.

Meaulnes fails to learn the lesson from Frantz's example of the inadvisability of falling madly in love with girls you don't know, and proceeds to do exactly the same (well they are French after all) with the elusive Yvonne de Galais.

The party breaks up and Meaulnes cadges a lift home in an

old berlin carriage. He finally gets back to school the next morning halfway through a lesson. His four-day bunk doesn't even earn him a detention from the headmaster, M. Seurel.

But Meaulnes has changed. He is no longer the charismatic playground ringleader. The strange fete has marked him and he has now become withdrawn, contemplative and friendless. While other kids are planning their careers he decides to devote his life to rediscovering the mysterious estate and its beautiful mistress who now haunts his dreams.

The Legacy

Le Grand Meaulnes became the classic tale of adolescent angst in France — a *Catcher in the Rye* of its day. As with J. D. Salinger it was pretty much the only thing its author ever wrote. Salinger lived to the age of ninety-one. Alain-Fournier had a better excuse: he was killed on the Western Front in 1914, the year after his novel's publication, aged just twenty-seven.

7

The Ball at Mansfield Park

LOCATION: NORTHAMPTONSHIRE, ENGLAND
HOSTS: SIR THOMAS AND LADY BERTRAM
DATE: 22 DECEMBER 1814

From *Mansfield Park* (1814) by Jane Austen

The Hosts

Sir Thomas Bertram of Mansfield Park in Northamptonshire is a wealthy landowner and Member of Parliament. Stern and patriarchal, he is perfectly comfortable with his fortune being derived from the slave plantations he owns in Antigua, but absolutely forbids his children to engage in anything as morally debased as amateur dramatics.

Lady Bertram is of humble stock, having started life as plain Miss Maria Ward, of Huntingdon, 'with only seven thousand pounds'. Since the upward social mobility brought on by her marriage to a baronet she spends her days 'sitting nicely dressed on a sofa, doing some long piece of needlework'. Outsourcing the upbringing of her four children to a governess and 'proper masters' she is freed up to devote all of her attentions to her pug dog. The words 'indolence' and 'indolent' are used in connection with Lady Bertram five times in the novel. To qualify as such by the standards of Jane Austen's world, where no one works for a living and the average person's maximum daily exertion is to walk round to tea with a neighbour or write a letter, is quite an achievement.

The Bertrams have decided to give a ball in honour of

their niece, Fanny Price, whom they adopted at the age of ten to rescue her from being brought up by her natural mother (the younger sister of Lady B) who had the misjudgement to marry a lieutenant of marines 'without education, fortune, or connections'. When their cousin arrived at Mansfield Park the four Bertram children 'could not but hold her cheap on finding that she had but two sashes, and had never learned French'.

Eight years of luxury and idleness have done wonders for Fanny and by the age of eighteen she has been transformed from a girl with 'no glow of complexion, nor any other striking beauty' into a 'pretty woman'. With her 'exceedingly timid and shy' nature she is now regarded as the model of humility. When her seafaring brother William comes to visit and expresses a desire to see his sister dance, Sir Thomas takes the opportunity to organize Fanny's coming out party.

The Invitation

'Invitations were sent with despatch, and many a young lady went to bed that night with her head full of happy cares'. In Regency England the receipt of an invitation to a ball was an indication of a young lady's status in the eyes of society. The ins and outs of whether a girl was 'in' or 'out' were rather complex.

'A girl not out, has always the same sort of dress; a close bonnet, for instance, looks very demure, and never says a word,' we are told. To do otherwise would confuse a young gentleman who might assume she was out and make the social gaffe of flirting with her. Sometimes girls who have come out commit the further offence to 'pass in such very little time from reserve to quite the opposite – to confidence!' which is in itself 'most objectionable'.

Fanny's combination of natural coyness and humble origins leave the other members of Mansfield society puzzled as to whether she is in or out. Fortunately she is kept ignorant as to the true purpose of the ball, 'had she known ... it would very much have lessened her comfort by increasing the fears she already had of doing wrong and being looked at'.

The Venue

The temptations of Northampton are resisted and it is decided that the ball will be held at home because for Lady Bertram the fatigue of leaving the sofa and her pug 'would be too much'. Mansfield Park is the Bertrams' ancestral pile, an elegant stately home surrounded by five miles of parkland, 'so well placed and well screened as to deserve to be in any collection of engravings of gentlemen's seats'.

The Guest List

Sir Thomas amuses himself with arranging the party: he decides on the date, chooses the rooms and draws up the guest list with 'young people enough to form twelve or fourteen couple' from a selection of acceptable local families.

These young people are just there to make up the numbers and we never find out their names, the action being focused on the complex love hexagon going on between the members of the two principal families in Mansfield: the Bertrams and the Crawfords. Fanny is in love with her cousin and trainee vicar, Edmund Bertram. Edmund is in love with Mary Crawford, a 'remarkably pretty' girl who lives at the vicarage with her brother Henry. The two Bertram daughters, Maria and Julia, are both in love with Henry Crawford ('not handsome' but with an estate in Norfolk and an income of £4,000 a year) and are playing hard to get by staying away from the ball. Maria has even gone so far as to marry Mr Rushworth (a man of little intelligence but with a stately home and £12,000 a year) just to spite Henry. Henry, who, despite his moneyed background, has a bit of a thing for wenches, has set himself the challenge of getting Fanny to fall in love with him.

The Dress Code

For Fanny 'with small means of choice, and no confidence in her own taste — the "how she should be dressed" was a point of painful solicitude'. Mary Crawford steps in as her stylist, but with a secret agenda. Fanny wears the gown she wore to her cousin Maria's wedding but her accessorizing options are limited, as the only item of jewellery she possesses is an amber cross from Sicily given to her by her brother William, but she lacks a chain to wear it on (William on his humble midshipman's wages couldn't afford one). Mary presses a gold chain on Fanny, which transpires to have been a gift from Henry. Fanny is saved from having to wear this token of her unwanted suitor by Edmund, who also gives her a gold chain. Edmund's chain fits Fanny's crucifix perfectly whereas Henry's is too big. If this wasn't Jane Austen we might think there was some sexual allusion going on here.

Just when Fanny is already fully dressed and heading downstairs to the ball, Lady Bertram 'with an unusual degree of wakefulness' springs into action and sends along her maid Mrs Chapman to assist her niece in her toilet.

The Entertainment

Violins strike up and the bashful Fanny is horrified to hear that she is expected to open the ball with the first dance: a prospect made even more unwelcome by the fact that Henry Crawford is to be her partner, having reserved the first two dances with her in advance (she accepted him out of fear that no one else would ask).

For those not wishing to dance, cards are also played, with whist and 'speculation' being the popular games. The card tables are organized by Fanny's other aunt, Mrs Norris, who aspires to be the 'doer of everything'. Aunts in literature frequently come in unmatched pairs and Fanny's are typical of the genre. The bumbling, dim and lazy Lady Bertram is complemented by Mrs Norris, her older sister, who is her diametric opposite: prickly, interfering and vindictive.*

---

* The sinister snooping cat belonging to Filch, the caretaker of Hogwarts School in the Harry Potter novels, is named Mrs Norris in honour of this nasty lady.

The Conversation

As Fanny is now officially 'out' she is entitled to receive the attentions of gentlemen: 'She was introduced here and there by her uncle, and forced to be spoken to, and to curtsey, and to speak again.' 'This was a hard duty', she reports, perhaps having more in common with her Aunt Bertram than we initially supposed.

The only conversation that does not daunt her is the one that she is due to have with her beloved Edmund when they have the two dances he has booked with her for later in the evening. When this moment arrives he informs her, a mite insensitively, 'I am worn out with civility ... I have been talking incessantly all night, and with nothing to say. But with you, Fanny, there may be peace. You will not want to be talked to. Let us have the luxury of silence.'

The Food and Drink

There is a 'supper hour' (for which Fanny is secured once more by Henry), but it seems rather meagre. The only refreshments we are informed the guests partake of are soup and negus (a hot drink of port, sugar, lemon and spices).

The Outcome

With none of the guests having to get up to do anything approaching gainful labour in the morning the ball goes on till late. It is after three o'clock in the morning when Fanny is sent to bed by her uncle, leaving 'five or six determined couples, who were still hard at work' and her brother William, who is planning to 'keep it up these two hours.' Fanny climbs the staircase 'sore-footed and fatigued, restless and agitated, yet feeling, in spite of everything, that a ball was indeed delightful'.

Henry and William are to leave for London early the next morning ('early' by Jane Austen standards: actually half-past nine). Fanny sees them off, crying '*con amore*' ('but it was con amore fraternal and no other'). It seems that Henry's plan has backfired on him and he has fallen in love with Fanny, though she continues to be indifferent to him and has eyes only for Edmund.

Despite he and Fanny being a perfectly matched pair of goody-two-shoes, Edmund still hankers after the shallow and snooty Mary Crawford. The ball was to be his final social engagement before his ordination as a priest and despite dancing twice with Mary she insists this will be the last time . . . 'She never has danced with a clergyman, she says, and she never *will*.' Men of the cloth are looked down on by posh ladies like her as they actually have to work for a living (delivering two sermons a week, paying the occasional visit to poor people etc).

The Legacy

Jane Austen had an ambivalent relationship with clergymen in her novels, probably due to the omnipresence of them in her life: she had seven in her extended family. Edmund however is so bland and wet as to make the vicars from other Austen novels (the unctuous Mr Elton in *Emma*, or even the ghastly Mr Collins in *Pride and Prejudice*) seem quite interesting in comparison. Cardinal Newman said of Austen's vicars 'what vile creatures her parsons are'.

Despite devoting all of her books to love and finding Mr Right, Austen failed to do so herself. Her romantic life is shrouded in mystery, which has provided modern biographers with plenty of latitude for lucrative speculation. She sup-posedly fell in love with a clergyman in her mid-twenties, who, depending on which theory you believe, either died or mar-ried someone else: which might go some way to explaining her later hostility to men of the cloth. In 1802 Harris Bigg-Wither, an affluent heir and the brother of one of her friends, proposed to her. She initially accepted, but thankfully for posterity she changed her mind the next morning. Could the literary world have taken seriously a Jane Bigg-Wither? Miss Austen died an old maid at the age of forty-one.

8

Belshazzar's Feast

LOCATION: BABYLON, MESOPOTAMIA
HOST: BELSHAZZAR
DATE: 12 OCTOBER 539 BC
From the Book of Daniel, the Bible

The Host

Belshazzar was the last King of Babylon (though he didn't know it at this point). He ruled over the ancient land of Mesopotamia, which was situated between the Tigris and Euphrates rivers, and is generally considered to be the cradle of Western civilization.

The Book of Daniel in the Old Testament is believed to have been written some time in the second century BC, over three hundred years after the historical events it recounts. However, modern scholars — viewing events from a more balanced 2,500-year distance — have decided they know better and have stripped Belshazzar of his kingly status. It seems he was merely the crown prince, who was acting as regent while his father, King Nabonidus, was away on a ten-year sabbatical in the oasis of Teima in Arabia.

The unknown author of Daniel also manages to get Belshazzar's parentage wrong (perhaps he was relying on some early prototype of Wikipedia) describing him as the son of Nebuchadnezzar. King Nebuchadnezzar II, the scourge of Judah, besieged Jerusalem twice and, on his second visit, burnt down its Holy Temple. In reality though three different kings reigned between his death and Nabonidus ascending the throne. Belshazzar wasn't even a blood relation.*

The Invitation

The art of writing is believed to have originated in Mesopotamia, although some scholars give the credit to Egypt. The Babylonians (also known as Chaldeans) used a cuneiform script etched with a reed onto clay tablets or cylinders. Archaeologists have unearthed tens of thousands of these artefacts, but sadly no party invitations seem to have survived.

So, although Daniel 5:1 tells us that 'Belshazzar the King held a great feast' we don't know what the occasion was. Perhaps it was to make up for the loss of the nation's most sacred holiday, the New Year festival of Akîtu. This eleven-day celebration, consisting of libations, sacrifices and sheep shearing, culminated in a holy procession leading to a great sacrificial meal of which all the people partook. Unfortunately only the king was entitled to lead the statue of Marduk, the patron god of Babylon, by the hand in the procession and so, with Nabonidus being away in Arabia, the festival could not take place.

This was a bit like Christmas being cancelled for a whole decade. Under the circumstances the Babylonian people weren't entirely opposed to the idea of a regime change and, with the Persian army already marching on their capital, they might not have to wait too long for it.

---

* It's possible that the writer of the Book of Daniel just got Nebuchadnezzar and Nabonidus confused. In Chapter 4 we are told that Nebuchadnezzar lost his mind and spent seven years living like a beast and 'eating grass like cattle'. The Dead Sea Scrolls imply that it was Nabonidus who went mad for seven years, which might explain why he spent all that time in rehab in Arabia.

The Venue

The ancient city of Babylon (described in Isaiah 13:19 as 'the glory of kingdoms') lay about sixty miles south-west of modern-day Baghdad on the River Euphrates. Belshazzar had a northern, southern and summer palace at his disposal. The feast was most likely held in the southern palace, the Babylonian kings' winter residence, which boasted five courtyards, richly ornamented with multi-coloured glazed bricks, and may also have contained the Hanging Gardens, one of the Seven Wonders of the Ancient World.

The Guest List

Belshazzar has a fairly limited social circle so his guest list consists of 'a thousand of his lords'. He also finds room to invite various other princes and his wives and concubines.

The Dress Code

The Bible doesn't supply any information on what was worn, but the Greek historian Herodotus gives us a few pointers on contemporary Babylonian fashion: 'The dress of the Babylonians is a linen tunic reaching to the feet, and above it another tunic made in wool, besides which they have a short white cloak around them, and shoes of a peculiar fashion ... They have long hair, wear turbans on their heads, and anoint their whole bodies with perfumes.'

The Food and Drink

It is only natural for a host to want to impress his guests by getting out his best tableware, so Belshazzar commands that the wine be served to his guests in gold and silver goblets which had been looted by Nebuchadnezzar from the Holy Temple in Jerusalem in 586 BC. The vessels are filled and the guests drink a toast in praise of 'the gods of gold, and of silver, of bronze, of iron, of wood and of stone'. This double heresy naturally arouses the wrath of the God of the Israelites.

The Entertainment

From Daniel 5 we know that Nebuchadnezzar was partial to the horn, flute, harp, zither, dulcimer and bagpipes. We're not told if Belshazzar carried on this musical tradition. The entertainment at his party comes from an unexpected source. 'In the same hour came forth fingers of a man's hand, and wrote over against the candlestick upon the plaister of the wall of the king's palace.' The disembodied digit writes on the wall the mysterious words: 'Mene Mene Tekel Upharsin'.

Belshazzar reacts to this apparition in very unkingly fashion: 'then the king's countenance was changed, and his thoughts troubled him, so that the joints of his loins were loosed, and his knees smote one against another.'

The Conversation

The ghostly graffiti causes consternation among the guests and much discussion as to its meaning. Belshazzar summons his magicians, astrologers and soothsayers and offers them a chain of gold, purple garments and a third part of his kingdom if they can decipher the message, but they profess themselves stumped. Under the circumstances you'd think one of them would have just made something up about the King embarking on a long voyage or beginning a new relationship, just so he could get his hands on that gold chain and a third of the kingdom.

The Queen (who for some reason has been left off the guest list) then enters the banqueting hall and remembers Daniel, who had interpreted a couple of tricky dreams for Nebuchadnezzar many years before. Daniel (who is confusingly also known as 'Belteshazzar') is quickly brought in and explains that the floating finger is an emissary of God and the words are an omen of the King's impending death and the overthrow of his kingdom. Belshazzar, quite generously considering the unflattering news, bestows the promised rewards.

The Outcome

Just as Daniel is being dressed in the purple clothes and having the gold chain hung round his neck the prophecy comes true: 'In that night was Belshazzar the king of the Chaldeans slain.

And Darius the Median took the kingdom, being about three-score and two years old,' the chapter concludes abruptly.

Though Darius was indeed to become a great king and commander of the Medes and Persians, it's unlikely that he was responsible for this act of regicide, as in 539 BC he was only eleven years old and it was probably past his bedtime. The culprit is more likely to have been Cyrus the Great (aged about sixty at the time) who was at the head of the invading Persian army and was welcomed by the people as a liberator come to release them from the neglect of Nabonidus. Mindful of a good PR opportunity, one of Cyrus's first acts on adding Babylon to his list of kingships was to reinstate the Akîtu festival, which he also improved upon by ensuring a plentiful supply of wine was distributed at the ceremony.

Daniel never gets his third of the kingdom but is kept on at the Persian court and appointed a high official. However, he falls victim to a conspiracy of jealous satraps who arraign him on a charge of heresy for which he is thrown into a lions' den. Daniel survives, thanks to his faith, and so the satraps with their families are instead fed to the lions (with a less happy outcome).

King Darius' greatest claim to modern fame was his botched invasion of Greece in 490 BC, leading to an embarrassing defeat for his army by a much smaller Greek force at the Battle of Marathon, which is to this day commemorated in the 26.2-mile road race.

The Legacy

Belshazzar's feast gave us the idiom 'the writing on the wall', which is still used today as a portent of doom. The future would bestow Nebuchadnezzar with two retrospective honours: his name is now more widely remembered as a bumper champagne bottle (containing twenty single bottles); and he was also the role model for Saddam Hussein, who saw himself as a reincarnation of the ancient king. When the Iraqi dictator initiated a project reconstructing parts of the city of Babylon, the bricks made to build the city walls all had the inscription 'To King Nebuchadnezzar in the reign of Saddam Hussein'.

9

The Duchess of Richmond's Ball

LOCATION: RUE DE LA BLANCHISSERIE, BRUSSELS

HOSTESS: THE DUCHESS OF RICHMOND

DATE: 15 JUNE 1815

From *Vanity Fair* (1848)
by William Makepeace Thackeray

The Hosts

The Duke and Duchess of Richmond could easily be mistaken for a couple of Thackeray's more over-the-top satirical creations, but they were actually real people and the ball was an actual event that took place on the eve of the outbreak of hostilities during Napoleon's 'Hundred Days' comeback appearance.

The duke had inherited his title (derived from an illegitimate son of Charles II) in 1809 along with an impressive property portfolio including stately homes in Surrey and London. Unfortunately also in the package was £180,000 of debt (about £8 million in today's money). Like many other impoverished British aristocrats the Richmonds had moved to Brussels in search of cheap continental living. 'Everybody in Vanity Fair must have remarked how well those live who are comfortably and thoroughly in debt', Thackeray observes.

Despite his pecuniary misfortunes the duke was described as 'irresistibly convivial'. He managed to father fourteen children with the duchess, seven boys and seven girls at annual intervals, and still found time to keep mistresses.

The duchess, née Lady Charlotte Gordon, was of a different mettle. Her son's tutor described her as 'one of the sourest most ill tempered personages I ever came across in my life'. A dedicated snob – her daughters were forbidden from dancing or talking familiarly with any man without a title and preferably nothing less than a duke or a lord – she would have been just another blue-blooded nonentity had not a total historical fluke converted her into one of the most legendary hostesses of all time.

The Venue

'There never was, since the days of Darius, such a brilliant train of camp-followers as hung round the Duke of Wellington's army in the Low Countries, in 1815'. Soldiers were the footballers of their day in terms of their celebrity status and their wives and girlfriends (WAGs) accompanied them on campaigns. 'People were going not so much to a war as to a fashionable tour.' This is how the dual heroines of this 'Novel without a Hero', Becky Sharp and Amelia Sedley, come to be in Brussels. Becky is married to Captain Rawdon Crawley of the Dragoons and Amelia is the wife of Captain George Osborne of 'His Majesty's –th regiment of foot'.

Brussels was 'one of the gayest and most brilliant little capitals in Europe' and with the ex-pat aristocratic community swelled by the influx of army officers it soon became 'a perpetual military festival' where parties were held almost every night.

Despite the retrospective fame of the Duchess of Richmond's ball there is still some dispute as to where exactly it took place. For many years afterwards rumour circulated that it was held in one of Brussels's palatial buildings like the Hôtel de Ville or the Maison du Roi. These whispers might have been nurtured by the cash-strapped duchess herself in a reluctance to admit that her grand ball was in fact an At Home. Unfortunately her daughter later broke ranks and confessed that the party was held in a large ground-floor room (which had previously been used by a coachbuilder to store coaches) in the house the Richmonds were renting on Rue de la Blanchisserie.*

The Invitation

Thackeray tells us that talk 'regarding the ball was much greater even than in respect of the enemy in their front. The struggles, intrigues, and prayers to get tickets were such as only English ladies will employ, in order to gain admission to the society of the great of their own nation.'

The duchess even checked in advance with the Duke of Wellington that he wasn't going to let any military distractions get in the way of her social plans. 'Duchess you may give your ball with the greatest safety, without fear of interruption,' the commander in chief reassured her magnanimously. The duchess swiftly turned her attention to coordinating the despatch of the invitations. Military precision was employed. The British ambassador's running footman was requisitioned as the duchess's postman and Captain Verner of the 7th Hussars hand-delivered cards to cavalry officers.

---

* Rue de la Blanchisserie means 'Laundry Street'. The Duke of Wellington referred to the Richmonds' residence scathingly as 'The Wash House'.

The Guest List

'There was everybody that every one knew, and only a very few nobodies in the whole room,' the social-climbing Becky Sharp observes approvingly. A guest list in the duchess's own hand survives and confirms Becky's verdict. It lists 228 names of whom only 22 don't have aristocratic titles or military rank. Prominent historical figures who attended the party include the Duke of Wellington, the Prince of Orange (future Dutch king), his brother Prince Frederick of Orange, the Duke of Brunswick and the Prince of Nassau.

The characters in *Vanity Fair* who manage to secure tickets are Captain and Mrs Rawdon Crawley, Captain and Mrs George Osborne and Captain William Dobbin. Major and Mrs O'Dowd and Amelia's brother Jos fail to make the cut.

Though Wellington had given the duchess his blessing for her ball to go ahead, Napoleon was more of a party pooper. The duke was dining at 5 p.m. when word reached him that French forces had crossed the Belgian border and attacked the Prussians near the Sambre. Though distant cannon fire could be heard in the capital Wellington announced his intention to go to the ball and passed word around that other officers should do the same to retain morale.

The Dress Code

British, Belgian and Dutch officers wore their dress uniforms. The Prince of Orange wore a British Army general's scarlet jacket with blue facing, while the Duke of Brunswick was in his jet-black uniform.

George Osborne 'commanded new dresses and ornaments of all sorts for Amelia', but her appearance at the ball 'was an utter failure (as her husband felt with a sort of rage)'. Becky's 'début was, on the contrary, very brilliant. She arrived very late. Her face was radiant, her dress perfection.'

The Food and Drink

The ball doesn't start until 10 p.m. so most guests have dined beforehand. There is a buffet and George Osborne drinks 'bumpers of wine' imploring Dobbin to join him, 'The Duke's wine is famous.' The Duke of Richmond had a particular liking for claret, available in Brussels at just two shillings per bottle. He was also renowned for his ability to sit down with a group of cronies and drink them all under the table.

The Conversation

Talk of the imminent conflict is the subject on everyone's lips, but the heroines of *Vanity Fair* fail to fit the bill of the weeping wives bidding adieu to their gallant husbands. The coquettish and manipulative Becky, oblivious to the military activities outside, patronizes soppy Amelia with fashion tips and a lecture on her husband's inveterate gambling habits. Amelia does shed some tears over George, though not in a dramatic farewell to the brave captain on the eve of battle, but because of his incessant flirting with Becky.

The Entertainment

Sitting miserable and alone in a corner, Amelia would not even have been distracted by the Duchess of Richmond's headline act – the Gordon Highlanders performing a traditional Scottish reel and sword dance.

An orchestra plays, despite the competition from the military drums and bugles sounding the alarm outside. The decadent and shocking new dance of 1815 was the waltz, but the ladies begin to run out of partners as news of the French advance spreads and more and more officers slip off to rejoin their regiments. At the exit they would have passed the frantic duchess imploring them to 'wait one little hour more' and 'not spoil her ball'.

The ebullient George needs no encouragement to stay. He dances with Becky 'twice or thrice – how many times Amelia scarcely knew' and manages to slip her a billet-doux concealed in a nosegay. Once his wife departs in dudgeon, he heads for the gaming tables 'wild with elation' and begins to bet frantically. He wins repeatedly, exclaiming: 'Everything succeeds with me tonight'.

The Outcome

'There was never such a Ball — so fine and sad. All the young men who appeared there shot dead a few days after,' as Lady Caroline Lamb (who didn't arrive in Brussels until a few weeks after the event) famously remarked. In fact she was totally wrong. Of the 103 military guests at the ball only 11 died in the two ensuing battles of Quatre Bras and Waterloo (and only four of these men were young). Lady Caroline's lover Lord Byron, equally unreliably, said in his description of the ball in *Childe Harold* that 'a thousand hearts beat happily'. There were about 225 people at the party. All of which goes to show that you can't trust writers.

So the probability of a military guest at the duchess's ball dying at Quatre Bras or Waterloo was only about 0.1068. But as George Osborne finds, fortune can be a fickle mistress. His lucky streak at the casino runs out and he is shot through the heart three days later at Waterloo.

The Legacy

The Duchess of Richmond's luck was in. She lived on until 1842, famous only for hosting this eve of battle ball. Napoleon too believed in luck. It is probable that he chose to attack on the 15th of June because that was the anniversary of two of his great victories (Marengo and Friedland). Had he invaded a day earlier then the duchess's ball would have been cancelled, her name would have been erased from history and her legendary status would have been assumed by Lady Elizabeth Conyngham, who gave a ball the previous evening (at which that notorious party animal Wellington was of course present).

10

The Onion Cellar

LOCATION: DÜSSELDORF, WEST GERMANY

HOST: FERDINAND SCHMUH

DATE: SPRING 1950

From *The Tin Drum* (1959) by Günter Grass

The Host

Ferdinand Schmuh is a restaurateur and nightclub owner in post-war West Germany. He is one of a new breed of entrepreneurs who 'had a keen eye for the society which had sprung up in Düsseldorf … since the currency reform'. This financial initiative was introduced by the Allies in 1948. It helped wipe out the black market and ensured that goods and services were now priced in the new Deutschmarks, rather than packets of American cigarettes.

Outside of working hours, Herr Schmuh finds respite from his busy schedule by driving down to the Rhine Meadows to shoot sparrows. 'Schmuh was a good marksman and perhaps a good man as well'. For reasons of sentimentality or superstition he never shoots more than twelve birds in a single outing. He assuages his guilt further by taking along a pocketful of birdseed to distribute among the surviving avian population.

The Venue

Schmuh's club, the Onion Cellar, is one of 'the newer night clubs which are distinguished from the older bars and cabarets by, among other things, their higher prices'.

Open six nights per week from 9 p.m. till 2 a.m., it competes with Düsseldorf's other arts venues the Ravioli Room, the Taboo and the Paprika. Outside is an enamel sign painted with the 'poignantly naive likeness of an onion' and the 'iron door, painted with red lead, had no doubt seen service outside an air-raid shelter in the war years.' Inside it boasts 'the note of authenticity essential to a successful night club' by being housed in an actual cellar, 'quite damp and chilly under foot', but minus the original ceiling, which has been removed to expose the former ground floor and a solitary window glazed with 'bottle-green bull's-eye panes.'

Guests descend into the basement via a 'dangerously steep' companionway with only 'two extremely original clotheslines to hold on to', which sways, evoking thoughts of an ocean voyage. Downstairs the 'original atmosphere' is created by crudely painted bare white walls, acetylene lamps, which emit a smell of carbide, plank tables and crates covered in onion sacks for seating. All these rudimentary features for no good reason, we are told, 'add to the price'.

The Invitation

Being a nightclub, no formal invitation is required, just the wherewithal to pay the entry fee of 'twelve marks eighty', a sum high enough to ensure exclusivity. A doorman dressed in 'rustic sheepskin' vets potential guests as they arrive. For their own good he rejects 'certain Old City characters, for whom the Onion Cellar was too expensive in the first place.' The people who pass his means test are perhaps surprised to come across a sign inside reading 'Please pay later'. This shows that the club is 'not only expensive but also and nevertheless high class'.

The Guest List

The doorman is clearly good at his job and the club's clientele consists of 'businessmen, doctors, lawyers, artists, journalists, theatre and movie people, well-known figures from the sporting world, and officials in the provincial and municipal government'.

This 'cross section of the world which nowadays calls itself intellectual' come with their 'wives, mistresses, secretaries, interior decorators, and occasional male mistresses'. Some of the more bizarre patrons include Gerhard and Gudrun (a bearded woman and man with a hairless chin), and Fräulein Pioch and Herr Wollmer, prisoners of an S&M relationship, whose romance began when he trod on her toe and which can only flourish if he keeps inflicting the same injury on her.

'The owner in person welcomed every single guest with elaborate gestures and mobile, expressive eyebrows, as though initiating him into a secret rite.' Only on Mondays does Schmuh deign to admit a less affluent demographic, when he offers half price entry, which inevitably attracts the city's student population.

The Dress Code

The only formality regarding dress pertains to the host himself. Once the cellar is full ('half-full was regarded as full') Schmuh disappears into the washroom to re-emerge wearing a cobalt blue silk shawl printed with a pattern of golden-yellow onions. 'The Onion Cellar was not really "open" until Schmuh had put on his shawl.'

Food and Drink

For a nightclub the fare at the Onion Cellar is rather limited. 'But what about the bar? No bar. Waiter, the menu please! Neither waiter nor menu ... there was nothing whatever to eat, and anyone who wanted to eat had to go elsewhere, to the "Fischl", for instance.' The only foodstuff on offer at the Onion Cellar is raw onions.

Schmuh emerges wearing his 'special shawl', and is welcomed by the guests 'like the Saviour, like the legendary uncle from Australia!' He carries a basket containing onions, sharp knives and little chopping boards in the shape of pigs or fish. Eagerly seizing these ritual accessories the patrons begin 'to cut their onions smaller and smaller until the juice – what did the onion juice do? It did what the world and the sorrows of the world could not do: it brought forth a round, human tear.' And not just one tear: 'the weepers poured out their hearts to their neighbors on the uncomfortable, burlap-covered crates, submitted to questioning, let themselves be turned inside-out like overcoats'.

The Conversation

Earlier the conversation had been 'subdued, forced, dispirited ... a stifled remark about a botched career, a broken marriage'. But now, under the influence of the onions, everyone opens up. Suddenly they are able to 'talk from their hearts, their bowels,

their entrails, to forget about their brains just this once, to lay bare the raw unvarnished truth, the man within'.

Tears, it turns out, are not the only effect of the onion juice. 'Homo lacrimans tends to be more generous than his dry-eyed counterpart', a consequence happily appreciated by the club's washroom attendant. Perhaps this is why Schmuh invites his guests to pay at the end of the evening.

The washroom attendant further cashes in on the general largesse by selling souvenir merchandise: onion-print handkerchiefs inscribed with the legend 'In the Onion Cellar' which habitués could dab their eyes with, wear on their heads or make into pennants to hang in the rear windows of their cars.

But for any readers wishing to experiment with onion chopping at home, Günter Grass provides a word of sage advice via the guests who have tried it. 'It wasn't the same. You needed an audience. It was so much easier to cry in company.' The students get best value for money and it was on half-price Mondays that the 'most violent weeping was done'.

The Entertainment

Once the customers have dried their eyes the house band, the Rhine River Three, takes over to provide 'a musical transition to normal, everyday conversation'. This outfit consists of Egon Klepp on flute and clarinet; Scholle (we never find out his first name) on guitar and banjo; and the novel's narrator Oskar Matzerath on his eponymous tin drum. At the age of three Oskar decided that he didn't want to become an adult and deliberately threw himself down the stairs of the cellar in his family grocery store to stunt his growth. Obsessed with nurses and tin drums, he displayed an early vocal talent for shattering glass by screaming. During the war he played with a concert party consisting entirely of dwarves and later worked as a tombstone engraver. Now aged twenty-five he has risen to the aggravatingly tall height of 4 feet 1 inch and finds himself once more down in a cellar.

The Outcome

Onion chopping at Schmuh's is a highly risky business. To partake of two onions in quick succession rouses carnal desires and en masse chopping could result in a dangerous outbreak of passion.

One evening Schmuh's 'vivacious wife' Billy turns up accompanied by a music critic and an architect: 'Both of them were regular customers, but their sorrows were of the most boring variety'. Under the influence of the onion juice Billy reveals some embarrassing stories about her husband (Oskar tactfully declines to give us details), but Schmuh is so upset that he hands out a free round of onions to the customers. This overdose of potent juices leads to an outbreak of hysterical, convulsive weeping and suddenly 'a lady of ripe years tore off her blouse before the eyes of her son-in-law'. Another guest 'bared his swarthy torso' and in no time the 'orgy was underway'. Sadly Oskar's decorousness comes to the fore again: 'But despite the violence with which it began, it was a dull, uninspired affair, hardly worth describing in detail'. And he doesn't.

Schmuh calls for music to 'counteract the stirrings of lewdness', but Klepp and Scholle are too busy laughing at the guests' cross-dressing antics to oblige. So Oskar takes up his tin drum for a solo performance and regresses the guests to 'Auntie Kauer's kindergarten' by banging out a medley of nursery rhymes and children's ditties ('I drummed my way back, I drummed up the world as a three-year-old sees it.'). Everyone forms a conga line and Oskar leads them round the club Pied Piper style until finally 'All the ladies and gentlemen, Schmuh the host, even the far-off washroom attendant, all the little children wet themselves'.

This evening is a turning point in the Onion Cellar and now its patrons begin to spurn the traditional offering of onions and call for Oskar's drumming instead, preferring to wet their pants rather than their cheeks. With his livelihood in danger Schmuh fires the Rhine River Three; but under the threat of a mass boycott by his regulars, he has to rehire them and even give them a pay rise to 20 Deutschmarks each, enabling Oskar to start a savings account.

Not long afterwards Schmuh, who eschews chopping onions in favour of weeping over slain sparrows, shoots that unlucky thirteenth bird and ends up dead when a flock of its vengeful kindred descends on his car. Oskar quits the Onion Cellar, goes solo and becomes a drumming superstar. He makes records that sell 'like hotcakes', accrues a fortune and ends up in a madhouse.

The Legacy

The tale of little Oskar and his tin drum was Günter Grass's first novel and it launched him on a literary career which would later earn him a Nobel Prize. Perhaps in tribute to Schmuh's club Grass's autobiographical memoir published in 2006 is called *Peeling the Onion*.

As a club promoter, I have hosted recreations of the Onion Cellar on many occasions under the title 'Loss – An Evening of Exquisite Misery'. It's particularly popular on Valentine's Night.

II
The Chief of Police's Reception

LOCATION: MIRGOROD, LITTLE RUSSIA

HOST: PYOTR FYODOROVICH

DATE: 1812

From *The Tale of How Ivan Ivanovich*
Quarrelled with Ivan Nikiforovich (1835) by Nikolai Gogol

The Host

Pytor Fyodorovich is the chief of police in Mirgorod, a provincial town in Little Russia (modern day Ukraine). He is a retired Cossack soldier with a fondness for recounting stories of his military days when he saw service as a lieutenant in the 42nd Chasseur regiment during the Napoleonic War. He was injured in service, receiving a bullet in the left leg, which has left him with a limp so debilitating that a step with the bad leg nearly cancels the advance made with the other. Fortunately the disability poses little threat to his function as police chief. The name Mirgorod translates as 'peace city' and the town lives up to its etymological roots: there is 'neither criminality nor thuggery and so everyone hangs out whatever they like on their lines'. The only unsolved mystery of recent times is what has become of the missing ninth button on Pyotr Fyodorovich's uniform which was 'torn off during the procession for the consecration of the church two years previously'.

The Venue

Mirgorod can also be translated as 'world city', making it sound like one of those allegorical locations from *The Pilgrim's Progress*. Surprisingly it is a real town, which is today situated in the Poltava province of central Ukraine.

'Mirgorod is a wonderful town! It has all sorts of buildings,' the narrator proudly tells us, 'some with thatched roofs, some with rush roofs, some even with wooden ones. There's a street to the right and a street to the left.' The town's most imposing feature however is its courthouse, which has 'eight windows in a row' overlooking the town square. The square itself boasts 'an amazing puddle. One which is unique and you'll never see anywhere else. It takes up almost the whole of the square. A beautiful puddle.'

In his enthusiasm for the town's water features the narrator fails to tell us whether the chief of police's party is an At Home or whether it is held at the police station.

The Invitation

We also don't know how the guests are invited to the party, but it is 'an extremely important event for the whole of Mirgorod' and on the day itself there is a 'chaos of wheels and boxes' as carriages and *britzkas** descend on the chief of police's courtyard.

The Guest List

Being a resident of this small town, the narrator knows every guest by name and begins to list them all: Taras Tarasovich, Evpl

---

* A *britzka* is a long, four-wheeled, two-horse carriage, a sort of nineteenth-century mobile home. Isambard Kingdom Brunel lived and worked in one.

Akinfovich, Evtikhy Evtikhievich, Ivan Ivanovich (two of them: the Ivan Ivanovich of the title, and another Ivan Ivanovich who only has one eye). The list goes on, but thankfully writer's cramp sets in and we are spared the entire roll call.

The one local dignitary who is not at the party is Ivan Nikiforovich, who suspects that his neighbour and enemy Ivan Ivanovich (the one with two eyes) will be there and has vowed never to be in the same room as that 'ruffian'. Two years ago, the pair were inseparable friends, but that was before the hurling of the fatal insult 'goose' led to a serious falling-out. The quarrel is too frivolous to warrant a full description in a book about parties, but the highlights include: the failed barter of a dun sow for a rifle; the offensive insult already mentioned above; the construction of a goose house; the nocturnal sabotage of the said house; a petition in court; a counter petition in court; the theft of the second petition by the above-mentioned dun sow belonging to the first petitioner; the filing away of the various depositions in the Mirgorod courthouse; and finally a year, and another that pass without a resolution.

The Dress Code

The men are dressed in traditional Cossack attire of balloon trousers, nankeen coats and tunics. Ivan Ivanovich wears his much-admired *bekesh*, a short coat made of astrakhan. When describing the wardrobe of the lady guests the narrator grows a little hysterical: 'So many bonnets! So many dresses! Red, yellow, coffee, green, blue, new, turned, re-cut; shawls, ribbons, handbags.' So overwhelmed is he by this parade of female fashion from Little Russia he fears the spectacle may impair his eyesight.

The Conversation

'How they all talked, what a noise they raised' the narrator tells us, before admitting that he doesn't know what they talked about, but can only suppose that it must have been about 'pleasant and useful things, such as: the weather, dogs, wheat, hats and stallions'.

Another conversational topic is the absence from the party of Ivan Nikiforovich. Ivan Ivanovich (the one with the blind eye) proposes a plan to reconcile the two quarrelling neighbours. His proposal is enthusiastically accepted by the other guests and they unanimously elect Anton Prokofievich Golopuz to go and fetch Ivan Nikiforovich and bring him to the party. Not everyone's choice of negotiator for such a delicate mission perhaps (we are told he once swapped his house for a gold brocade tobacco pouch), and wearing trousers that tend to get him attacked by dogs, Anton Prokofievich nevertheless manages to achieve the desired objective.

The Food and Drink

'I won't try to describe the food,' the narrator says, but luckily he does. On the menu were *mnishki* (fried cottage cheese patties) with sour cream, borscht with tripe, turkey with plums and raisins, fish with horseradish and an unnamed dish resembling boots soaked in *kvass* (fermented rye drink). The old-world chef has prepared his swansong, 'a sauce served all enveloped in flame, which amused and at the same time frightened the ladies'. Eventually the narrator makes good on his earlier promise: 'I will not speak of these dishes, because I much prefer eating them to holding forth on them in conversation.'

The opulence of the fare means that both Ivan Ivanovich

and the newly arrived Ivan Nikiforovich are too busy eating to notice each other's presence. It's only in the process of placing discarded fishbones on his plate that Ivan Ivanovich glances across the table and meets the eyes of his adversary.

The Entertainment

In the absence of any formal entertainment, the attempted reconciliation takes centre stage and the guests bar the doors preventing any attempt at escape. The two Ivans are literally pushed together by the other partygoers (this we are told is the standard method of appeasing squabbles in Mirgorod). The strategy seems to bear fruit and after years of enmity the old friends appear to be on the point of reconciliation with Ivan Ivanovich even going as far as to admit that he cannot remember the origin of their disagreement. This admission unfortunately proves to be the fly in the ointment. At the mere mention of the G-word again 'everything went to the devil'. Ivan Ivanovich storms out and locks himself in his house, appearing in society again only to spend his ancestral roubles on a legion of pettifoggers who escalate the case of Ivan vs Ivan to the state court.

The Outcome

On a damp melancholy autumn day, some dozen years after the party, the narrator happens to pass through Mirgorod. He finds that several of the guests from that event have since passed away and that the two Ivans, now wrinkled, white-haired and unrecognizable, are still embroiled in litigation against each other. But both have good news for him: 'My case will be decided tomorrow without fail. The court says it's certain.' They have of course been told the same thing for the past ten years.

As his carriage trudges onwards through the provincial mud the narrator concludes with the famous observation: 'It's a dreary world, gentlemen.'

The Legacy

Those celebrated last words seemed to haunt Gogol's life, even though he enjoyed all the trappings of success. His early stories based on his childhood in the Ukraine brought him recognition, enabling him to move to St Petersburg. He was befriended by Russia's greatest writer, Pushkin (who provided the ideas for two of his most famous works), and became affluent enough to swan around Europe for twelve years where he studied art in Rome and patronized the opera. Yet he still managed to have a pretty miserable death. Faced with great pressure to follow up his novel *Dead Souls* he fell under the influence of a spiritual elder, Matvey Konstantinovsky, who persuaded him that writing fiction was sinful. Gogol burnt his manuscript of the second part of *Dead Souls* and eventually starved himself to death in a religious frenzy at the age of forty-two.

12

The Beverly Hills Party

LOCATION: LOS ANGELES, CALIFORNIA

HOSTS: ELAINE AND ROSS CONTI

DATE: 1980S

From *Hollywood Wives* (1983) by Jackie Collins

The Invitation

In Hollywood physical party invitations are superfluous: word of mouth amongst the 'right' people is the best guarantee of attendance and 'If the people weren't right then you may as well not bother'. Society hostess, gossip and former Parisian hooker Bibi Sutton is the conduit via whom such invitations are disseminated; provided you are important enough for her to return your calls in the first place.

The Hosts

Ross Conti is an ageing and faded movie star and 'first class shit', whose one remaining attribute is his legendary schlong. Elaine Conti is an upwardly mobile shoplifter from the Bronx (née Etta Grodinski, aka Etta the Elephant), who has risen via plastic surgery to become one of the Hollywood Wives of the title.

The Contis reckon that the only way to resurrect Ross's career is for him to land the starring role in *Street People*, a film in development which is tipped to be the next blockbuster. They plan to achieve this by throwing a lavish party to which they will invite the movie industry elite (despite Ross being so cash-strapped that he can't even afford to pay off a photographer who is blackmailing him).

Initially rebuffed by Bibi Sutton, Elaine sagely reminds herself that the 'worse star-fucks were the stars themselves' and enlists her best friend's father, the Hollywood legend George Lancaster, to be the party's honorary host. The gambit pays off. Her subsequent call to Miss Sutton is returned within eleven minutes and the party quickly becomes the talk of the town with everyone (including *Street People*'s production team) begging for an invite. Elaine's masseur even initiates an affair with her to get himself on the guest list.

The Guest List

The hostess's other guiding principle in organizing the party is 'the very rich are only really comfortable with the very rich' and so she ensures that no poor people are invited (masseur excepted).

The guest list includes most of the cast of the novel, with a generous smattering of the real life Hollywood 'A' List, including James Caan, Elliott Gould, Liza Minnelli, Richard Gere, Ann-Margret, Clint Eastwood, Dyan Cannon, Burt Reynolds, Warren Beatty and Jack Nicholson. Some guests are recorded as arriving with their spouses (Michael and Shakira Caine, Rod Stewart with his 'striking wife' Alana). Other celebrities are referred to in the plural ('The Sean Connerys', 'The Roger Moores'). Perhaps this is the Hollywood equivalent of the Royal We; or maybe Jackie Collins's researcher didn't get round to checking who the movie stars in question were currently married to.

The Venue

'The House of Conti' is a 'six bedroomed, seven bathroomed, goddamn Beverly Hills palace' with a mosaic-tiled swimming pool, immaculately manicured lawns and an encampment of paparazzi at the bottom of the drive. Arriving guests are greeted by 'female and male valets wearing white T-shirts' emblazoned with 'Superjock'.*

The party is a product placement paradise: guests arrive in Cadillacs, Lincolns, DeLoreans, Rolls-Royces, Porsches, Ferraris, Bentleys and Excaliburs. The glassware is Baccarat, the napkins are Porthault and the vases are Waterford.

The centrepiece of the evening is a sit-down dinner for 240 held in a specially erected marquee on the patio. We are told that 'Elaine had spent hours poring over the guest list deciding where to seat everyone'. Hardly surprising. This is a Jackie Collins novel, which means almost everyone is having an affair with just about everyone else, and so the probability of not managing to sit at least one pair of covert lovers next to each other would be tiny.

The Dress Code

The hostess's party preparations are hampered by her being arrested for shoplifting on the morning of the do and spending the afternoon in the custody of store detectives rather than with her hairdresser and manicurist. But this is nothing that popping a couple of pills and slipping into a seventeen-hundred-dollar Galanos frock can't fix.

---

* Superjock was a toy brand of the 1970s, a range of plastic sports figures which would kick a football/hit a baseball when their heads were pressed. The valets are presumably just as obliging, cheap and disposable.

The party is a paean to the 'Groomed, and plasticized' Beverly Hills look. Outfits on display include gold lamé harem pyjamas; snakeskin cowboy boots; white silk jodhpurs tucked into knee-length boots with a white silk blouse and leather vest fringed with Indian beads; and a velvet suit with a ruffled shirt and embroidered evening slippers.

The Food and Drink

This being Hollywood the guests are more interested in gossip than food. The author gives us plenty of details about the sexual orientation of the chefs, Sergio and Eugenio, but very little of the canapés they prepare. We know guacamole is involved somehow. The guests' beverage of choice seems to be Valium washed down with Pernod.

The Entertainment

At 8 p.m. the Zancussi Trio strike up with a selection of cheesy Italian love songs, closing with a rendition of the theme from *The Godfather*.

They are followed by Ric and Phil, two ex-rock stars in tight jeans, who after the failure of their recording career are now reduced to peddling their live disco show round society parties. They spin Donna Summer and Kool & the Gang hits and the guests willingly oblige with the request to 'Get Down On It'. These days it would have a certain ironic retro chic. Back then it would have been just horrible.

Sammy Cahn, the lyricist of 'Three Coins in the Fountain' and 'Come Fly with Me', is present and, we are told, has promised to sing one of his famous parodies on George Lancaster. But, like the rest of the impressive array of real life Hollywood talent

on display at the party, he has a non-speaking role. Guests talk to the celebs, but they never reply. Perhaps they are too grand; or more likely it is just an authorial device to avoid libel actions. As a result we never get to hear what the wordsmith who penned the immortal lines 'In llama land there's a one-man band and he'll toot his flute for you' might have crafted for the occasion.

The Conversation

Thankfully we are permitted to eavesdrop on the conversations of the lesser guests and the Beverly Hills bons mots are gloriously snide and graphic:

'Go sleep with your ego.'

'She's like a Barbie doll – you wind her up and she buys new clothes.'

'The biggest prick I knew had the smallest!'

'If it cost him a nickel to shit he'd vomit.'

'Every day she comes to my office, locks the door, gets under the desk and sucks my cock.'

Or the ubiquitous put-down at Hollywood soirées: 'Don't get dramatic on me. Keep it for the cameras.'

The Outcome

Superficially the occasion is a great success. 'Hollywood was basically an early town, and past twelve was late.' The last guests don't depart until five past two: tardy for stars who have to be on filmsets or at sessions with personal trainers at the crack of dawn.

But the Contis' hard work is for nothing. Ross's dreams of landing the coveted role in *Street People* are scuppered when the guest of honour, George Lancaster, announces that *he* has been awarded the part. If Ross expects to gain any sympathy from his wife for having bankrupted himself by hosting the bash, it is not to be. She boots him out of the house, having earlier in the day discovered that he is having an affair with her best friend.

Worst of all, the guests who make the headlines the next day are the two who failed to show up. Neil Gray, the director of *Street People*, and Gina Germaine, actress and 'America's Second Top Blonde' were engaged in a ménage à trois with a bogus Eurasian geisha. Neil's sexual exertions (he climaxes 'Thick, salty spurts of life's essence' Ms Collins tells us in an early bid for the Bad Sex Award) cause him to have a heart attack; Gina simultaneously undergoes severe vaginal contractions and they are rushed to the Emergency Room locked together in an inseparable coitus.

Altogether just another day in Tinseltown.

The Legacy

Hollywood Wives became Jackie Collins's most successful novel. Marketed as a 'scandalous exposé' of Tinseltown, it reached number one in the *New York Times* Best Seller list. The following twenty years saw the publication of various spin-off books including *Hollywood Husbands*, *Hollywood Kids*, *Hollywood Wives: The New Generation* and *Hollywood Divorces*. One can only hope that *Hollywood Dogs* is in the pipeline.

13

Bilbo Baggins's Eleventy-First Birthday Party

LOCATION: BAG END, HOBBITON,
THE SHIRE, MIDDLE-EARTH
HOST: BILBO BAGGINS
DATE: THURSDAY, 22 SEPTEMBER 1401 (SHIRE
RECKONING) OR YEAR 3001 OF THE THIRD AGE
(ACCORDING TO THE RECKONING OF
THE ELVES AND THE DÚNEDAIN)

From *The Fellowship of the Ring* (1954)
by J. R. R. Tolkien

The Invitation

'When Mr Bilbo Baggins of Bag End announced that he would shortly be celebrating his eleventy-first birthday with a party of special magnificence, there was much talk and excitement in Hobbiton.'

To receive one of Bilbo's invitations, written in gold ink, would have been the ultimate status symbol among the local hobbitry, if it weren't for the fact that just about everyone who lived in the area had been sent one. So in the event it just means that 'the Hobbiton post-office was blocked, and the Bywater post-office was snowed under, and voluntary assistant postmen were called for'.

The Host

Hobbits (aka halflings) are 'an unobtrusive but very ancient people' whose height ranges between two feet and four feet. They are 'quick of hearing and sharp of eye', beardless and 'inclined to be fat'.

Bilbo Baggins is the most famous hobbit in the Shire, the small province of north-west Middle-Earth where the species dwells, mainly because he is one of the very few ever to have left the place. Some sixty years earlier he had embarked on an adventure which involved dwarves, trolls, wizards and a dragon, as a result of which he is still regarded as eccentric, if not plain mad, by his fellow hobbits.

Contrary to expectations at the time, he returned from his trip and has now reached the ripe old age of eleventy-one (III) in remarkably fine fettle. His powers of preservation he owes to the effects of a magic ring which he had brought back from the Misty Mountains.

Bilbo's co-host is his nephew and heir Frodo Baggins, who shares his birthday. Frodo is turning thirty-three, which is when a hobbit traditionally comes of age.

The Venue

Hobbits of old lived in holes in the ground, but these days it is a custom maintained only by the poorest and the richest of the breed. Bilbo belongs to the latter category and Bag End, built by his father, Bungo Baggins, is 'the most luxurious hobbit hole ... that was to be found either under the Hill or over the Hill or across the Water'. It has bedrooms, bathrooms, larders, cellars and a study, with 'panelled walls, and floors tiled and carpeted'. Rumour among the regulars at the Ivy Bush inn on the Bywater

Road holds that the Baggins residence is 'full of tunnels packed with chests of gold and silver, and jools'. However, they still hold that 'Bag End's a queer place, and its folk are queerer'.

For the occasion of Bilbo and Frodo's birthday celebrations tents have been erected in an adjoining field. The main pavilion is so large that an entire tree can fit right inside it.

The Guest List

The guest list includes representatives of all the families in the Shire: the Bagginses, Boffins, Tooks, Brandybucks, Grubbs, Chubbs, Burrowses, Hornblowers, Bolgers, Bracegirdles, Good-bodies, Bockhouses and Proudfoots.

As we have already heard 'Practically everybody living near was invited. A very few were overlooked by accident, but as they turned up all the same, that did not matter.' Even Otho and Lobelia Sackville-Baggins, Bilbo's relatives and would-be heirs, with whom he shares a mutual antipathy, are on the guest list. 'Many people from other parts of the Shire were also asked; and there were even a few from outside the borders.' The most out-landish of these being Gandalf, a weirdo wandering wizard.

Guests are not required to bring presents, as hobbit trad-ition dictates that it is the duty of the person celebrating their birthday to give gifts to everyone else. So any hobbit with a decent social profile could hope to receive a present from some-one else at least once a week.

This custom had led to the coining of the term 'mathom', which denotes 'anything that Hobbits had no immediate use for but were unwilling to throw away'. Mathoms would frequently be unwanted gifts which had been recycled and handed on from person to person until they 'had circulated all round the district'.

Arriving guests are met by Bilbo at his new white gate where he hands them their presents in person. Some hobbits are so excited by the quality of the produce on offer (which includes exquisite dwarf-made toys all the way from the Lonely Mountain) that they sneak out by a back way and return to join the receiving line a second time.

The Dress Code

We are not told if there were any sartorial rules for the occasion, but hobbits usually 'dressed in bright colours, being notably fond of yellow and green'. Plus 'they seldom wore shoes, since their feet had tough leathery soles and were clad in a thick curling hair, much like the hair of their heads'. Bilbo himself is resplendent at the occasion in an embroidered silk waistcoat with golden buttons.

The Food and Drink

Hobbits were 'fond of … six meals a day (when they could get them)' and so in order to lay on adequate provender for his guests 'Bilbo's catering had depleted the stocks of most stores, cellars and warehouses for miles around'. At the party there 'were three official meals: lunch, tea and dinner (or supper)', but in fact guests were 'eating and drinking – continuously from elevenses until six-thirty, when the fireworks started.'

Amid the general gluttony Bilbo hosts a private dinner for friends and family in the pavilion. Invitations to this are restricted to a gross of guests (a gross being 144, which equates to the combined total of Bilbo and Frodo's ages). The Sackville-Bagginses take offence, 'feeling sure they had only been asked to fill up the required number, like goods in a package.'

The Conversation

The hobbits seemingly apply themselves too diligently to eating and drinking to find any other use for their mouths.

The Entertainment

The main feature on the entertainments programme is a firework display, courtesy of Gandalf, whose dwarf-candles, elf-fountains and goblin-barkers burst into representations of birds and butterflies, forests and mountains, with the finale being a 'terribly life-like' red-golden fire-breathing dragon which swoops down over the terrified hobbits before exploding.

After dinner an impromptu orchestra strikes up 'a merry dance-tune', playing musical instruments that came out of crackers bearing the stamp of Dale, the lakeside town far away beyond the Misty Mountains. These include trumpets, horns, pipes and flutes: 'small, but of perfect make and enchanting tones'. Master Everard Took and Miss Melilot Brandybuck take to the floor in the Springle-ring: 'a pretty dance, but rather vigorous'.

The least eagerly anticipated part of the evening's entertainment is Bilbo's speech of thanks. 'They rather dreaded the after-dinner speech of their host (an inevitable item). He was liable to drag in bits of what he called poetry'. Bilbo sensibly waits until his guests are well refreshed, and by the time he gets to his furry feet 'Most of the company were, however, now in a tolerant mood, at that delightful stage which they called "filling up the corners" ... They were prepared to listen to anything, and to cheer at every full stop.'

Though the speech starts well with 'the sort of stuff they liked: short and obvious', before long, just as his audience feared,

Bilbo starts to 'allude to the absurd adventures of his mysterious journey'. As he reminisces about his 'arrival by barrel in Esgaroth on the Long Lake' on his fifty-first birthday his listeners ask themselves (as we all have at formal dinners) 'Why couldn't he stop talking and let them drink his health?'

The Outcome

Bilbo's speech finishes more quickly than any of the guests could have hoped. He abruptly announces that he is leaving, there is a blinding flash of light and Bilbo vanishes and 'was never seen by any hobbit in Hobbiton again'.

Once the hobbits' befuddlement has died down it 'was generally agreed that the joke was in very bad taste, and more food and drink were needed to cure the guests of shock and annoyance'. But at least the stunt has the effect of kickstarting the hitherto absent conversation, which now centres on 'Bilbo Baggins's oddities, past and present'. In fact his disappearance has 'given the whole Shire something to talk about for nine days, or ninety-nine more likely'.

By and large the guests are content to see the back of him, especially as he 'hasn't taken the vittles with him', and they guzzle on merrily into the evening. Carriages arrive at midnight for the important folk. 'Gardeners came by arrangement, and removed in wheelbarrows those that had inadvertently remained behind.'

The next day many of the guests descend once again on Bag End, in search of more food and Bilbo's legendary gold. Various gifts of an everyday nature have been left for them, but there is no sign of any of the loot. Lobelia Sackville-Baggins, furious at receiving only a case of silver spoons instead of Bilbo's entire estate as she had been hoping, leaves, 'driving a pony-trap towards Bywater with a face that would have curdled new milk'.

Frodo gets the only bit of genuine treasure that is handed out: Bilbo's magic golden ring. This ring confers invisibility on anyone who puts it on their finger and had enabled Bilbo to pull off his spectacular exit from the party (with a little help from Gandalf's pyrotechnics).

Though hardly a mathom, the ring has a history of being passed on to people as a present. Its previous owner, Sméagol (aka Gollum), had requested it as his birthday present from his cousin Déagol 538 years earlier and then strangled him when he refused to hand it over. Bilbo in his turn had stumbled across the ring in an underground cave, but had always claimed that Gollum had given it to him as a gift. Gollum begged to differ with this version of events and embarked on a seventy-eight-year quest to get it back (the ring confers great longevity on its bearers).

Of course it turns out that this is no common gewgaw, but a Ring of Doom; and is something Frodo might have happily passed on to the Sackville-Bagginses had he known all the aggro and bother it would cause him over the next thousand pages or so of the trilogy.

The Legacy

Inspired by a phrase that Professor Tolkien scribbled on a blank page in a student's exam book that he was marking – 'In a hole in the ground there lived a hobbit' – came the trilogy of novels which still, to the enduring frustration and fury of the literary establishment, wins just about every poll of the greatest book ever written. *The Lord of the Rings* pretty much founded the fantasy literature genre and has sold over 150 million copies worldwide. One wonders if Professor Tolkien's books would have been quite so popular if he hadn't had a weird name, like one of the characters from his own stories, but had been called something dull instead, like his friend and fellow Oxford don and writer Clive Lewis (better known as C. S. Lewis).

14
The Ponteleone Ball

LOCATION: PALAZZO PONTELEONE, PALERMO, SICILY
HOSTS: DON DIEGO AND DONNA
MARGHERITA PONTELEONE
DATE: NOVEMBER 1862

From *The Leopard* (1958)
by Giuseppe Tomasi di Lampedusa

The Hosts

Don Diego and Donna Margherita Ponteleone are an elderly couple, representatives of the ruling class of Sicily. Their party (in the metaphorical sense) had been spoilt by the arrival two years earlier of Giuseppe Garibaldi and his Redshirts on their campaign to reunify Italy and overthrow the old social order. Their invasion of Sicily had put an end to Spanish rule on the island under the Bourbon family.

White-haired and patchy, Don Diego symbolizes the precarious state of their class, 'saved from looking plebeian only by his caustic eyes'. His wife offers no greater hope, 'between coruscating tiara and triple rows of emeralds, the hooked features of an old priest'.

The Invitation

After two years of keeping a low profile, Palermo's landed gentry have re-emerged with a tour de force of revelry: a social whirl of 'various, yet identical parties'. The Ponteleones' 'gleaming invitation card' has been sent out to 'the few hundred people who made up "the world" … and never tired of meeting each other to exchange congratulations on still existing'.

The Venue

'The Ponteleone ball was to be one of the most important of that short season' and the hosts' palace is a suitably splendid setting. Its golden ballroom is 'a jewel-case' with smoothed-on cornices, stippled-on door frames, chandeliers and panels with knots of rococo flowers. The dining room is equally opulent with a long table 'lit by the famous twelve silver-gilt candelabra given to Diego's grandfather by the Court of Madrid at the end of his embassy in Spain', evidence of a past collaboration with the old ruling masters.

'The Sicilians never want to improve for the simple reason that they think themselves perfect.' This perhaps explains why the decor of Palazzo Ponteleone has remained untouched since the time of Queen Maria Carolina seventy years before. Painted gods smile down on the guests from a mural on the ceiling. 'They thought themselves eternal; but a bomb manufactured in Pittsburgh, Penn., was to prove the contrary in 1943.'[*]

The Guest List

We view the party through the eyes of the hero of the novel: Don Fabrizio Corbera, Prince of Salina and the eponymous Leopard – an amateur astronomer and womanizer with a death fixation. Aged somewhere in his late forties, he is the epitome

---

[*] The author's family palace had met a similar fate at the hands of the Allies in the Second World War.

of that 'unlucky generation, swung between the old world and the new'. Or as he puts it elsewhere: 'we were the Leopards and the Lions; those who'll take our place will be little jackals, hyenas'.

Representing the jackal and hyena contingent at the party is Don Calogero Sedàra, the mayor of the provincial town of Donnafugata – a prosperous self-made businessman and budding property tycoon. Initially he is not on the guest list until Don Fabrizio gets his wife to have a discreet word with the hosts to obtain an invitation for Calogero and his daughter, even though they did not feature on the Ponteleones' social radar ('no one knew them'.).

Having secured Calogero's attendance at the ball Don Fabrizio has to get there early, just in case the parvenu mayor is gauche enough to actually turn up at the time specified on the invitation ('they don't know yet, poor things').

Don Calogero returns the compliment by viewing his blue-blooded fellow guests as 'sheep-like creatures, who existed merely in order to give up their wool to his shears and their names and incomprehensible prestige to his daughter'. Sure enough his seventeen-year-old offspring Angelica – 'a voluptuous maiden' with a mass of raven hair, strawberry lips and emerald eyes – is engaged to be married to Tancredi Falconeri, the gadabout nephew of Don Fabrizio.

Far from trying to oust the old order, Don Calogero is quietly sucking up to them and has engaged heraldologists to delve into his family tree and concoct an aristocratic title for his daughter. 'Baronessina Sedàra del Biscotto' ('biscotto' means biscuit in Italian) is the best they can cook up. Calogero has even begun to grasp society mores sufficiently to arrive fashionably late at the ball.

The guest of honour of the evening is the only real-life

character in the novel, Colonel Pallavicino, the commander of the Italian army division which had defeated Garibaldi's troops at the Battle of Aspromonte in August of that year.

The Dress Code

Frocks are commissioned from Naples as the female guests prepare for the ball with 'an hysterical coming and going of milliners, hairdressers and shoemakers'.

The fashion style on the evening is set by Colonel Palla-vicino, who arrives 'amid a tinkle of epaulettes, chains and spurs in his well-padded, double-breasted uniform, a plumed hat under his arm and his left wrist propped on a curved sabre'.

Angelica Sedàra is in pink crinoline with long kid gloves, satin slippers and 'intentionally modest pearls.' Her father, 'a rat escorting a rose', has been discreetly taken to the tailors for a fitting (after his tailcoat at a previous party had been a 'disastrous failure'), and 'though his clothes had no elegance this time they were at least decent'.

Despite their extravagant toilettes the women at the party do not meet with Don Fabrizio's approval. 'Two or three among the older ones had been his mistresses' and, seeing them twenty years on, he is 'annoyed at the thought of having thrown away his best years in chasing (and catching) such slatterns'. As for the younger women, he finds them too inbred to be presentable and the 'three or four lovely creatures' in the room are like 'swans over a frog-filled pool'. Later he extrapolates his zoological analogy and imagines the women as monkeys swinging from the chandeliers by their tails.

The male guests fare little better in his world-weary eyes. In their black clothes they look like 'crows veering to and fro above lost valleys in search of putrid prey'. As for his own evening dress, Fabrizio gloomily imagines himself being laid out in his coffin wearing it.

The Conversation

Colonel Pallavicino regales anyone who will listen with the story of his triumph at the Battle of Aspromonte and how he shot Garibaldi in the foot. In reality the battle was not much of a contest, as Garibaldi, mindful of the fact that his mission was to unify the Italian peninsula, refused to allow his troops to fight their fellow countrymen.

The nouveau riche Don Calogero's 'quick eyes were moving over the room, insensible to its charm, intent on its monetary value' and his conversational repertoire is restricted to discussing recent fluctuations in the price of cheese and wheat.

The Entertainment

Polkas, mazurkas and waltzes are danced to an orchestra in the ballroom. Tancredi has engaged Angelica for every dance and they provide 'the most moving sight there, two young people in love'. The Palermitans, we learn, are particularly responsive 'to the appeal of beauty and the prestige of money'. Angelica has both the qualities required to fit this particular bill: 'so lovely an amphora brimming with coin'. 'No Tancredi could have resisted that beauty united to that income.' Tancredi (though 'a perfect sieve with money') has brought the aristocratic pedigree to their union.

Don Fabrizio views the happy couple with his usual sepulchral cynicism. Love is, in his opinion, 'Flames for a year, ashes for thirty.' The young dancers are just 'ephemeral beings out to enjoy the tiny ray of light granted them between two

shades, before the cradle, after the last spasms', poor wretches condemned to die, cattle on their way to the slaughterhouse.

Thankfully Fabrizio is self-aware enough to realize what a downer these sentiments would be for the general party mood and so, after dancing a mazurka with Angelica, he politely declines the young couple's invitation for him to join them at dinner.

The Food and Drink

It takes an Italian writer to give us a proper description of the food and Tomasi di Lampedusa, like Petronius before him, does not disappoint. The Ponteleones serve 'coraline lobsters boiled alive, waxy *chaud-froids* of veal, steely-lined fish immersed in sauce, turkeys gilded by the ovens' heat, rosy *foie-gras* under gelatine armour, boned woodcocks reclining on amber toast decorated with their own chopped guts, dawn tinted galantine, and a dozen other cruel, coloured delights.' The Sicilian national dish of macaroni, otherwise omnipresent in the novel, does not appear to have made it onto the menu.

The desserts merit a paragraph of their own. Signature Sicilian dishes include 'Triumphs of Gluttony' and 'Virgin's Cakes' shaped like breasts ('Saint Agatha's sliced-off teats sold by convents, devoured at dances!'). Don Fabrizio wonders how these puddings, which suggest at least two deadly sins, have managed to escape prohibition by the Holy Office.

In recognition of the Roman-style opulence of the feast the hosts have even provided 'twenty vast vats' in a 'disordered little room near the band alcove' which seem to be for guests to throw up into.

The Outcome

The ball goes on till six in the morning. Everyone wishes they'd gone home three hours earlier, but it would have been an insult to the host and hostess 'who had taken such a lot of trouble, poor dears.'

Don Calogero crashes out in an armchair before the end, his trousers rucked up revealing his underwear. Don Fabrizio decides to walk home alone so he can take in a few more emblems of death before bedtime. Sure enough he comes across a wagonload of bulls fresh from the slaughterhouse. Only the stars and planets in the night sky give him comfort. He looks up at Venus, his companion on his early morning shooting outings. 'When would she decide to give him an appointment less ephemeral, far from stumps and blood, in her own region of perennial certitude?' he wonders. The next chapter in the book is entitled 'The Death of a Prince' and set twenty-one years later, so we can only imagine how depressingly morbid he must have become in the long wait for his own final end.

The Legacy

'If we want things to stay as they are, things will have to change,' Tancredi Falconeri says in *The Leopard*'s most enigmatic quote. The convenient compromise between the old and new orders achieved by Garibaldi still seems to have been in force in mid-twentieth-century Italy, where Giuseppe Tomasi di Lampedusa, the author of *The Leopard*, could rejoice in the title of Duke of Palma and Prince of Lampedusa.

Tomasi di Lampedusa didn't get round to starting work on his only novel until he was in his late fifties. The constant musings on mortality by his hero and alter-ego Don Fabrizio become clear when we realize that the author himself died in 1957 shortly after completing the book. At the time he had only a couple of rejection letters from Italy's leading publishing houses to show for his work. The novel, published a year later, was hailed as a classic by the likes of E. M. Forster and L. P. Hartley, and won the Strega Prize, Italy's most prestigious literary award, in 1959.

15

The Symposium

LOCATION: ATHENS

HOST: AGATHON

DATE: JANUARY—FEBRUARY 415 OR 416 BC

From *The Symposium* (*c*. 385–380 BC) by Plato

The Invitation

This party was supposedly a real historical event, but our invitation to it is at several steps' remove. Plato would have been only about eight years old when it took place, so the story is recounted through a narrator, Apollodorus, who in turn was told about it by Aristodemus, who was present at the party.* He wasn't actually invited but just tagged along with Socrates, on the grounds that 'good men come uninvited to lesser men's feasts'.

Plato offers apologies for any inaccuracies in his account which might be due to lapses in his narrators' memories. This distancing device recalls one of his most famous allegories: that human beings are like prisoners chained up in a cave and perceiving the reality of the outside world as flickering shadows cast on the wall.

---

* If you factor in the fact that this is my take on Tom Griffith's translation of Plato's text, then what you're reading here is a fifth-hand account of the actual party.

The Host

Remembered as a man of remarkable beauty and noted effeminacy, Agathon was a celebrated writer of tragedies in Ancient Greece. His ultimate tragedy was that his plays have been lost to posterity and only about forty lines of his total writings have survived. Today he is mainly remembered for being the host of this symposium, which he held to celebrate his first victory at the Lenaean festival. This annual festivity honoured Dionysus, the god of wine. It featured sacrifices of bulls, drinking (naturally) and five days of dramatic performances, after which prizes were given for the best plays (to win one was the Hellenic equivalent of getting an Oscar).

The Guest List

Men and women socialized separately in Ancient Greece (judging by the ribald scenes depicted on pottery of the time this was probably a wise move). So Agathon's guest list is entirely male and features several Athenian celebrities of the day. It includes:

ARISTODEMUS – the narrator, who hails from Cydathenaeum. Plato tells us he is a 'small man, never wears shoes'.

PHAEDRUS, son of Pythocles. He appears in other Platonic Dialogues including the eponymous *Phaedrus*, where his chief characteristic is his ardent interest in erotic oratory.

PAUSANIAS – Agathon's lover.

ERYXIMACHUS – a doctor. The historian Xenophon described him as an authority on diet.

ARISTOPHANES – the poet and comic playwright. He had lampooned Socrates in his play *The Clouds* seven years previously, yet the two of them appear to be on friendly terms at this gathering.

SOCRATES — one of the founders of Western philosophical thought. He was a wandering teacher who refused to take payment for his lessons. A rationalist, yet highly eccentric, he is here described as being impervious to the effects of cold or alcohol.

Several other guests are present, but unfortunately Aristodemus doesn't give us their names and couldn't remember anything about their contribution to the evening, so they miss their shot at immortality.

The Venue

Agathon's house in Athens. In the fifth century BC, symposia were a regular feature of Athenian nightlife. Well-appointed houses were equipped with a special room called an *andron*, which often had a mosaic floor and walls decorated with erotic frescoes, where men could spend the evening drinking and talking. Guests would recline on *klinai* (couches) arranged around the perimeter of the room in the shape of a square. Two guests shared each couch, from which they would eat off small three-legged tables.

The Dress Code

'Agathon always looks elegant' so his guests feel certain sartorial obligations. Even Socrates, when he finally arrives (having gone to the wrong house), is 'all washed and brushed, and wearing shoes (a thing he hardly ever did).'

The Food and Drink

To the modern reader a symposium suggests a gathering of professors reading dry academic papers to each other, but in Plato's time it meant a booze-up (the Greek word literally means 'drink together'). On this occasion, however, Agathon's guests are feeling a little fragile after a big session the night before. 'Whatever else we do, we don't want to let ourselves in for another evening's hard drinking', Aristophanes advises the others. Eryximachus further warns them that 'getting drunk is bad for you'. Being a doctor he naturally draws their attention to the fact that they have exceeded their alcohol units for the week.

Dinner is served, but Plato is too keen to get on to the hard-core rhetoric to bother giving us any details of the fare.

The Entertainment

A flute girl in attendance is dismissed by Eryximachus to ensure there is no female intrusion on this male gathering: 'She can play to herself, or to the women upstairs,' he suggests.

The Conversation

The modern reader might wonder if a bunch of men who had carefully arranged for their womenfolk to be absent might not have booked some strippers or were intending to sing a few bawdy songs. But this company is looking forward to nothing more debauched than an evening of conversation and philosophy.

Just to show they're not totally without hormones, Eryximachus, who seems to have been appointed the *symposiarch* (the master of ceremonies) for the evening, decides that the topic for debate should be love. Each guest, going round the room anticlockwise, will be required to make a speech in praise of Eros, the Greek god of love. The guests unanimously accept this proposal, with Socrates adding, 'I'm certainly not going to refuse, since love is the only thing I ever claim to know anything about.'

First up is Phaedrus, who puts forward a notion that armies should be made up of pairs of gay lovers, on the grounds that they would fight bravely and be prepared to die for each other. Considering that homophobia is still an issue in today's armed forces, this was obviously an idea well ahead of its time.

Next to speak is Pausanias, Phaedrus's lover. He argues that Eros is divided into two separate gods: common Eros, who symbolizes carnal desires, including man's love for women; and heavenly Eros who represents the only pure form of love: that between men and boys. According to him it's OK for boys to sexually gratify their lovers as long as it's done in a quest for self-improvement.

Aristophanes has hiccups, so Eryximachus gives the next speech. He waffles on about how love has the ability to unite opposites and that medicine, sport, agriculture, cooking and music are all governed by the laws of Eros.

Aristophanes then takes his turn and tells us that there were originally three sexes: male, female and hermaphrodite, and humans had four arms, four legs and two faces. After a rebellion against the gods Zeus split each person in half to form two separate beings. This explains our quest for love, as we are all looking for our lost other halves to complete us.

The host Agathon speaks next and says that Eros is the youngest of the gods. He is also the most sensitive, as he abides in the most tender parts of our bodies, but at the same time he is stronger even than Ares, the god of war (who fell in love with Aphrodite, thus succumbing to Eros). Eros calms arguments between the gods, brings humans together and is the source of all our good and positive qualities. Agathon declaims this bunch of platitudes in a high rhetorical style, which earns him a round of applause from his guests.

Socrates is the final speaker and he uses semantic sleight of hand to prove that Eros is neither good nor beautiful. He then relays some teachings from the prophetess Diotima, his instructress in erotica. In a nutshell: we all begin with physical love and aspire eventually to the love of beauty itself; and it is only through love, physical or spiritual, that we can achieve immortality, via our offspring or our ideas.

The Outcome

Before the speeches can be properly debated, there is a commotion in the courtyard. Alcibiades, a young handsome playboy politician, wearing 'a luxuriant garland of ivy and violets', has turned up drunk with a group of companions. He is welcomed in and joins Agathon and Socrates on their couch. Appalled by the general sobriety, he appoints himself master of ceremonies and makes the guests drink several forfeits in the form of an ice bucket of wine.

He is called on to give a speech but, too drunk to remember that he is supposed to be talking about Eros, he delivers a eulogy on Socrates instead. He tells us how he failed to bed the great man and warns Agathon, whom he suspects of also having designs in that direction, that the same will happen with him. Socrates would have been in his mid-fifties at the time of this party and according to contemporary sources he was strikingly ugly. His pulling power with dishy young men was apparently down to his ability to discourse. 'When I hear him, it's like the worst kind of religious hysteria', Alcibiades gushes. 'My heart pounds, and I find myself in floods of tears'.

Soon Agathon and Alcibiades are squabbling over who gets to sit next to Socrates, acting more like a couple of six-year-olds than a pair of noted Athenian intellectuals.

Another band of drunken gatecrashers arrives to further lower the academic tone of the evening. Some of the guests leave and the remainder succumb one by one to the drink and drop off to sleep. By dawn Socrates is the last man standing, so he heads off to the Lyceum and then takes a bath.

The Legacy

Socrates didn't write any of his teachings down and so most of our knowledge of him is based on the works of his students, of whom Plato was one. Socrates appears as a character in all but one of Plato's *Dialogues*.

Despite the indifference he shows here to the charms of handsome youths, Socrates was nevertheless put on trial for 'impiety and corrupting the minds of the young' in 399 BC. He was found guilty and sentenced to commit suicide. Like with Petronius (see chapter 1), a few friends dropped round to watch him take the lethal dose of hemlock — a solemn affair commemorated by Plato in his dialogue *Phaedo*.

Plato is perhaps best remembered these days in the term 'platonic love', but, as we see from Socrates' speech, he didn't rule out a bit of rumpy-pumpy on the path to enlightenment.

16

The Marquise de Saint-Euverte's Musical Soirée

LOCATION: FAUBOURG SAINT-GERMAIN, PARIS

HOSTESS: MADAME LA MARQUISE
DE SAINT-EUVERTE

DATE: EARLY 1880S

From *Swann's Way* (1913) by Marcel Proust
from *In Search of Lost Time*

The Invitation

Wealthy art collector, man about town, friend to the Prince of Wales and member of Paris's exclusive Jockey Club, Charles Swann is yet another one of those literary heroes who doesn't have a job. Once a great socialite he has of late become something of a recluse, occupying himself with an obsessive, miserable, jealousy-racked love affair with Odette de Crécy.

Odette is not exactly his type. Though she is 'one of the best-dressed women in Paris' she is of obscure origins, lives in a new development in the unfashionable 16th arrondissement and is a self-proclaimed 'ignoramus with a taste for pretty things' who has never heard of Vermeer, about whom Swann has been half-heartedly attempting to write a monograph for a number of years. When she first throws herself at him one evening at the theatre he is indifferent to her beauty, 'which aroused no desire in him and actually caused him a sort of physical repulsion.' He only falls in love with her later when he decides that she looks like the wife of Moses in a painting by Botticelli.

Swann has recently begun to find ways to put Odette out of his head 'but his meticulous prudence was undone one evening when he went out into society'.

The Host

Madame La Marquise de Saint-Euverte is a perennial party-giver throughout the seven volumes of *In Search of Lost Time*. But, despite having a brother and brother-in-law who are archbishops, she is rather looked down on by the fashionable Parisian elite of Faubourg Saint-Germain. One of them, the Baron de Charlus, says that the Marquise opening her mouth to issue an invitation would make him think his 'cesspit had ruptured'. And if he had the misfortune to go along to one of her parties 'the cesspit would become a great sewage wagon.' This may have something to do with the marquise's gauche habit of sending her guest list to the newspapers and her tendency to issue invitations to absolutely everyone rather than flattering her guests' egos by inviting only a select few.

This is to be her last social occasion of the season: a chamber music recital at which 'she allowed people to hear the artistes who would later feature in her charity concerts'.

The Venue

Grooms 'hatted and booted' are stationed on the gravelled drive and in front of the stables of the marquise's house: the first in a long receiving line of footmen, ushers and valets who process the arriving guests.

As Swann is out of the habit of attending society functions, he pays attention to these flunkeys for the first time. Being Swann, he sees them not as human beings, but in terms of their resemblance to characters from the classical paintings of Mantegna, Goya, Dürer and Cellini.

He trudges up the grand marble staircase (which he manages to compare to the Staircase of the Giants at the Doge's Palace in Venice) in a state of melancholy indifference, haunted 'with the sad thought that Odette had never climbed it', and dreams of 'the old dressmaker's pestilential and longed-for staircase' where Odette currently is.

The Guest List

'Swann quickly regained his sense of masculine ugliness when, on the other side of the hanging tapestry, the spectacle of the servants was followed by that of the guests.'

Despite all the snooty comments and professed reservations about attending the marquise's parties there are 300 people there including such representatives of the grande monde of La Belle Epoque as the Général de Froberville, the Marquis de Bréaute, the Marquise de Cambremer, the Vicomtesse de Franquetot, the Marquise de Gallardon and the Comtesse de Monteriender. The Baron de Charlus is only not present because Swann has commandeered him to go and check up on Odette.

The normally reclusive Swann isn't the only surprise appearance at the soirée. The Princesse des Laumes, possessor of the oldest and purest blood in France (she's even married to her cousin to keep it that way), arrives at the party 'as an act of condescension' and to enhance her reputation for doing the unexpected.

The Dress Code

Monocles of various styles and sizes are the de rigueur fashion accessory for male guests at the party. This spectacle provokes another burst of classical allusions in Swann. One guest's particularly well-endowed eyepiece makes him look like a Cyclops while another resembles a Giotto.

The fad among the ladies is for rustic-themed headdresses. The Princesse des Laumes crowns her 'simple and charming coiffure' with an ensemble of plums and hawthorn berries, while the Marquise de Cambremer has a bunch of black grapes nestled in her hairdo.

The Entertainment

The evening's musical programme opens with a flute solo from Gluck's *Orpheé et Eurydice*, moving on to a piano intermezzo from Liszt's 'Saint Francis Preaching to the Birds', followed by a prelude and polonaise by Chopin.

The members of the audience are divided into those who show a self-consciously demonstrative appreciation of the music, like the Princess des Laumes ('With her fan she beat time for an instant, but so as not to abdicate her independence, on the off-beat.'); and those who use the dead time to plan how to catch the eye of people they want to network with or deliver snubs to those they have been slighted by.

The Food and Drink

A servant passes out refreshments during the polonaise and clicks the spoons noisily, attracting urgent signals from the hostess for him to go away. But perhaps the servant is merely trying to distract the more aesthetically sensitive guests. Chopin was very out of fashion at the end of the nineteenth century ('even those whose taste was bad never took more than an unavowed and limited pleasure in it'). Mme de Cambremer's daughter-in-law 'despised Chopin and suffered when she heard it played'.

The Conversation

The guests dispense snide observations about mutual acquaintances, dismissing one for her Empire furniture ('that horrible style – chests of drawers with swans' heads, like bathtubs') and sniggering at Mme de Cambremer for her name (which sounds a bit like *merde*). The hostess is not immune, with speculation rife about whether she might have hired her guests 'along with the musicians and the chairs and the food' from Belloir's (a party supplier from where the temporary seats for the less important attendees were rented).

Charles Swann finds a conversational soulmate in the Princesse des Laumes. Not only do they have neighbouring country estates, but they share 'a similar way of looking at the little things in life'. They agree that 'Life is a dreadful thing'. Swann is much invigorated by their concurrence on this point and tells her 'what's nice about being with you is that you're not cheerful. We could spend an evening together.'

The Outcome

The Princesse des Laumes offers to take Swann on to the Princesse of Parma's birthday party, but he is anxious to get home for fear of missing the note he had been waiting for all evening: an update on Odette from the Baron de Charlus. Before he can make his exit the Général de Froberville intercedes with

a request for an introduction to a pretty girl, the Marquise de Cambremer. Swann complies, but finds himself trapped in the salon as the music begins again. The violin rises to a series of high notes and 'suddenly it was as if she had entered and this apparition caused him such a wrench of suffering that his hand rose instinctively to his heart'.

The musicians have begun to play the andante from Vinteuil's sonata for violin and piano in F sharp, which for Swann and Odette was 'the national anthem of their love'.* Swann would insist on Odette playing the theme from it to him on the piano whenever he went to her house, a bit like a child who always wants to be read the same bedtime story.

The unexpected appearance of the melody sends Proust off

---

* Vinteuil's haunting theme recurs throughout the seven-book series and becomes a metaphor for unrequited love and the recollection of lost time. In a letter to a friend Proust said it was inspired by 'the charming but infinitely mediocre phrase of a sonata for piano and violin by Saint-Saëns, a musician I don't like'.

on an eight-page digression about the nature of music ('emotional accretion ... espoused our mortal condition ... destiny was linked to the future ... the reality of our soul ...' etc., etc.), which means he never gets back to telling us what happened at the end of the party. So we have no idea about what the musicians played for their encore, what was served for dessert, or who went home with whom.

A few days later Swann receives an anonymous letter telling him that Odette is not only a prostitute, who has been the mistress of several of his friends, but that she is also a lesbian who takes part in orgies. Naturally he ends up marrying her.

The Legacy

In his twenties, Marcel Proust was a social butterfly, doing the round of Parisian salons and soirées, where he met the society figures who would later serve as models for his fictional cast.

By his mid-thirties he had become a recluse, devoting himself to writing and rarely emerging from the cork-lined walls of his flat on the Boulevard Haussmann. He couldn't find a publisher for *Swann's Way* (one editor complained 'I cannot understand how a man can take thirty pages to describe how he turns about in his bed before he finally falls asleep.') so paid himself for it to be published in 1913.

In Search of Lost Time was originally planned as a modest trilogy, but due to the paper shortage in the First World War Proust had to wait six years for the publication of the second volume and occupied himself in the meantime in sketching out four more novels in the series.

Proust was a heavy drug user and consumed a prodigious daily intake of caffeine (one host recalls him drinking seventeen cups of coffee in a single evening). This may explain his manic inability to confine himself to short sentences. The longest sentence in *In Search of Lost Time* clocks in at a brain-numbing 942 words.

Not long before his death in 1922 Proust made one of his rare social forays to attend a dinner party at the Majestic Hotel. The other guests included Picasso, Stravinsky, Cocteau, Diaghilev and James Joyce. Ironically Proust and Joyce, the two giants of Modernism, were ignorant of each other's work. The only common conversational ground they could find was their bowel complaints.

17
Satan's Rout

LOCATION: APARTMENT NO. 50,
302A SADOVAYA STREET, MOSCOW
HOST: THE DEVIL
DATE: 1930S

From *The Master and Margarita* (1967)
by Mikhail Bulgakov

The Host

Fictional parties offer few hosts as original as Satan, here going under the nom de guerre of Professor Woland, a travelling conjuror. The occasion is *Walpurgisnacht*: a traditional night of revelry for witches and demons, which the Devil marks with an annual festivity known as The Springtime Ball of the Full Moon (aka The Ball of a Hundred Kings), where the denizens of hell are allowed the evening off from eternal damnation to engage in earthly excesses. Due to the host's perennial bachelor status, a woman, whose name must be Margarita, is plucked from the local populace to act as hostess. In return for providing this satanic escort service she is granted any wish her heart desires.

The Invitation

A mysterious encounter on a park bench is an invitation normally reserved for spy novels: especially when the park happens to be in Moscow, the solicitation on behalf of a foreign gentleman and the recipient in need of escape. More bizarrely, this invitation is delivered by Azazello, a strange man with fiery red hair, a wall eye and a protruding fang, who proffers a small solid gold box filled with ointment and the instructions that the invitee should strip naked, wait by the telephone and rub it all over herself at exactly half past eight in the evening. The recipient is a young Muscovite, Margarita Nikolayevna, and it is an indication of how unhappy she is in her marriage that she accepts immediately.

Margarita doesn't yet know it, but she has just received the most desirable invitation in literature. The cream, despite smelling of swamp mud, has the magical effect of restoring her youth and beauty with the additional benefit of making her hair curly and her skin shine like satin. The cream transforms more than her appearance. 'Now everywhere, in every last part of her body, joy welled up and she felt as if little bubbles were pricking her all over. Margarita felt free, free of everything.' Metamorphosis complete, Margarita pauses only to dash off a quick note to her husband telling him that she is leaving him for ever before flying off on a broomstick across Moscow to an unknown destination, stopping off en route to trash the flat of a critic who gave her boyfriend's novel a bad review.

The Venue

Satan has commandeered an apartment on Sadovaya Street for the occasion which is accessed discreetly via the fifth dimension. Every estate agent's dream, this outwardly modest residence transpires to contain a vast staircase leading to a tropical forest inhabited by scarlet-breasted parrots; two grand ballrooms, one lined with columns of iridescent stone; the other with walls of roses and Japanese camellias; kitchens with blazing furnaces beneath a glass floor; huge stone troughs filled with 'mountains of oysters' and 'dark cellars where candelabra were burning'. Overhead 'live satin butterflies swooped down on the dancing masses, flowers fluttered down from the ceilings. Whenever the electricity went off, the tops of the columns were lit up by myriad glowworms and will-o'-the-wisps floated in the air.'

The Guest List

As befits the ample address book of His Satanic Majesty the guest list is a *Who's Who* of damned souls from history, including: kings, dukes, knights, suicides, poisoners, cut-throats, gallows-birds, procuresses, jailers, cardsharpers, hangmen, informers, traitors, seducers and vampires.

Amongst the infamous invitees are:

CALIGULA, mad and despotic Roman Emperor, murdered by his own bodyguards in AD 41.

MESSALINA, Empress of Rome, noted for her sex parties, executed by her husband, Claudius, in AD 48.

SIGNORA TOFANA, retailer of bespoke poisons to Italian ladies who wished to murder their husbands. Strangled in prison in 1709.

M. JACQUES COEUR, fifteenth-century French proto-capitalist who was imprisoned for the murder of Agnés Sorel, the mistress of Charles VII – accompanied by his wife.*

EARL ROBERT DUDLEY, who reputedly murdered his wife to free himself for an amorous liaison with Queen Elizabeth I.

MADAME DE BRINVILLIERS, a seventeenth-century poisoner who killed her entire family to inherit their estate and was subsequently beheaded.

---

* The Devil clearly hasn't done his homework here: Monsieur Coeur was posthumously pardoned by Charles VII's son Louis XI.

LADY MINKINA, rumoured to be a witch, who branded her maid's face with a pair of curling tongs and was murdered by a mob of her own peasants in 1825.

RUDOLPH II OF AUSTRIA — Holy Roman Emperor, astrologer, alchemist and lunatic.

The Dress Code

The guests make their entrance as decayed corpses that drop down through the chimney into a grand marble fireplace. On arrival they are magically made over: the men resurrected in immaculate black tie and tails with starched white shirts; the women naked except for shoes and feather headdresses.

As Queen of the Ball, Margarita's toilette involves being washed in blood, then laid out on a crystal couch and dried with large green leaves. She wears nothing, apart from shoes woven from pale rose petals, a diamond-inlaid crown and a heavy necklace bearing the image of a black poodle. 'This adornment severely burdened the queen. The chain immediately started to chafe her neck and the weight of the image caused her to stoop.'

Ever the maverick, the host, Satan, appears, incongruously amid all this reincarnated splendour, attired in a dirty, stained nightshirt and down-at-heel slippers, offset with a sword which he uses as a walking stick.

The Food and Drink

Satan skimps a bit on the food (which is seemingly only to be found in a basement, where 'waitresses served sizzling meat on red-hot coals') but he makes up for it on the alcohol front. Margarita is advised to drink nothing but water, despite being surrounded by a dipsomaniac's paradise. Three ornamental fountains spurt champagne, a cascade of wine falls into a basin of ice and lissom female guests frolic in a pool of pink champagne that later turns to cognac.

The Entertainment

Satan's house conductor turns out to be Johann Strauss II, though what diabolic associations 'the King of the Waltz' might have had in his lifetime to merit him getting the gig are unclear. His 150-piece orchestra plays a roistering polonaise that competes with a jazz band pounding away in the adjoining ballroom. Later in the evening the human players are replaced by a musical menagerie, which includes a jazz ensemble of frenetic apes, a salamander magician, dancing polar bears who play the accordion and tigers in the bar whose roaring gives the Devil a migraine.

Such is the energy of the dancers' exertions that 'the massive marble mosaic and crystal floors of this remarkable hall pulsed rhythmically' but due to some form of supernatural soundproofing, all this noise is inaudible to the neighbouring flats and even to the intelligence spooks secretly observing the building.

The Conversation

Margarita finds the conversational options a little limited. As hostess, she is obliged to spend the first three hours of the ball greeting the stream of arriving guests, professing herself 'overjoyed' to meet each one of them. She has been given strict instructions to show no favouritism to any of the assorted murderers, traitors, adulterers and heretics she is introduced to. The

dead, it seems, are highly susceptible to slights and any neglect by her of them is likely to cause them to 'waste away'.

The unwilling guest of honour is Mikhail Berlioz: the recently deceased Chairman of the Moscow Writers' Union, whose head is temporarily reincarnated and brought in on a salver. This is so that Woland can continue a discussion they were having earlier in the novel on the subject of religion and the afterlife, which was cut off (literally) by the untimely death of Berlioz from falling under the wheels of a tram. Woland now wishes to ascertain whether the late Comrade Berlioz still holds to his belief in atheism. Berlioz is given no chance to state his opinion before his head shrivels into a skull.

The only living guest at the ball is Baron Maigel, an official from the State Tourist Board, whom Woland engages in a short one-sided conversation in which he accuses him of being a spy and an informer. Again, Woland rudely (but what do you expect from the Devil?) gives his guest no right to reply before having him summarily executed. Margarita is then forced to renounce her earlier teetotal pledge and join Woland in drinking a cup of the baron's blood, which luckily, by a spot of inverse transub-stantiation, has turned into wine.

The Outcome

No problems with lingering unwanted guests at this event as the dead souls all promptly evaporate into powder at the first cock crow.

The Devil's retinue adjudge the party to have been a great success, whereas Woland himself describes it as 'tiresome'. After a restorative shot of pure spirits, Margarita is granted her heart's desire; but rather than requesting to be reunited with her lover, the Master, she instead selflessly asks for Frieda, one of the damned souls, to be released from torment. The Devil, somewhat to his annoyance, feeling that charity is outside his remit, obliges and finds himself having to grant her a second wish. This time she obtains the release of the Master from the state asylum and the Devil even throws in another good deed for free by restoring the manuscript of the Master's novel, which he had earlier burned.

The Legacy

On 24 April 1935 Mikhail Bulgakov was a guest at the 'Spring Festival' at Spaso House, the residence of the first US ambassador to the USSR, William Bullitt. This lavish party provided the model for Satan's Rout. With Soviet propagandists already demonizing America, Bullitt's evening of decadence and excess didn't do his country's reputation any favours.

Bulgakov burnt the first draft of *The Master and Margarita* and even when he finished it he knew that his novel, combining religious themes with a vicious satire on Soviet bureaucrats, could never be published under Stalin's regime. His wife Yelena (and possibly the inspiration for Margarita) kept the manuscript in a drawer until it was finally serialized in *Moskva* magazine in 1966 and 1967, twenty-six years after the author's death.

18

The Lord Mayor's Ball

LOCATION: THE MANSION HOUSE,
THE CITY OF LONDON
HOST: THE LORD MAYOR OF LONDON
DATE: 7 MAY 1888

From *The Diary of a Nobody* (1892)
by George and Weedon Grossmith

The Invitation

Shortly after moving into a new house in Holloway, Charles Pooter, City bank clerk and the eponymous Nobody, decides it is time the wider world is made aware of his existence, so he starts to keep a diary. He duly fills it with details of household improvements he has undertaken, arguments with the grocer's boy, confusion over a misplaced walking stick and games of dominoes played with his neighbours. But just a few weeks into his journal, on April 30th, Mr Pooter admits himself 'Perfectly astounded' to find that he has inexplicably become a Somebody. 'My heart beat like that of a schoolboy's', he confesses, on receiving an invitation from the Lord and Lady Mayoress to a reception at the Mansion House to 'meet the Representatives of Trades and Commerce.'

However, his reverie of social triumph is quickly dashed and he feels that his invitation is 'considerably discounted' on discovering that not only was his name put forward by Mr Perkupp, his boss at the bank where he works, but that a fellow clerk, Spotch ('a vulgar man'), was also invited and has had the temerity to say no.

Mr Pooter sends notes to his friends Mr Cummings and Mr Gowing informing them that he will be out on the evening in question. His wife Carrie posts the prized invite to her mother for her inspection, but to Mr Pooter's fury that lady manages to upset a glass of port over it.

The Host

The Lord Mayor of the City of London presides over the world's oldest municipal corporation, which, despite being only a fraction larger than a square mile in size, commands a business turnover greater than many sovereign nations. The post of Lord Mayor is unpaid, so its chief attractions are the various perks to which the incumbent can lay claim: he gets to be styled 'The Right Honourable' and also holds the position of Chief Magistrate of the City, Head of the Lieutenancy, Admiral of the Port of London and Chancellor of the City University. He is entitled to any sturgeon caught below London Bridge, to drive sheep over it and to take possession of any cattle that fall off it, as well as being entrusted with the password to the Tower of London.

The normally impressionable Mr Pooter fails to provide us with any details of his illustrious host, but we know that the Lord Mayor in May 1888 was the splendidly named Polydore de Keyser, a Belgian-born hotelier, a Freemason and the first Catholic to be elected to the position since the Reformation. A profile from the *Illustrated London News* in 1882 tells us that M. de Keyser 'can shoot, fish, play the piano, sing a tenor song, has a taste for geography and statistics and is an industrious collector of pictures and bronzes'.

The Venue

The Mansion House is the Lord Mayor's official residence, though it was not actually built until 550 years after the first Mayor took office. It was designed by George Dance the Elder (with a few amendments by his son George Dance the Younger) at a cost of £70,000 (of which £20,000 was provided by fines levied against Aldermen who refused to act as Sheriffs).

The Egyptian Hall, where the reception would have been held, is decorated in the Palladian style, with statues and stained-glass windows depicting inspirational scenes from English history, including Sir William Walworth killing Watt Tyler, from the days when Lord Mayors were drawn from the ranks of proper men of action instead of lawyers and accountants.

The Dress Code

Mr Pooter wears a white tie (having prudently purchased two ties 'in case one got spoiled in the tying') and lavender kid gloves. His ensemble manages to survive an accident involving the grocer's boy and the weekly coal delivery. Carrie, 'looking like a queen', wears a satin dress of sky-blue, accessorized with an ivory fan decorated with red feathers from the extinct 'Kachu eagle'.

There was little chance of any guest managing to upstage the Lord Mayor himself, to whom tradition bequeaths a strict directive in regards to his formal wardrobe. At official banquets he would be attired in a black and gold entertaining gown made of stiff silk weighted with gold thread, on top of his traditional court dress of black knee breeches, silk stockings and buckled shoes. Round his neck he would wear the insignia of mayoralty: the gold 'collar of esses' set with twenty-four rose-cut diamonds around a cameo decorated with roses, thistles and shamrocks;

all ensuring he would have looked almost as silly by the standards of the Victorian age as his successors do today.

The Guest List

'Crowds arrived and I shall never forget the grand sight. My humble pen can never describe it,' Mr Pooter gushes. It is up to his wife to provide us with a more prosaic explanation for his fogginess about the attendees: 'Isn't it a pity we don't know anybody?' she repeatedly says. When the Pooters are finally rescued from their social isolation, to their horror it is by Mr Farmerson, the local ironmonger. This gentleman seems to be very well connected and is even intimate with one of the sheriffs, leaving Mr Pooter appalled 'To think that a man who mends our scraper should know any member of our aristocracy!'

The Conversation

Mr Pooter reports that the Lord Mayor 'graciously condescended to talk with me some minutes' but he fails to provide any details of their discourse. Perhaps he was too nervous to recall it, or possibly, like for many of the rest of us, a conversation with a Belgian about geography and statistics was not that memorable.

The Food and Drink

'There was an immense crowd in the supper room, and, my stars! it was a splendid supper, any amount of champagne.' Mrs Pooter makes 'for a most hearty supper' while her husband claims he is too thirsty to eat and concentrates on the champagne. Mr Pooter is scant on details of the menu, but we find out that it features lobster mayonnaise (which seems to be literary short-hand for posh nosh).

The Entertainment

Dancing is on the evening's programme, perhaps to the String Band of the Royal Artillery, who played at Polydore de Keyser's banquet at Guildhall on the Lord Mayor's Day 1887, performing selections from *Coppélia* and Gilbert and Sullivan's *Ruddigore*.

The Pooters themselves contribute unwittingly to the evening's entertainment. They commence a waltz, but Mr Pooter has ignored his wife's advice and failed to make precautionary scratches on the soles of the shiny new boots he has donned for the occasion. He skids on the polished floor of the ballroom, bringing himself and his wife crashing ignominiously to the ground.

The Outcome

After their 'unfortunate mishap' on the dance floor the Pooters opt for an early exit, but are buttonholed on their way out by the enterprising Mr Farmerson, who manages to cadge a lift home in their hansom cab.

The repercussions continue for some days afterwards. Mr Pooter is too hungover the next day to notice that his wife is not talking to him. He occupies himself with conducting an increasingly frosty correspondence with the *Blackfriars Bi-Weekly News* over its failure to include the Pooters' names on the published guest list of attendees at the ball.

Mrs Pooter, it turns out, is sulking at having been forced to socialize with the 'vulgar man, who made a bungle out of repairing our scraper'.

Pooter laughs at tradesmen and servants because he believes in his vain, deluded, small-minded way that he is somehow superior to them. And naturally we laugh at Pooter.

The Legacy

George Grossmith was a member of the D'Oyly Carte Opera company and created many famous comic roles for Gilbert and Sullivan's popular operettas, including the Major General in *The Pirates of Penzance* and Ko-Ko, the Lord High Executioner, in *The Mikado*. He was famously portrayed in the Mike Leigh film *Topsy-Turvy* as a morphine-addicted depressive.

Mr Pooter's self-important musings first appeared as a serialization in the comic magazine *Punch* in 1888. At the time it was considered immensely satirical that such an utter nonentity would think that his drab life was of any interest to the outside world. In the modern age of blogs and social networking sites the joke may be rather lost on us. These days Charles Pooter even has his own Twitter account.

19

The Bacchanal of the Century

LOCATION: RUE JOUBERT, PARIS
HOST: JEAN-FRÉDÉRIC TAILLEFER
DATE: OCTOBER 1830

From *La Peau de chagrin* (*The Wild Ass's Skin*) (1831)
by Honoré de Balzac

The Invitation

A twenty-five-year-old impoverished writer, Raphaël de Valentin, wanders into a gambling house in the Palais-Royal and stakes his last gold napoleon on black. When red comes up the young man picks up his hat and heads off to drown himself in the Seine. But on getting to the river he decides that 'death in broad daylight is tacky' and so takes a detour to browse in a curiosity shop while he waits for nightfall. Here the 102-year-old shopkeeper shows him a *shagreen* (an ass's skin) with a mysterious Sanskrit inscription: 'if you possess me, you will possess everything, but your life will belong to me.' This talisman has the power to make its possessor's every wish come true, but with the caveat: 'With each wish I will shrink, like your days. Do you want me?'

No customer has ever been brave enough to accept the skin's dare, but Raphaël, who is only planning to live a few hours longer, has little to lose. He takes the talisman and his first wish is 'for a banquet of royal splendour, a bacchanal worthy of this century in which everything has supposedly been perfected'. He also requests there to be enough wine to bring about 'three days of delirium' and for the occasion to be graced with 'hot women'. 'I need to embrace the pleasures of heaven and earth in a final clinch and so die.' Outside the shop by happy coincidence, or dark arts, he runs into three friends who invite him along to just such a party.

The Host

The host who supplies Raphaël's dream party is Jean-Frédéric Taillefer, a retired financier, who is a representative of France's new 'aristocracy of bankers and lawyers'. Taillefer, 'not knowing what to do with his gold, wants to convert it into ideas'. So, in an age where 'power has shifted from the monarchy to the press' and journalism has become 'the religion of modern societies'* he has decided to found a newspaper. To supply the content for his first edition he throws a party for 'the most remarkable young men in Paris'. This event, he pledges, will 'surpass the tame saturnalias of our little modern Luculluses'.†

If immense wealth often entails a few skeletons in the closet then our host certainly has them. Taillefer also appears in *The Red Inn* (*L'Auberge rouge*) – a novel which Balzac wrote in parallel with the *The Wild Ass's Skin*. Here we learn that he began his career as an army surgeon and acquired the start-up capital on which he founded his subsequent fortune by murdering a wealthy industrialist. But, as Taillefer proudly maintains, the rich make their own laws and 'there are no scaffolds, no executioners for millionaires'.

---

* For journalism read 'media' and Balzac could have been talking about our own age.
† Lucius Licinius Lucullus was a Roman general and statesman, whose military and political achievements have been overshadowed by his reputation as a gastronome, which lives on in the word 'lucullan' meaning excessively extravagant.

The Venue

Taillefer's palatial mansion is on the Rue Joubert in the IXe arrondissement of Paris. 'Luxury beyond the portico is rare in France' and as soon as Raphaël sets foot on the rich carpet he knows that 'his wish has unquestionably been fully granted'. The bottom of the Seine is now far from his thoughts as he checks out the opulent interior: rooms appointed in silk and gold, rich candelabras, gilded friezes, bronze sculptures, sumptuous furniture and sweetly scented rare flowers. 'Everything, even the curtains, exuded an elegance without pretension, and in all there was a sort of poetic grace whose prestige could not fail to stimulate the imagination of a man without money.'

The Guest List

'Thirty men of talent and spirit' comprising painters, sculptors, writers, poets, journalists, critics, politicians, lawyers, scholars, doctors, comedians, a famous musician, a cartoonist and a political philosopher provide the potential font of wit for Taillefer's organ. Balzac does not miss the opportunity to have a swipe at his rivals on the Paris literary scene. 'Young authors without style stood alongside young authors without ideas, prose writers full of poetry next to prosaic poets.' He concludes scathingly 'among these guests, five had a future, ten or so would achieve passing glory', while the rest were 'mediocrities' who would soon be forgotten.

The Dress Code

Aside from Raphaël's frock coat and a cravat 'on terms so intimate with his waistcoat no one could suspect him of underlinen', Balzac fails to take the opportunity to provide an insight into the couture of nineteenth-century Paris.

The Food and Drink

'Prepare your stomach,' Raphaël is told by his friend Emile, as they behold the 'majestic, thrice-blessed and reassuring spectacle presented by their capitalist benefactor's dining room'.

In addition to Lucullus, two legendary French gastronomes – Brillat-Savarin and Cambacérès – are namechecked in relation to the splendour of the feast, but the only items from the main course mentioned are 'delicious green peas' and asparagus. The dessert, however, is a *pièce de résistance* worthy of Trimalchio: 'The table was laid with a huge centrepiece of gilded bronze' featuring carved figures holding baskets of 'strawberries, pineapples, fresh dates, yellow grapes, pale peaches, oranges brought in from Setubal by steamer, pomegranates, fruits from China; in short, all manner of luxurious surprises, miracles of the confectioner's art, the most desirable delicacies, the most seductive dainties.'

The wines, Taillefer's intended lubricant of wit, are detailed in full. There is Madeira, white and red Bordeaux and Burgundy, champagne in lavish quantities and 'the splendid wines of the Rhone, with warm Tokay, and heady old Roussillon'. Not to mention the 'powerful philtres' of the dessert wines and punch. Before very long drunkenness breaks over the guests like a premature dawn: 'pale foreheads reddened, noses began to turn purple, faces lit up'.

The Conversation

Once lubricated this 'coven of intellects' comes to life and 'witticisms and bons mots gradually began to escape everyone's lips'. Soon 'the orgy deployed its great voice, its voice composed of a hundred confused clamours which swelled like a Rossini crescendo'. 'Everyone ate as he spoke, spoke while he ate' with every philosophy, religion and moral code being discussed. These are just a few of the soundbites that emerge from the babel of opinions.

THE MONARCHIST – 'Despotism does great things illegally, while liberty can't even be bothered to do small ones legally.'

THE REPUBLICAN (between hiccups) – 'Men and events count for nothing … in politics and philosophy there are only principles and ideas.'

THE NOTARY – 'There is no science nor virtue worth shedding a drop of blood for.'

THE ABSOLUTIST – 'All individuality will disappear in a people levelled by instruction.'

THE MISANTHROPE – 'Public opinion? The most vicious of all prostitutes.'

THE FATALIST (asking for the asparagus) – 'Liberty begets anarchy, anarchy leads to despotism, and despotism brings us back to liberty.'

THE BANKER – 'Let us drink to the imbecility of power, which gives us such power over imbeciles!'

THE CYNIC – 'Man is a buffoon dancing on the precipice.'

THE CRITIC – 'I'd happily give a hundred sous to the mathematician who can prove with an algebraic equation the existence of hell.'

RAPHAËL (not wishing to be outdone) – 'Man is corrupted by the exercise of reason and purified by ignorance.'

The Entertainment

With the guests already in 'that exquisite limbo where the lights of the intellect are extinguished and, relieved of its tyranny, the body gives itself up to the delirious joys of freedom' the maître d' appears and invites them to revive themselves in the drawing room. The traditional restorative, coffee, is promised but the revellers are instead greeted by a more potent stimulant, a group of women whose 'ravishing beauty eclipsed all the marvels of the palace'. Raphaël's wish has now been completely fulfilled and he and Emile quickly fall into conversation with two sirens named Aquilina and Euphrasie.

No cheap hookers this pair. Aquilina is 'the queen of pleasure, like an image of human joy, that joy which squanders wealth built up over three generations'. Euphrasie is 'the most gentle little creature that a fairy's wand had ever conjured from a magic egg' with 'an innocent face that hides the deepest depravations, the most refined vices, beneath a forehead as soft and tender as a daisy'.

They both have the names of saints, though this is where the resemblance ends: 'the first was the soul of sin; the second, sin without a soul in it'. 'Virtue? We leave that to the ugly girls and the hunchbacks,' Euphrasie says. 'What would they be without it, the poor things?'

The seraglio offers 'seductions for every eye and pleasures for every whim' and the guests are quickly reinvigorated for a second bout of revelry. 'The blue flame of the punch lent a hellish tint to the faces of those who could still drink. Mad dances animated by a wild energy provoked laughs and cries which burst like fireworks.' Neighbours appear at the window, complaining of the racket, but Taillefer simply advises them to soundproof their doors with straw.

The Outcome

The dinner party metamorphoses into a slumber party and the rooms of Taillefer's mansion, metaphorically 'strewn with the dead and the dying … resembled a battlefield'. Although most of his fellow guests are now out cold, Raphaël is somehow still compos mentis enough to give Emile a detailed account

(which runs to 120 pages) of the source of the misery which had earlier driven him towards suicide: the hardships of a writer's life, a tyrannical father, and inevitably a woman: the heartless Countess Fœdora, who 'trampled on my hopes, shattered my life and destroyed my future with the cold insouciance and the innocent cruelty of a child who, out of curiosity, rips the wings off a butterfly'.

At the end of his story Raphaël remembers the talisman, draws it from his pocket and half-jesting, half-earnestly wishes for 200,000 livres a year, before he and Emile finally pass out.

The revellers present a sorry spectacle when they wake up towards midday 'the morning after the debauch'. 'The men disowned their mistresses of the night before, seeing them all faded and withered like flowers trampled underfoot in the street after a procession has passed.' But 'these disdainful men looked more horrible still'.

Breakfast is served in the same dining room that had hosted the previous night's supper. As the guests reconvene around the table, the notary reappears 'on serious business'. His announcement 'I bring six million for one of you' silences the guests. The lucky benefactor and sole heir to the fortune of the late Major O'Flaharty of Calcutta proves to be none other than Raphaël. He reacts to this news 'as if he had been shot'. Checking the magic skin and finding that it has perceptibly shrunk he 'could see that every desire of his must cost him days of his life'.

The Legacy

The young Balzac craved two things: creative recognition and love. *The Wild Ass's Skin* proved to be his own magic *shagreen*. Not only did the novel's commercial success set him on the path to literary stardom, but it inspired the first letter in a seventeen-year correspondence with Ewelina Hanska, his future wife. A series of complications, including her marriage to another man and inheritance issues, delayed their wedding until March 1850. Balzac died just five months later, his wild ass's skin having finally shrunk to zero.

20

Dick Hawk-Monitor's 21st Birthday Party

LOCATION: THE ASSEMBLY ROOMS,
GODMERE, SUSSEX
HOSTESS: MRS HAWK-MONITOR
DATE: 21 APRIL 1951*

From *Cold Comfort Farm* (1932) by Stella Gibbons

The Hostess

Mrs Hawk-Monitor is a handsome widow of some sixty years and a 'darling old bird whose hobby was the Higher Thought'. She lives at Hautcouture Hall (pronounced Hochiker in the local manner) in rural Sussex with her two children: 'a son who was easy on the eye but slow on the uptake, and a healthy sort of daughter named Joan'. The occasion is her firstborn, Richard's, coming-of-age party.

The Invitation

Dick's 21st is a celebration to which 'all the county will be asked', except that is for the Starkadders, the eccentric residents of Cold

---

* *Cold Comfort Farm* is set in an unspecified year of the near future from 1932. We are told the party takes place on Saturday the 21st of April and we know that the action happens some time after 1946, so the year was probably 1951, assuming they had the same calendar as us. Though as midsummer's day is apparently celebrated on June 14th, perhaps they didn't.

Comfort Farm in the nearby village of Howling. Only invitations to 'funerals or the churching of women' are permitted in this family, ruled over by domineering, bedridden matriarch Ada Doom. Sixty-nine years previously she went doolally following a traumatic childhood experience, which she endlessly references in her mantra 'I saw something nasty in the woodshed.'

The Venue

The Assembly Rooms in the fictional town of Godmere, Sussex, were built by Mr Aubrey Featherweight in 1830, some 120 years prior to 'the near future' in which Stella Gibbons sets her novel. Video phones and air taxis are now part of everyday life, but interior design remains strictly conventional. A classic red carpet is laid out, two flambeaux illuminate the entrance where a large crowd of sightseers has gathered. The interior of the ballroom boasts florid crimson walls with dark green foliage nestled in the alcoves, slender white pillars capped by gold acanthus leaves and tables decorated with spring wreaths and flowers.

The Guest List

Despite Aunt Ada's injunction, her niece Flora Poste, a recently orphaned London socialite and new resident at Cold Comfort, is determined to see Elfine Starkadder's name on the guest list. Elfine, a seventeen-year-old devotee of St Francis of Assisi, 'wild and shy as a Pharisee of the woods', is in love with Richard and desperate to attend his birthday celebrations. Flora, who has appointed herself the task of sorting out the lives of her relatives on the farm, has to get down to 'the serious business of arranging Elfine's future.' Marriage to Richard is the only way to save

Elfine from a dismal life of inbreeding with her cousin Urk (to whom she has been promised since birth) or a possibly worse fate in Horsham working in an arts and crafts shop and doing barbola work in her spare time.

Flora puts her London connections to use and makes a video phone call (a precocious predecessor to Skype) to Claud Hart-Harris. He knows 'positive herds of people who live in country houses' including the Hawk-Monitors and successfully secures four invitations: for himself, Flora and Elfine, whose walker is to be her brother Seth – a handsome, highly sexed fan of 'the talkies'.

The rest of the guest list is made up of 'young persons of both sexes, most of them handsome and all of them happy.' 'Perhaps it was more by luck than by judgement that Mrs Hawk-Monitor had combined two of the essentials for a successful ball (too many guests in a smallish room)'.

One person who thankfully fails to secure an invitation is Flora's unwelcome admirer, Mr Meyerburg (more commonly known as Mr Mybug). He is 'rather fat and his clothes were not very good' but his main detraction is the fact that he is a writer. As Flora observes: 'You know how dreadful intelligent people are when you take them to dances'.

The Dress Code

Securing a spot on the guest list is only the first step towards arranging Elfine's marital bliss; a makeover is also necessary, both in dress and manners. The Hawk-Monitors are members of the hunting gentry and they 'liked dogs to be well trained and girls to be well turned out'. Flora lavishes £80 (four-fifths of her annual allowance) on taking Elfine to Lambeth, the fashionable area of this future London (in which Mayfair is now a slum), for a 'fiendishly expensive' haircut from Maison Viol and a fifty-guinea bespoke snow-coloured gown from Maison Solide. Elfine's education in social mores is supplied by a copy of *Vogue* and a lingerie catalogue. 'Only over poetry was there a little struggle.' Elfine is reluctant to sacrifice her passion for composing verse, but as Flora succinctly warns her: 'most young men are alarmed on hearing that a young woman writes poetry.'

With the help of a hip bath belonging to the cleaner Mrs Beetle (the farm lacks a bathroom) Elfine is successfully transformed. Flora, eager not to outshine her cousin, wears a dress in 'harmonious tones of pale and dark green', pale green gloves and a long coat of viridian velvet. Seth in an off-the-peg dinner jacket resembles 'a panther in evening dress', but Elfine's 'triumphant beauty' steals the limelight. Flora 'had done what she had hoped to do. She had made Elfine look groomed and normal, yet had preserved in her personality a suggestion of

cool, smoothly-blowing winds and of pine trees and the smell of wild flowers.'

The male guests are in black tie with Claud Hart-Harris looking dashing in 'tail coat and white waistcoat'.

The Conversation

'Gay voices rose every second above the roar of the general conversation like individual trills of water from the rush of a stream in spate.' The strong and silent Seth, a parody of a lusty swain from the works of Thomas Hardy and D. H. Lawrence, attracts a tribe of female admirers and drawls 'ay' and 'nay' in answer to their questions. The birthday boy, Dick Hawk-Monitor, on the other hand seems to have escaped from a P. G. Wodehouse novel: he refers to his mother as 'the mater' and comes out with expressions like 'I say, this is jolly, isn't it?' The Angry Young Men clearly did not feature in Stella Gibbons's crystal ball.

The Food and Drink

This being England we are told of the 'elegance and lavishness of the supper-tables' but the only dish named is crab mousse, washed down with the de rigueur champagne. Stella Gibbons fails to break the mould of deficient culinary enthusiasm among British writers.

The Entertainment

The guests dance until 'every cheek was crimson and the floor was scattered with fans, hairpins, shoe-buttons and wilting flowers'. The orchestra's repertoire includes the 'Twelve

Sweet Hours' waltz, 'a gay polka' and 'a jolly tune to which the "Lancers" could be danced'. Rock and roll was still a long way off in this version of the 1950s.

Elfine, who claims to 'hate dancing unless it's in the woods with the wind-flowers and the birds', proves an unexpected hit on the dance floor and her beauty inspires a 'group of eager young men' to gather about her every time the music stops.

As 'Flora knew by observing the antics of her friends', young men frequently need to be reminded that they are in love and Richard indeed realizes 'not that Elfine was beautiful, but that he loved Elfine'. He proposes to her on the spot and wastes no time in announcing to his guests how much jollier his engagement has made his already jolly evening.

The Outcome

'Flora had every reason to feel smug and satisfied with her evening's work'. Not only has she saved her cousin from the dreadful Urk, but Elfine would now 'bear children and found a line of pleasant, ordinary English people who were blazing with poetry in their secret souls'. Mrs Hawk-Monitor is a little less certain of the party's success, being understandably apprehensive of her son's engagement to this flower child.

Flora, Elfine and Seth return to Cold Comfort Farm at half past one in the morning to find an unexpected after-party taking place. Once a year Ada Doom spontaneously descends from her bedroom for 'the Counting' – a sort of census of the Starkadder clan – and she has chosen this particular night to convene the gathering. Aunt Ada rules over the assembly with a rod of iron (actually a copy of *The Milk Producer's Weekly and Cowkeeper's Guide* – but equally vicious). Her constant worry is that the family will break up, leaving her all alone in her metaphorical woodshed, and this triggers her other mantra – 'There have always been Starkadders at Cold Comfort.'

When Flora confirms her aunt's worst fears by announcing the news of Elfine and Richard's engagement, Urk shrieks and collapses 'face downwards in the beef sandwiches' only to re-appear moments later and declare his love for Meriam, the hired help. Then Amos Starkadder, paterfamilias and lay preacher at the Church of the Quivering Brethren, announces his intention to join the family exodus and tour the country in a Ford van spreading the Gospel (another of Flora's machinations).

For Flora the whole occasion resembles 'the Chamber of Horrors at Madame Tussauds' and she anticipates a sleepless night, feeling 'as though she were at one of Eugene O'Neill's plays; the kind that goes on for hours and hours and hours'.

The Legacy

Stella Gibbons wrote *Cold Comfort Farm,* her first book, when she was in her late twenties. She went on to produce thirty-one further novels, pretty much all of them now forgotten. Despite this prodigious prose output she, like Thomas Hardy (whose novels of arcadia she was parodying), considered herself to be primarily a poet. Sadly she was destined to be forever remembered as the author of a single, light comic novel.

21

The Blossom Viewing Party

LOCATION: THE HEIAN PALACE, KYOTO, JAPAN
HOST: HIS IMPERIAL MAJESTY
KIRITSUBO NO MIKADO
DATE: THE END OF THE SECOND MONTH,
EARLY ELEVENTH CENTURY

From *The Tale of Genji* (before 1021)
by Murasaki Shikibu

The Host

Kiritsubo no Mikado is a fictional emperor of the Heian period in eleventh-century Japan. *Heian* means 'peace and tranquillity' and this was a time when the Imperial Japanese court was at its cultural zenith. Needless to say, the emperor had long since been stripped of any political power (which had been assumed by the Fujiwara clan) and relegated to a largely ceremonial role. As the direct descendant of the Sun Goddess he had to officiate at religious ceremonies, including the Obeisance of the Four Directions, the Presentation of the Full Moon Gruel and the Washing of the Buddha.

The Invitation

Hosting the *hanami*, the annual festival to observe the appearance of the blossom on the cherry trees, was another of the emperor's official functions. We don't know what form the invitation to the viewing party would have taken, but as the trees could blossom at any point from the beginning of March to early May guests couldn't have had much notice.*

The Venue

The Great Imperial Palace in Heian Ky■ (modern day Kyoto). Though much of the palace was built in imposing and grandiose style copied from the Chinese, the gardens were simple and Japanese in feel with raked white gravel and trees planted in tubs. Apartments in the palace often derived their names from these trees. In front of the Ceremonial Palace (*Shishenden*) stood two of the two most famous trees in the capital: the Cherry of the Left and the Orange of the Right.

The Guest List

In Heian Japan it was impolite to refer to aristocratic personages by their real names, so the characters in *The Tale of Genji* are known by soubriquets which allude to their position at the court or some incident concerning them. The emperor himself is called after a wing of the Imperial Palace, which in turn derives its name from the paulownia tree.

To make the guest list even more confusing the emperor had various grades of female companions. In medieval Japan the greatest compliment that could be paid to a gentleman of rank was for the Mikado to sleep with his daughter; so in addition to the empress (*Chugu*), the emperor would have several consorts (*Nyogo*) and a number of lower-ranking intimates or concubines

---

* *Hanami* is still celebrated in Japan today. The blossom forecast (*sakurazensen*) is announced each year by the weather bureau, and the progress of the blossom across the country is followed as eagerly as inhabitants of Miami follow the development of Atlantic hurricanes.

(*Koi*); well he didn't have any governing to do so he had to be kept busy somehow.

The current empress is named after another wing of the palace – Fujitsubo. She is twenty-five and a woman of unrivalled beauty, though her name translates into English as Lady Wisteria Tub, which makes her sound like an elderly matriarch from an Oscar Wilde play.

For the blossom viewing festivity, tented enclosures (*tsubone*), consisting of curtains and screens, have been erected for the imperial guests and 'The empress and the crown prince were seated to the left and right of the throne.'

The Consort Kokiden (named after yet another wing of the palace 'the Hall of Great Light') is the daughter of the Minister of the Right and believes that she should be empress, especially as, for complex reasons, her son is the Crown prince and heir apparent. She is riled by the fact that Fujitsubo is sitting to the left of the emperor and so occupying a more prestigious position than her son: 'This arrangement of course displeased Kokiden, but she put in an appearance all the same, unable to let such an occasion pass.'

Genji – the hero of the novel, here aged twenty – is handsome, charming, talented and eloquent. 'Genji's looks had an indescribably fresh sweetness ... and this moved people to call him the Shining Lord.' He is the emperor's son and favourite, but as his mother was a mere intimate she wasn't of sufficient rank to be made empress. Genji is also secretly the father of Fujitsubo's infant son (the future emperor Suzaku), making him both Genji's stepbrother and son.

Also present is Genji's father-in-law: His Excellency, the Minister of the Left. He is one of the two senior ministers of the state, his job title being derived from where he sits in court in relation to the emperor's throne. He outranks his colleague the

Minister of the Right (which puts paid to our Western notions of 'the right hand man').

The Secretary Captain (Tō no Chūjō) is Genji's best friend (and, as pretty much everyone was related in the Imperial Court, also his brother-in-law).

Also present are various court officials and some professors 'who took such occasions in their stride, though their court dress may have been a little shabby'. A millennium on, academics' dress sense hasn't changed.

The Dress Code

The life of ladies at court in Imperial Japan could be very dull as they were encouraged to stay indoors most of the time with only the odd festivity to distract them. To stop time hanging heavy on their hands formal attire was elaborate and cumbersome, consisting of a heavy outer costume and multiple layers of unlined silk undergarments (twelve was the standard number).

Women of rank would beautify themselves by whitening

their faces with powder, plucking their eyebrows and then repainting them, and blackening their teeth with a type of dye made by soaking iron and powdered gallnut in vinegar or tea. In later times the blackening of teeth became confined to married women: to denote their marital status and dissuade potential adulterers (not that the unattractive dentistry of the ladies in *The Tale of Genji* seems to lead to any shortage of male courtiers willing to jump into bed with them).

The Food and Drink

No details are given, but Genji is described as being drunk after the party, so we can assume that *sake* was served.

The Conversation

The guests are too lost in contemplation of the ineffable beauty of the cherry blossom to engage in any small talk.

The Entertainment

Chinese culture was all the rage in eleventh-century Japan and the day begins with a poetry-writing competition. This is a bit like a game of charades: gentlemen assemble in order of rank and draw a Chinese character from a lottery, around which they have to configure the rhymes for their poem. Genji draws the character representing 'Spring', which sounds like a bit of a fix for the emperor's favourite, considering that this is a party dedicated to celebrating the coming of spring.

The high courtiers are nervous. 'They came stiffly out into the radiant garden, awed by the company in which they found themselves.' And this is just the bit where they have to formally announce which character they have drawn in the lottery (for which performance they are also awarded marks).

Next there are dances, which are in the Chinese *bugaku* style. Genji dances 'The Song of the Spring Warbler' and his 'uncommonly fine' performance wins him 'a sprig of blossoms for his cap' from the Crown prince, who requests an encore, which Genji obligingly provides. The 'quiet waving of his sleeves as he came to the climax was incomparable. The Minister of the Left forgot his anger at his negligent son-in-law. There were tears in his eyes.'

Tō no Chūjō manages to trump his brother-in-law's routine with his own dance, 'The Garden of Willows and Flowers', and receives a robe from the emperor as a token of his appreciation. Then the 'other senior courtiers danced, but as it was growing dark one could not easily tell who were the better dancers.'

At the end of the evening, an official reader declaims everyone's poems. 'Genji's was so remarkable that the reader paused to comment upon each line. The professors were deeply moved.' All in all the occasion is something of a triumph for the emperor's favourite.

The Outcome

'The festivities ended late in the night' and Genji, as befits the playboy son of an emperor, wanders drunkenly off into the palace to try to get laid. His first port of call is his stepmother's apartments, but her handmaiden Omyobu's door is closed and so there is no one to show him up (protocol has to be observed even in cuckolding the emperor). Instead he pops through an open door where he hears a girl reciting a Chinese poem: 'What can compare with a misty moon of spring?' 'It was a sweet young voice, so delicate that its owner could be no ordinary serving woman.'

The couple have a passionate night of . . . well, we're not sure exactly what, but it seems to involve quoting a lot of poems to each other. With dawn approaching they both become nervous about being caught and so 'they exchanged fans and he was on his way'.

Genji is unable to sleep for speculating on the identity of his mysterious lover. He thinks she might be one of the younger daughters of the Minister of the Right. 'He rather hoped she was not the sixth daughter, whom the minister had thoughts of marrying to the crown prince.'

The next day he attends 'a lesser spring banquet' and plays 'the thirteen-stringed koto, his performance if anything subtler and richer than that of the day before'. But he is preoccupied with his inability to find the 'lady of that dawn encounter' again. He has her 'three-ply cherry' fan depicting 'a misty moon reflected on water' and he dashes off a quick poem on it, in the same way that we today might jot a few reminder notes on the business card of a person we'd met.

It is only two months later at a Wisteria Banquet that he succeeds in finding her again. For the sake of added plot complexity Oborozukiyo ('Night with a Misty Moon') does indeed transpire to be the sixth daughter of the Minister of the Right, the Crown prince's betrothed and sister of Genji's sworn enemy Kokiden.

The Legacy

Known to have been completed before 1021, *The Tale of Genji* has a strong claim to being the world's first novel. And it was written by a woman.

A leitmotif of the book is the concept of *mono no aware* — an untranslatable Japanese expression that means something like 'sadness at the ephemeral nature of all things'. The Blossom Viewing Party is a good example: celebrating the transient beauty of the flowers on the cherry trees, which appear for just a couple of short weeks each spring. Ironically the term can also be applied to the author of *Genji*, whose identity has been totally lost.

We know that she was an attendant in the service of the Empress Akiko in the early eleventh century. The problem is that, as already mentioned, in Heian Japan it was bad manners to refer to well-born people by their names, so we have no idea what she was actually called. The name she is normally known by — Murasaki Shikibu — is an honorific title: the first name means 'purple' and the second derives from the official position held by her father.

22

Mrs Leo Hunter's Costume Breakfast

LOCATION: 'THE DEN', EATANSWILL, SUFFOLK

HOSTS: MR AND MRS LEO HUNTER

DATE: AUGUST 1827

From *The Pickwick Papers* (1837) by Charles Dickens

The Venue

The peripatetic branch of the Pickwick Club, comprising Messrs Pickwick, Snodgrass, Tupman and Winkle, four gentlemen unburdened by wives, children or any seeming necessity to earn the money to fund their travels, has been sojourning in the Suffolk town of Eatanswill in order to observe the local election. Two political parties divide the town: the Blues and the Buffs. Both employ an equally scandalous roster of political chicanery: drugging opposition voters with laudanum, drowning out rival candidates' speeches with impromptu brass band performances and bribing coach drivers to deliberately dump passengers in the canal to prevent them getting to the polls.

As to the identity of Eatanswill, Mr Pickwick has 'purposefully substituted a fictitious designation for the real name of the place, in which his observations were made'. The town is generally believed to be modelled on Sudbury in Suffolk, where as a young reporter Dickens had covered the 1834 parliamentary by-election for the *Morning Chronicle*. The notorious corruption of the borough led to it being disenfranchised in 1844.

Sudbury's most famous sons are the painter Thomas Gainsborough and Simon of Sudbury, who was Archbishop of Canterbury and Lord Chancellor during the Peasants' Revolt of 1381.*

The Invitation

On the third morning after the election Mr Pickwick is surprised to find the business card of one Mrs Leo Hunter placed in his hand by his manservant, Sam Weller. It has been presented by Mr Leo Hunter, 'a grave man' who is awaiting him downstairs in the drawing room to extend an invitation to the Pickwickians: 'To-morrow morning, sir, we give a public breakfast – a *fête champêtre*'.

A *fête champêtre* was a type of garden party popular at the court of Versailles. Meaning literally 'pastoral festival' it would often involve its aristocratic guests donning fancy dress and affecting a rustic ethos while they were serenaded by orchestras hidden amid the trees.

The *Eatanswill Gazette*, the official organ of the Blue Party, has no ethical qualms over printing a review of the fete before it has even taken place. The occasion 'would present a scene of varied and delicious enchantment' the newspaper confidently predicts, 'a bewildering coruscation of beauty and talent – a lavish and prodigal display of hospitality – above all, a degree of splendour softened by the most exquisite taste; and adornment refined with perfect harmony and the chastest good keeping'.

---

* Simon of Sudbury took refuge in the Tower of London during the uprising. However, he was so unpopular that the guards, ignoring both the sanctuary of the Tower and his ecclesiastical status, allowed the mob to enter and drag the luckless archbishop off to Tower Hill where they beheaded him.

The Hosts

Dickens does not provide us with a portrait of Mrs Leo Hunter, apart from quoting the *Eatanswill Gazette*'s description of her as a 'virtuous and highly distinguished lady'. From the fulsomeness of the compliments paid to her by her male guests and their gallant professions to find her indistinguishable from her daughters, we can conclude that she is a lady of a certain age.

Mrs Hunter's reputation as a hostess is enhanced by her literary credentials as a poetess. Her most famous work is 'Ode to an Expiring Frog', which created 'an immense sensation' when it appeared in a lady's magazine.

Her co-host, Mr Leo Hunter, acts as his better half's subservient intermediary. In addition to delivering invitations, his role is to flatter his wife in public and occupy her less important guests in conversation so that she is free to ignore them.

The mild Mr Leo Hunter does not seem like the big game sportsman his name implies. The chapter describing the party is full of leonine imagery: the hosts' house is called 'The Den', guests are described as lions and lionesses, etc. Dickens here is playing on the phrase 'lion hunter' which in nineteenth-century parlance denoted a social climber who tried to cultivate celebrities.

The Guest List

'Mrs. Leo Hunter – is proud to number among her acquaintance all those who have rendered themselves celebrated by their works and talents', her grave husband informs Mr Pickwick when he proffers the invitation, 'it is her ambition, sir, to have no other acquaintance'.

The party is indeed a 'blaze of beauty, fashion and literature'. The Hunters have managed to snare 'half a dozen lions from London — authors, real authors, who had written whole books, and printed them afterwards'.

The local intelligentsia is represented by Mr Pott, the editor of the *Eatanswill Gazette*, an august and pompous gentleman, accompanied by his high-handed wife. Other members of the *Gazette*'s literary staff are also in attendance.

To give the gathering an international flavour there is Count Smorltork — a comic all-purpose foreigner, who amuses us with his malapropisms and by mispronouncing the names of everyone he is introduced to.

The Dress Code

The ever-dignified Mr Pickwick is exempted from the obligation to don fancy dress. His three companions hire costumes from Solomon Lucas's shop on the High Street. Mr Lucas's wardrobe, we are told, did not contain 'any one garment made precisely after the fashion of any age or time'. Everything is 'more or less spangled' — somewhat pointless at a breakfast garden party.

The members of the Pickwick Club choose costumes which reflect their characters. Mr Tupman, the amorous adventurer, dresses as a bandit in a green jacket with a two-inch tail, velvet shorts, a sugar loaf hat and with bandages on his legs 'to which all Brigands are peculiarly attached.' Mr Snodgrass, the poet, dons blue satin trunks and cloak, white silk tights and shoes, and a Grecian helmet, 'which everybody knows (and if they do not, Mr. Solomon Lucas did) to have been the regular, authentic, everyday costume of a Troubadour'. The athletic Mr Winkle wears a light-red coat and 'could not possibly have been mistaken for anything but a sportsman, if he had not borne an equal resemblance to a general postman.'

Having some visual means of distinguishing between Mr Pickwick's companions is useful as Dickens doesn't bother fleshing out the three gentlemen's characters and they are pretty much interchangeable. Mr Snodgrass is not observed to read or write any poetry in the 850 plus pages of the novel, Mr Winkle seems to have no interest in or aptitude for sport and Mr Tupman's lady-killing is confined to pursuing a fifty-year-old spinster aunt, in which endeavour he is easily outsmarted by the nefarious Mr Alfred Jingle.

Mr Pott, the 'slumbering lion of the *Eatanswill Gazette*', arrives at the party as a Russian officer of justice with knout in hand. Mrs Pott is garbed as Apollo, perhaps suggesting who wears the toga in that relationship. Other guests come as field marshals, Turks, sultanas, officers, cavaliers and Charles the Seconds. The hostess herself presides over the assembly dressed as Minerva 'overflowing with pride and gratification at the notion of having called such distinguished individuals together.'

Mr Pickwick, despite being attired in his everyday clothes, arouses 'delight and ecstasy' in the people who have gathered at the gates to watch the guests arrive and who are 'under the impression that his tights and gaiters were some remnants of the dark ages'.

The Conversation

The literary lions from London are to be found 'walking about like ordinary men, smiling and talking – aye, and talking pretty considerable nonsense too, no doubt with the benign intention of rendering themselves intelligible to the common people about them.' Count Smorltork takes copious notes on all details of the proceedings as he is 'gathering materials for his great work on England'.

The Entertainment

Quadrilles are danced, despite the early hour, to a 'band of music in pasteboard caps'. The musicians, like Count Smorltork, are foreigners of no fixed nationality: an ensemble of 'four something-ean singers in the costume of their country' who sing their national songs, which comprise grunts offset by a howling soloist.

Their 'interesting performance' is followed by a peculiar dance involving a boy and a chair, 'After which, the voice of Mrs. Pott was heard to chirp faintly forth, something which courtesy interpreted into a song'.

This is all a prelude to Mrs Leo Hunter's 'Ode to an Expiring Frog' declaimed by the authoress herself, which is immediately followed by an encore. Indeed the hostess is only prevented from undertaking a third rendition of her magnum opus by her guests' heartfelt insistence that she should not exert herself further.

The Food and Drink

Breakfast consists of lobster salad and champagne. Regular attendees scramble for the table aware of their hostess's parsimonious inclination 'to issue cards for a hundred, and breakfast for fifty, or in other words to feed only the very particular lions, and let the smaller animals take care of themselves'. Sam Weller makes his own private catering arrangements, abstracting a bottle of Madeira from the breakfast table for a surreptitious tipple in the garden.

Needless to say, Count Smorltork notes down particulars of all the fare for his book.

The Outcome

All proceeds swimmingly and Mr Pickwick makes himself 'universally agreeable' until the arrival of a certain Mr Charles Fitz-Marshall, who is attired as a naval officer. This gentleman turns out to be none other than the 'faithless Jingle', who had incurred the enmity of the Pickwick Club during their earlier stay in Dingley Dell by running off with Miss Rachel Wardle, the above-mentioned spinster aunt. Jingle had compounded the offence by borrowing ten pounds off Mr Tupman to fund the elopement. However, his greatest crime in the Pickwickians' eyes was to have abbreviated his love rival's name to 'Tuppy'. This was enough to cause the normally mild-mannered Mr Pickwick to hurl an ink-stand at him.

Jingle flees and Mr Pickwick leaps into his post-chaise in hot pursuit. Perhaps in his haste to run this notorious villain to ground Mrs Hunter's words are still fresh in his ears: 'I must make you promise not to stir from my side the whole day. There are hundreds of people here, that I must positively introduce you to.'

The Legacy

Dickens was a twenty-four-year-old unknown, writing under the name of Boz, when he was commissioned to provide the text to accompany a monthly series of illustrations by the artist Robert Seymour depicting the adventures of a club of Cockney sportsmen. Shortly before the second number was published Seymour committed suicide. Rather than drop the serial, Dickens, who confessed to knowing very little about sport (as illustrated by his chapter on the cricket match at Dingley Dell), persuaded his publishers to make the words the focus of the series and allow him to expand its satirical remit. It quickly made his name, especially after the introduction of Mr Pickwick's worldly manservant Samuel Weller in the tenth number, and spawned a merchandising empire which included Pickwick cigars, Weller corduroys and Boz cabs.

23

The Masque of the Red Death

LOCATION: PRINCE PROSPERO'S REALM
HOST: PRINCE PROSPERO
DATE: UNKNOWN

From 'The Masque of the Red Death' (1842)
by Edgar Allan Poe

The Host

Prince Prospero is the 'happy and dauntless and sagacious' ruler of an unnamed country in an unspecified era. His domains are being ravaged by a virulent plague known as the Red Death: a combination of the worst bits of tuberculosis and bubonic plague. Its victims die in thirty minutes accompanied by agonizing pain and profuse bleeding from the pores. 'Blood was its Avatar and its seal – the redness and the horror of blood.'

With no known cure to the Red Death the Prince decides to seal himself into an abbey until it abates. He takes with him 'a thousand hale and light-hearted friends from among the knights and dames of his court'. In casual neglect of his duties to the remainder of his subjects he decides that 'The external world could take care of itself.' Not exactly the most enlightened ruler by today's standards.

With no engineers or navvies to do the job for them the courtiers, having entered the iron gates of the abbey, 'brought furnaces and massy hammers and welded the bolts. They resolved to leave means neither of ingress or egress to the sudden impulses of despair or of frenzy from within.'

We don't know much about what happened next but all those aristocrats must have got pretty bored stuck in there on their own with no poor people to lord it over. So in the fifth or sixth month of their seclusion in the abbey the prince decides to cheer everyone up by throwing 'a masked ball of the most unusual magnificence'.

The Invitation

No formal invitation is required as all the inmates of the abbey are invited. Considering they have all been incarcerated together for six months it would have been pretty hard even for a person as heartless as Prince Prospero to leave someone off the list.

The Venue

A suite of seven interconnecting rooms in the castellated abbey which was 'the creation of the prince's own eccentric yet august taste.' Each room is themed in a different colour, enhanced by a stained-glass window through which light shines from a brazier outside and refracts off a 'profusion of golden ornaments that lay scattered to and fro or depended from the roof.'

The decor of the first six rooms is respectively: blue, purple, green, orange, white and violet. The seventh room is draped in black velvet hangings and lit by a blood-red light – a sort of glorified teenager's bedroom. In it is a gigantic clock of ebony whose 'pendulum swung to and fro with a dull, heavy, monotonous clang'. As the idea of the party is to help take guests' minds off the grimness outside the abbey none of them much cares to venture into this scary final chamber.

The significance of the seven colour-coded rooms has been much discussed. Some critics have suggested they represent the seven deadly sins, the seven ages of man or even the seven days of the week (some sort of anticipation by Poe of twentieth-century pop music perhaps: Blue Monday to Black Sabbath?).

More likely it is an allusion to the Book of Revelation where everything comes in sevens: the book of seven seals is opened by a lamb which has seven eyes and seven horns and leads to the appearance of seven angels bearing seven trumpets. And of course it all has a suitably apocalyptic finale.

The Guest List

The guest list comprises everyone who is anyone in the abbey. Which of course literally means everyone, as all the nobodies have been left outside to die of the plague.

The Dress Code

Under the sartorial direction of Prince Prospero the masqueraders are garbed in costumes inspired by the grotesque. 'There were arabesque figures with unsuited limbs and appointments. There were delirious fancies such as the madman fashions. There were much of the beautiful, much of the wanton, much of the *bizarre*, something of the terrible, and not a little of that which might have excited disgust.'

The Food and Drink

In all his gloomy gothicism Poe doesn't bother us with the niceties of the menu. All we know is that there is wine. We have no idea who was serving it, as all the sommeliers and maître d's have long ago succumbed to the Red Death outside. Possibly it was a self-service buffet.

The Entertainment

It turns out that a few common people have been allowed into the abbey after all: there are buffoons, improvisatori, ballet dancers and musicians. Improvisatori were the stand-up comedians of the Renaissance, strolling poets who improvised verses on topics of contemporary relevance.

'It was a gay and magnificent revel,' we are told. Waltzes are danced to the 'wild music' played by the orchestra. The only interruption to the general jocularity comes every hour when the great ebony clock in the seventh chamber strikes, causing the waltzers to freeze in their gyrations and the orchestra to fall temporarily silent. There's definitely a feeling in the air that something really quite bad is going to happen.

The Conversation

Again the apocalyptic tone of the story doesn't give much licence to dwell on anything as mundane as the guests' conversation. Or perhaps it's just that these people who'd been cooped up with one another for six months had totally run out of small talk.

The Outcome

'And the revel went whirlingly on, until at length there commenced the sounding of midnight upon the clock.' As the chimes boom out and the habitual spooked silence falls on the dancers and musicians a mystery guest makes his appearance. 'The figure was tall and gaunt, and shrouded from head to foot in the habiliments of the grave' and has 'out-Heroded Herod'* by wearing a mask in the form of the 'countenance of a stiffened corpse' daubed with blood. A deadly terror seizes anyone who attempts to apprehend this ghoulish gatecrasher. Only Prince Prospero has courage enough to pursue the apparition to the final chamber. Here it turns suddenly to face him and the prince falls to the ground stone dead. The guests seize the mummer but its costume proves be 'untenanted by any tangible form'. The plague has symbolically entered the castle and one by one the revellers perish. 'And Darkness and Decay and the Red Death held illimitable dominion over all' concludes Poe as the party ends on a distinct downer.

The Legacy

Alfred Hitchcock once said, 'It's because I like Edgar Allan Poe's stories so much that I began to make suspense films.' (Though oddly enough he never filmed any of Poe's stories.) Despite Poe's early death at the age of forty in 1849 he made a huge posthumous contribution to the horror movie industry. The Internet Movie Database lists 254 films based on his works dating from 1908 to 2013. The actor Vincent Price owed much of his career to

---

* Out-Heroding Herod would actually be pretty tough. King Herod of Israel (c.74–4 BC) was not only responsible for the biblical Massacre of the Innocents, but also had three of his own sons executed, not to mention his wife and numerous rabbis.

Poe adaptations, starring in eight of them, including *The Masque of the Red Death* made by legendary B-movie director Roger Corman. In order to pad out an eight-page story to movie length lots of gratuitous new elements were added, including devil worship, virgin sacrifices and some satanic S&M.

24

The Feddens'
25th Wedding Anniversary Party

LOCATION: 48 KENSINGTON PARK GARDENS,
NOTTING HILL, LONDON
HOSTS: GERALD AND RACHEL FEDDEN
DATE: 5 NOVEMBER 1986

From *The Line of Beauty* (2004) by Alan Hollinghurst

The Hosts

Officially designated 'The Right Hon Mr and the Hon Mrs Gerald Fedden', Gerald owes his title to being a Member of Parliament, and his wife Rachel because she is the daughter of a baron. Being an 'Honourable' is of course (to those who care about such things) more honourable than being a mere Right Honourable.

Gerald is a 'bon viveur' who is keen on wine, his wife, power, Wensleydale cheese and the music of Richard Strauss. He is Conservative MP for Barwick, a grim provincial town somewhere in the Midlands, 'which still had a regular livestock market and loose straw blowing in the street' which he loathes. He is deeply competitive and when his parliamentary duties oblige him to attend the summer fete in his constituency he insists on winning the 'welly-whanging' competition.[*]

An 'amusing speaker from the floor of the House', Gerald

[*] Welly whanging (also spelled 'wellie wanging') is a sport developed in the North of England where competitors attempt to throw a wellington boot as far as possible. The

manages his workload by relying 'on briefings by hard-working secretaries and assistants'. He is a pro-European because he owns a large property in the Dordogne where he spends the summer. He collects art and political cartoons (well, any ones that feature himself) and dreams of receiving the ultimate fillip to the ego of a 1980s politician – having 'a *Spitting Image* puppet in his likeness'.

There are two women in his life: his wife, Rachel Fedden, née Kessler, older and posher than himself; and the prime minister, Margaret Thatcher. Their photos sit side by side on his desk and Gerald hopes that the occasion of twenty-five years of marriage to one will give him the perfect social excuse to have the honour of receiving the other in his home.

The Invitation

Invitations crowd the Feddens' mantelpiece, irrespective of their date (prestige over practicality determines their shelf life), overlapping to form 'almost one long curlicued social sentence, Mr and Mrs Geoffrey – & Countess of Hexam – Lady Carbury "At Home" for – Michael and Jean – The Secretary of State …' The invite to the Feddens' own silver wedding anniversary is presumably adorning the mantelpieces of an equally prestigious selection of the great and the good.

The Venue

The Feddens' residence is a 'big white Notting Hill house' where the porcelain is Sèvres, the curvy French furniture oyster and the painting above the fireplace a Guardi. The drawing room,

---

welly must be a standard Dunlop green, size 9, non steel toecap, though competitors may select whether they use a left or right boot.

'devised and laid out for entertaining, on a generous scale', hosts occasional piano recitals. For the anniversary party a marquee has been erected in the garden, 'a dreamlike extension to the house-plan'. Lights and candles and the smell of lilies give 'a sense almost of being in church'.

Gerald frets that his house might betray some evidence of political backsliding on his part. An assemblage of early photographs of himself and Rachel, including one of him in his hippy phase, which 'had reached its counter-cultural extreme in a pair of mutton-chop whiskers and a floral tie', gives him cause for unease. Even the house's 'eternally green front door' is repainted in 'a fierce Tory blue' so as not seen to be espousing any covert environmentalist sympathies.

The Guest List

Gerald, who is having difficulty seeing the party as a family occasion rather than a career-advancement opportunity, nevertheless finds himself obliged to invite some members of his household: his son, Toby, a Hooray Henry Oxford graduate, and daughter, Catherine, a manic-depressive with a history of self-harm, who has a horror of the 'au' sound and the colour maroon. The domestic guest list is completed by their appropriately named lodger, Nick Guest, Toby's friend from university and the novel's de facto narrator. Nick has a sinecure as art director on his millionaire boyfriend's style magazine (which runs to one issue) and is the putative producer of a doomed film version of an obscure Henry James novel, *The Spoils of Poynton*. In reality he spends most of his time partying in London's gay scene.

All Gerald's wettest dreams have come true and the guest of honour of the evening is to be the prime minister, Mrs Margaret

Thatcher, aka 'The Lady'. She is the only real life person who attends the party (apart from her unobtrusive husband, Denis). The rest of the guests are a backdrop of Central Office central casting, with silly Tory names like Badger Brogan and Jonty Stafford; though a guest in white tuxedo with grey curls 'oiled back in deep crinkly waves' seems to bear a distinct resemblance to Douglas Hurd.

Mrs T 'came in at her gracious scuttle' inspiring a frenzy of adoration and sycophancy among the gathered party faithful, with their faces taking on 'a look beyond pride, a kind of rapture' as she graces them with her presence. They instinctively realize that 'she'd be piqued if there wasn't a throng, a popular demonstration' and form themselves into 'a sort of unplanned receiving line when the Lady came into the room'.

The Dress Code

Though not explicitly stated, the dress code seems to be black tie, so we are spared any eighties power dressing or even Gerald's penchant for pink shirts with white collars. Rachel and Catherine are 'transformed by silk and velvet, jewels and make up' but Mrs Thatcher is the sartorial star of the gathering: 'Her hair was so perfect ... a fine if improbable fusion of the Vorticist and the Baroque': a tribute to Aqua Net in those innocent days before ozone depletion concerns. 'She was wearing a long black skirt and a wide-shouldered white-and-gold jacket, amazingly embroidered, like a Ruritanian uniform, and cut low at the front to display a magnificent pearl necklace.' Catherine tartly observes that 'she looks like a country and western singer'.

The Conversation

All the guests are desperate for their 'twelve seconds with the PM'. The men, endeavouring to lose their clinging wives, jostle for their chance to pull 'a hot date with the Lady'. The outcome proves generally tepid though, with most granted 'an audience of a minute or two before being amicably dislodged'. Mrs T's preferred conversational topic of the Common Agricultural Policy is her secret weapon for deflecting unwanted social attentions. Despite her general affability, Nick Guest suspects that in place of a conversation 'There was something in the PM that seemed to say she'd have preferred an argument, it was what she was best at'.

The Food and Drink

The dining room is set up for a sit-down dinner 'crowded like a restaurant with separate tables'. Unfortunately we are obliged for our description of events to Nick, and his prodigious cocaine intake throughout the evening has suppressed his appetite to the extent that he shows no interest in the food. But he does note the mitred napkins, black-inked cards (untitled of course) and champagne flutes the size of tubas.

Even the effect of the drink on offer, 'champagne, claret, Sauternes, and more champagne', is neutralized by all the 'laughing powder' he has ingested.

The Entertainment

Nick doesn't find the official line-up – big band jazz, early rock and roll and a speech by Toby – of much interest and instead arranges his own programme of entertainment. He goes cottaging in a public lavatory before the party and then spends much of the evening snorting lines of charlie upstairs in his bedroom. When he finally stumbles back down to the party, he has acquired enough chemically induced chutzpah to ask Mrs Thatcher for a dance. She, being 'fairly sozzled', accepts. They take to the parquet dance floor 'to the thump of "Get Off of My Cloud" ' and the Iron Lady starts 'getting down rather sexily with Nick'. With 'the PM breathless in his grip' it is up to Gerald to step in, interrupt their cavorting and restore decorum.

The Outcome

Nick heads back upstairs for a gay threesome with his Lebanese playboy boyfriend and an obliging doe-eyed Portuguese waiter. Gerald manages to dance with the PM 'for almost ten minutes', which he has always planned as the 'climax of the evening'. As things turn out it also proves to be the last hurrah of his political career. As his guest of honour leaves, he sees her to her Daimler with 'the glow of intimacy and lightness of success about him'.

'The 80s are going on for ever', Catherine surmises later. Just a week before the Feddens' party, on 27 October 1986, the UK's financial markets had been deregulated, ushering in the true beginning of what we now think of as the Thatcherite era (yuppies, greed, corporate excess, etc), which reigned for two decades before coming so spectacularly unstuck in 2007/8. At the time of writing Gerald and Rachel would be celebrating their golden wedding anniversary (in the unlikely event that their marriage survived his financial ruin and political downfall).

The Legacy

Margaret Thatcher went on to win the 1987 election and eventually notched up 11 years and 209 days in office, to become the longest-serving British prime minister since Lord Salisbury. Well in demand for cameo roles in literature, she also appears in several novels by Frederick Forsyth, *XPD* by Len Deighton, and *The Child in Time* by Ian McEwan.

25

The College Summer Ball

LOCATION: A NAMELESS PROVINCIAL UNIVERSITY
HOST: ITS EQUALLY NAMELESS PRINCIPAL
DATE: THE EARLY 1950S

From *Lucky Jim* (1954) by Kingsley Amis

The Invitation

Twenty-five shillings for a ticket to the College Summer Ball is a fairly steep price for a junior lecturer to have to fork out in the post-war austerity years, especially one who professes himself to have 'never been much of a dancing man'. However, blackmail can be persuasive and James Dixon, the eponymous 'Lucky Jim', finds himself trapped into taking his fellow lecturer Margaret Peel to the ball. She is recovering from a suicide attempt after her previous boyfriend dumped her and makes cunning use of pity and the occasional fit of hysteria to trap Dixon in an ambiguous and sexless relationship.

The Host

The principal is a 'small, ventricose man with a polished, rosy bald head' and a 'loud homicidal-maniac laugh' notorious for its ability to silence conversation in the common room. His hosting duties are confined to his more upmarket guests. As Margaret tells us: 'The Principal holds court on these occasions in a room at the other end of the dance-floor – he doesn't mix with the rabble in here.'

The Venue

The dysfunctional university at which the novel is set is never named, nor is any hint given as to its location, apart from its being 'provincial'. Over the years various seats of learning have been put forward as possible models, usually by rival establishments.

The annual summer ball is held in a room whose 'walls were decorated with scenes from the remoter past, portrayed in what was no doubt an advanced style' though Dixon, despite being a history lecturer, is unable to identify what period or ethnicity the depicted warriors represent.

The Guest List

Pretty much all of the dramatis personae of the novel are at the ball, apart from Dixon's feckless medieval-music-loving supervisor, Professor Ned Welch, who is unaccountably absent. However, he is ably represented at the event by his pretentious artist son Bertrand. Bertrand has a braying voice, affects a beret and describes the ball as a 'species of dancing festivity'. Dixon entertains regular fantasies involving extreme violence on both father and son.

Bertrand has come up to the ball from London accompanied by his gorgeous nineteen-year-old girlfriend Christine Callaghan. To the northern, bespectacled Dixon the 'notion that women like this were never on view except as the property of men like Bertrand was so familiar to him that it had long since ceased to appear an injustice'.

Short of being grateful for his good fortune, Bertrand keeps a mistress, Carol Goldsmith, who is also at the ball, her husband being conveniently absent at a conference in Leeds. Bertrand's justification for his serial philandering is, according to Carol, 'if he can have a lot of women that makes him a great artist, never mind what his pictures are like'. On this occasion his women have competition for his attentions in the form of Julian Gore-Urquhart, Christine's uncle and 'a rich devotee of the arts ... who was a fish that Welch had more than once vainly tried to land'. Bertrand is angling for a job as Mr Gore-Urquhart's private secretary.

Other members of the university staff also present include the sexagenarian Professor of Philosophy, the fifteen-stone Senior Lecturer in Economics, the Professor of Music, Barclay, with his horsey wife and Alfred Beesley, a member of the English department, 'notorious for his inability to get to know women' who nevertheless always attends such occasions in the hope that his luck will change.

Among the students are Miss O'Shaughnessy, another inaccessible beauty, whom Dixon is eagerly trying to procure for his special subject class next year, and her boyfriend Michie, an annoyingly keen ex-serviceman, whom Dixon is equally eagerly trying to dissuade from joining the class.

The Dress Code

Margaret's 'sort of minimal prettiness was in evidence' with well-applied lipstick (her usual cosmetic efforts were prodigal to distraction) and a royal-blue taffeta gown with a quadruple row of pearls. Dixon finds himself uncomfortably affected by the sight of Miss O'Shaughnessy's low-cut frock and Christine's yellow dress with bare shoulders. He reminds himself that 'somebody like Aristotle or I. A. Richards had said that the sight of beauty makes us want to move towards it'. However, his reaction to these visions of unattainable femininity is to want to

'pull the collar of his dinner-jacket over his head and run out into the street'.

The men are in evening dress, and even the bearded bohemian Bertrand from whom Dixon had earlier required 'an apology, humbly offered, for his personal appearance' manages to look 'quite presentable'.

The Entertainment

Dixon overcomes the temptation to flee from Christine's beauty and instead asks her to dance. When she accepts he feels like a 'special agent, a picaroon, a Chicago war-lord', but still finds it hard to believe that she will allow him to touch her and that 'the men near them wouldn't spontaneously intervene to prevent him'.

Dixon's warnings about not being much of a dancing man prove well founded, but he is in good company. The dance floor is like 'a C. and A. sale', full of 'jigging, lurching couples, who every few seconds lurched all one way together, bearing one along like a crowd that knows a baton charge is imminent'. The entertainment is provided by a band with a singer who has an 'enormous, half-incoherent voice, like that of an ogre at the onset of aphasia'. Their slightly retro repertoire includes 'The Darktown Strutters' Ball' and 'The Hokey-Cokey'.

The Food and Drink

The bar is 'a small room not designed for the purpose'. The tradition of a 'wet' summer ball had only recently been implemented in the hope of discouraging students from continuous visits to the pub by providing 'cheap non-spirituous liquors on the premises'. The strategy proves sound, though rations are meagre with beer and cider being served only in half-pint glasses. Beesley describes the quality of the ale on offer 'by a monosyllable not in decent use'.

Maconochie, the college porter, is doubling up as head barman for the evening, with the requirement 'to prevent the importation of spirits'. Gore-Urquhart manages to bond with him over their shared Scottish nationalist sympathies and as a result his group is supplied not only with beer in pints, but also double measures of gin.

The Conversation

There are 'talking groups on one side and the mutes lining the walls on the other'. Bertrand is firmly in the former category and devotes his energies to sucking up to Mr Gore-Urquhart with a 'frenzy of self-advertisement' about his art, including its 'contrapuntal tone-values'. Dixon silently wishes for a 'vomiting-basin'.

Unable to bear Bertrand any longer, Dixon and Carol Goldsmith dance and she offers some of her blunter observations about the nature of love, which she defines as 'Ignorance of the other person topped up with deprivation'. She diagnoses Dixon, to his guilty surprise, as suffering from a bad case of this condition with respect to Christine Callaghan, on the grounds that 'You want to go to bed with her and can't, and you don't know her very well.'

The Outcome

Emboldened by his dance with Christine and Bertrand's neglect of her, Dixon offers her a lift home in his taxi which she accepts. When his cab fails to show up he resorts to stealing Professor Barclay's and conducts Christine back to Professor Welch's house 'filled with awe at the thought that she seemed, not only not to dislike him to any significant extent, but to trust him as well'. He even manages to get a furtive kiss and a date to meet up for tea off her.

'For once in his life Dixon resolved to bet on his luck' and as the book's title suggests, it comes good. He subsequently beats Bertrand in a fight, steals Christine off him and even lands that lucrative job as Mr Gore-Urquhart's private secretary.

His triumph is inevitably someone else's misfortune. 'It was all very bad luck on Margaret, and probably derived, as he'd thought before, from the anterior bad luck of being sexually unattractive.' With this sentence Kingsley Amis irrevocably alienated feminists everywhere.

The Legacy

Lucky Jim was Kingsley Amis's first published novel; it was an immediate success, won the Somerset Maugham Award for Fiction and was filmed by the Boulting Brothers in 1957. Having a young family, Amis wasn't immediately able to give up his teaching job at the University of Wales in Swansea and spent four more years there, constantly denying it was the model for his fictional university.

26

The Anubis Orgy

LOCATION: A YACHT ON THE RIVER ODER, POLAND

HOSTS: ANTONI AND STEFANIA PROCALOWSCY

DATE: SUMMER 1945

From *Gravity's Rainbow* (1973) by Thomas Pynchon

The Invitation

Following the German surrender in the Second World War, Lieutenant Tyrone Slothrop, Harvard graduate and American GI, is on a renegade solo mission through liberated Europe in search of the last of Hitler's V2 rockets (think Captain Ahab and Moby Dick). This device (serial number 00000) 'was used in the last desperate battle for Berlin – an abortive firing, a warhead that didn't explode'.

Slothrop, the possessor of a uniquely talented penis, had been stationed in London the previous year where his erections served as an early warning system for incoming V2 rockets (which also always fell on the sites of his numerous sexual conquests).

Unfortunately, his phallic clairvoyance provides minimal assistance in the hunt for the missing missile. On Mount Brocken he picks up a lead from Geli Trippling, an 'apprentice witch', who advises him that the Schwarzgerät (black device), the propulsive hardware used in the rocket, can be found in the port of Swinemünde in Soviet-occupied Poland. For someone on a secret mission who has to pass through many checkpoints he chooses an odd costume, deciding to dress as 'Rocketman'

(Racketemensch) in an improvised superhero outfit, comprising a helmet from a looted stash of Wagnerian opera costumes and a green velvet cape with a red R sewn on. But this is rather an odd novel.

Also on her way to Swinemünde is Margherita Erdmann, an ageing German film actress who starred in 'dozens of vaguely pornographic horror movies.' She is looking for her daughter Bianca who she left on a yacht called the *Anubis*. Margherita and Slothrop had shared a brief S&M relationship in Berlin and they set off together by barge along the Spree–Oder Canal. They are in the jokily named resort town of Bad Karma when the *Anubis* heaves into view.

Waving passengers beckon the couple aboard, but as Slothrop is in the process of embarking someone mischievously pulls away the gangplank, tipping him into the river. He tries to haul himself onboard via a rope, whereupon a drunken lady in a tiara on the deck produces a meat cleaver: 'Let's cut it … and see him fall *in* again!' These guests are clearly sadists after his own heart. It promises to be a good party.

The Hosts

Slothrop is rescued from a second involuntary bath by the hostess, Stefania Procalowska, who pulls him through the porthole of her cabin and gives him a shower instead. *Gravity's Rainbow* has almost 400 named characters which doesn't leave Pynchon much room for description. All we know about the hosts ('cloud-man' and 'fogwife') is that Stefania is eighteen, blonde and the possessor of 'the first cheekbones Slothrop can recall getting a hardon looking at', while her husband, Antoni, is 'an enormous figure in Polish cavalry fatigues and with a lot of maniacal teeth' who owns the *Anubis*.

The Venue

The *Anubis*, 'an ocean-going yacht, nearly the color of the mist', has been sailing the German lowlands all summer, 'just as Viking ships did a thousand years ago, though passively, not marauding: seeking an escape it has not yet defined clearly'. The vessel's figurehead is 'a gilded winged jackal' and its additional seafaring comforts include a bar 'hung with festive garlands of flowers and light bulbs' and bedecked with 'a cheerful array of lights, red, green and white'.

The Guest List

The *Anubis* is a 'moving village', with its weather-decks 'crowded with chattering affluent in evening dress' – a melting pot of representatives of previously warring nationalities. With the arrival of the American Slothrop, the host reflects 'We are the ship of all nations now.' There is even a Japanese gentleman – Ensign Morituri, an ex-liaison officer from Berlin who 'didn't quite get out by way of Russia'.

Also on board are Miklos Thanatz, Margherita's husband, and her daughter Bianca. The identity of Bianca's father is uncertain. She was conceived on a movie set, during the filming of legendary director Gerhardt von Göll's *Alpdrücken* (Nightmare). In the role of a captive baroness Margherita was ravished by a hoard of jackal men dressed in animal masks and black hoods. The resulting footage was reserved for the director's cut (and of course 'found its way into Goebbels's private collection').

Slothrop's arrival on deck is greeted with a song. 'Welcome aboard, gee, it's a fabulous or-gy that you just dropped in on, my friend' the assembled guests serenade him in a cordial chorus, detailing the forthcoming entertainment available on the *Anubis*. 'The behavior is bestial, hardly Marie-Celestial, but you'll fit right in with the crowd,' they assure him.

The Dress Code

The 'elegantly-decked guests' are attired in tiaras, pearl chokers, white gloves, pink magnolias and satin, velvet and voile gowns, with a few jackboots thrown in for a bit of period kinkiness.

Bianca is a 'knockout ... wearing a red chiffon gown, silk stockings and high-heeled slippers, her hair swept up elaborate and flawless and interwoven with a string of pearls to show pendant earrings of crystal twinkling from her tiny lobes.' Slothrop, courtesy of the hostess, has swapped his wet superhero outfit for a tuxedo.

The Food and Drink

Though no food seems to be on offer there is little sign of postwar austerity when it comes to drinks and other stimulants: 'Waiters with brown skins and doe eyes circulate with trays on which you are likely to find any number of substances and paraphernalia.' The drinks list includes absinthe, Irish whiskey and highballs mixed 'with a sinister white powder'.

The Conversation

Even an orgy needs a bit of ice-breaking small talk. The ladies gossip about Margherita's use of Oneirine, a 'celebrated intoxicant' synthesized by Laszlo Jamf* – a hallucinogen which also has the handy property of modulating time. The men discuss

---

* The versatile Dr Jamf also sexually conditioned Slothrop as a child and invented Imipolex G, a polymer used in the V2.

military hardware and particularly Slothrop's favourite subject, V2 rockets, in suitably macho terms ('Cruel, hard, thrusting into the virgin-blue robes of the sky').

The Entertainment

The reunited Margherita and Bianca are already 'playing stage mother and reluctant child'. The precocious starlet treats the guests to a rendition of 'On the Good Ship Lollipop' 'in perfect mimicry of young Shirley Temple – each straining baby-pig inflection, each curl-toss, unmotivated smile, and stumbling toe-tap.' Her performance earns her 'much applause and alcoholic bravo-ing', but it's the next act that really gets the audience going. Bianca sulkily refuses to perform 'Animal Crackers in My Soup' as an encore, at which Margherita, armed with a steel ruler, throws her daughter across her lap and 'pushing up frock and petticoats, yanking down white lace knickers' proceeds to give her a good spanking.

This bit of gratuitous S&M provides just the catalyst the passengers need to commence the promised orgy. Soon they are engaged in some group sex which is as meticulously choreographed as an Olympics opening ceremony – a sort of priapic conga line involving the entire guest list (minus the hosts and Ensign Morituri, who prefers to play the voyeur).* Two of the waiters satisfy a 'juicy blonde', who is 'licking ardently the tall and shiny French heels of an elderly lady in lemon organza', who is 'busy fastening felt-lined silver manacles to the wrists of her escort, a major of the Yugoslav artillery', who in turn is using his tongue to investigate the 'bruised buttocks of a long-legged ballerina from Paris', whose companion, 'a tall Swiss divorcée',

---

* Stefania thus becomes one of the rare female characters in the book that Slothrop doesn't manage to have sex with.

is employing half a dozen roses to flagellate her friend's breasts, the blood from which splashes into the mouth of a Wend . . . and so on and on, until we get back to the two waiters.

The Outcome

'It *feels*, at least, like everybody came together, though how could that be?' the author wonders (possibly the influence of that time-manipulating drug?). 'There is a general withdrawing from orifices after a while, drinking, doping and gabbing resume, and many begin to drift away to catch some sleep.' Among the last few standing is a girl with 'an enormous glass dildo inside which baby piranhas are swimming in some kind of decadent lavender', a saxophone player who uses his horn as a sex aid on 'a pretty matron in sunglasses' and a pair of robust octogenarians 'who wear only jackboots and are carrying on some sort of technical discussion in what seems to be ecclesiastical Latin' while servicing the navel and chignon of a Montenegrin countess.

Slothrop retires to his bunk and oddly dreams about a

wet weekend in Llandudno 'drinking bitter in bed with a tug skipper's daughter'. He wakes to find Bianca in his cabin, who in traditional *Gravity's Rainbow* fashion hops into bed with him, providing further employment for his 'metropolitan organ'.

The Legacy

Gravity's Rainbow has acquired a reputation for being dense and difficult to understand, but it's really just a picaresque romp in which the good soldier Slothrop sleeps his way through liberated Europe. You could say that it's not rocket science (except that much of it is).

The novel won the National Book Award in the USA in 1974, but the famously reclusive Thomas Pynchon failed to show up to the presentation ceremony. He sent the comedian 'Professor' Irwin Corey in his place who gave a nonsensical acceptance speech on behalf of 'Richard Python' accompanied by a male streaker who ran across the stage as he spoke.

The Pulitzer Prize award of that year proved equally farcical. Though the three members of the jury voted unanimously in favour of *Gravity's Rainbow*, they were overruled by the board, who deemed the book 'unreadable' and 'overwritten'. Consequently no prize was awarded, a verdict repeated in 2012 when none of the three books on the shortlist was deemed worthy of the trophy.

27

Lady Metroland's Party

LOCATION: PASTMASTER HOUSE, MAYFAIR, LONDON

HOSTESS: LADY METROLAND

DATE: 12 NOVEMBER EARLY 1930S

From *Vile Bodies* (1930) by Evelyn Waugh

The Hostess

Lady Metroland 'has for many years been a prominent hostess in the fashionable world' of the Bright Young People, the blue-blooded socialites of 1920s London. 'Regarded as one of the most beautiful women in Society' we first met her as plain the Honourable Mrs Margot Beste-Chetwynde in Waugh's previous novel, *Decline and Fall*. Initially described as South American, pretty soon she appears to have transmogrified into a standard upper-class English lady with 'the high invariable voice that may be heard in any Ritz hotel from New York to Budapest'.

She owes her social position to two advantageous marriages. Rumour holds that she murdered her first husband and father of her son, Lord Pastmaster: a whisper no doubt exacerbated by her penchant for toyboys. Her first ten years of widowhood were spent in the company of various popular dancing men of Mayfair to whom she pays monthly remittances for undisclosed services. She also has a series of young gentleman companions, including Chokey, a black American jazz musician, and the Honourable Alistair Digby-Vane-Trumpington. She once almost made the mistake of marrying one of her escorts,

Paul Pennyfeather, a schoolmaster, before she was spared this social indignity by his convenient arrest on the day of their wedding.

Her second, and current, husband is the former Sir Humphrey Maltravers, working-class lad made good and ex-Home Secretary. When kicked upstairs to the peerage his chosen title Lord Metroland is a nod to his past position in government as Minister of Transportation (which by this stage of Britain's proud history meant being responsible for buses and trams rather than sending convicts to Australia).

Unlike the idle rich of her social set, Margot Metroland works for a living, being the European agent for her family business, The Latin American Entertainment Co. Ltd., a chain of 'night time' establishments along the coast of her native continent, to which she ships out a procession of well-favoured young ladies. It is likely that this shady avenue of finance has provided her with rather more income than any of the Hons or Lords she has married. As she says: 'I wouldn't be poor, or even moderately well off, for all the ease in the world.'

Lady Metroland is a somewhat unpredictable hostess. In *Decline and Fall* she holds a weekend party at her country residence during which time none of her guests lay eyes on her due to her spending three solid days sound asleep in bed after taking a heavy dose of Veronal.

The Invitation

The Bright Young People had to endure a punishing social schedule of almost nightly parties (Archie Schwert's 'Savage party' was only two nights before Lady Metroland's) and Mayfair's post office must have been well staffed to accommodate the flow of invitations and RSVPs.

Invites of the era could be a simple 'At Home' card or, in the case of one party given by the Bright Young People, fourteen inches high and inspired by a Futurist manifesto. Adam Fenwick-Symes, aspiring novelist and the closest thing *Vile Bodies* has to a hero, receives his invitation to Lady Metroland's in the modest form of a telegram on the morning of the party, though he finds that the enclosed prepaid reply envelope has been appropriated by his landlady to send off her betting slip.

The Venue

Pastmaster House, Hill Street, Mayfair, is 'by universal consent, the most beautiful building between Bond Street and Park Lane'. This seventeenth-century mansion resplendent with a magnificent ballroom represents only a fraction of Margot's property portfolio, which also includes a country pile in Hampshire, villas in Cannes and Corfu and a castle in Ireland.

Mayfair was the only London address for the social elite of the time. Bertie Wooster resided just a stone's throw away on Half Moon Street. The area was also associated with Margot's other line of business. Shepherd Market was a well-known haunt of prostitutes and was where Jeffrey Archer famously engaged the services of Monica Coghlan in the 1980s.

The Guest List

Lady Metroland has the ability to attract both men of state and the fashionable Bright Young People to her soirées, which 'testified to her success ... it is only a very confident hostess who will invite both these sets together at the same time'. This particular gathering gives Waugh the opportunity to bring together many of his very silliest-named characters, including the Duchess of

Stayle, Miss Mouse, Mr Malpractice, Lady Circumference and Lady Throbbing.

The most prestigious guest is 'this week's Prime Minister', the Right Honourable Walter Outrage, who during the course of the novel seesaws with Sir James Brown in occupancy of No 10 Downing Street – in a parody of the revolving door premierships of Ramsay MacDonald and Stanley Baldwin in the 1920s.

Also present are the press baron Lord Monomark (a thinly veiled Lord Beaverbrook), the Maharajah of Pukkapore and various other titled folk. 'The Bright Young People came popping all together, out of someone's electric brougham like a litter of pigs, and ran squealing up the steps.'

The guest of honour is the American evangelist Mrs Melrose Ape, who is on a fundraising European tour with her entourage of performing angels, who bear names such as Chastity, Divine Discontent, Humility, Temperance and Creative Endeavour. The angels' social status causes perplexity among the staff at Pastmaster House, who finally conclude that they should be classified as nurses.

One person who is expressly excluded from the party is gossip columnist Lord Simon Balcairn (aka Mr Chatterbox of *The Daily Excess*), about whom Lady Metroland grumbles 'He's written things about me in the papers'. Simon, who only gets paid by writing things about the likes of Lady M in the papers, is desperate to secure an invitation.

The Dress Code

Unusually for a party to which the BYPs are invited, there isn't a dress code. Their standard social whirl included 'Masked parties, Savage parties, Victorian parties, Greek parties, Wild West parties, Russian parties, Circus parties, parties where one had to dress as somebody else, almost naked parties in St. John's Wood'. Lady Metroland's cunning break with tradition has confused a bunch of gatecrashers who arrive attired in Victorian fancy dress and are immediately 'detected and repulsed'. They hurry home 'to change for a second assault.'

The only other person to make a special effort with his outfit is the banned Simon Balcairn, who infiltrates the party decked out in a false beard and the Order of St Michael and St George.

Mrs Ape, resplendent in a gown of heavy gold brocade embroidered with biblical texts, and her angels with white shifts, gold sashes and wings take centre stage.

The Conversation

Much of the conversation that Simon Balcairn is so desperate to eavesdrop on is provided by elderly twin sisters Lady Throbbing and Mrs Blackwater. They speculate on whether Nina Blount has recently lost her virginity (she has), discuss whether Lady Metroland's son, Peter Pastmaster, drinks too much (he does) and wonder whether a past dalliance between Lady Metroland and Lord Monomark might be continuing (we wouldn't put it past her). The Bright Young People, who talk in a 'coterie' language in which everything is either 'divine' or 'dreary', decide this gathering falls into the latter category and proclaim themselves bored.

The Food and Drink

There is no mention of any alcoholic consumption (a not very 'drunk-making' occasion, as the Bright Young People would say). Perhaps this abstemiousness is a nod to the religious sensibilities of the guest of honour (one of her angels is called Temperance after all). The only reference to drink is when Mrs Ape promises champagne to her chapter if they 'sing nice', but this is revoked after a squabble breaks out.

The Entertainment

Upon an orchid-banked stage, her angels sitting behind her, Mrs Ape rises to deliver 'her oration about Hope', which is normally guaranteed to stir up 'a tornado of emotion' in her audience. She invites the assembled aristocrats and socialites to '*Just you look at yourselves*' and succeeds in evincing a few seconds of self-doubt in them before Lady Circumference lets out 'a resounding snort of disapproval'. This is enough to dispel the 'fashionable piety' that was in danger of breaking out and 'Margot Metroland for the first time in her many parties was glad to realize that the guest of the evening was going to be a failure.' As quickly as it had begun Mrs Ape's social debut is over, without even time for the angels to give a rendition of her signature hymn, 'There ain't no flies on the Lamb of God'.

The Outcome

Lady Metroland is quick to take advantage of Mrs Ape's social *échec* and has soon headhunted a couple of the more comely angels to alternative careers in her South American franchise.

Simon Balcairn, caught red-handed attempting to phone through his copy to the *Daily Excess*, is unmasked and ejected from the party. To have failed to file a story on a Margo Metroland party is a shame too great to bear for a society diarist. He phones the night editor and dictates a totally bogus* account of the evening's events. 'It was his swan-song. Lie after monstrous lie bubbled up in his brain' as he describes scenes of religious ecstasy breaking out at Pastmaster House. He then retires to his kitchen and puts his head in the gas oven.

The *Daily Excess* receives sixty-two writs for libel in an 'orgy of litigation such as they had not seen since the war'. Many of the cases are settled out of court and the Bright Young People use their damages to fund another party at which they also get bored, this time on an airship.

The Legacy

In the introduction to *Vile Bodies* Evelyn Waugh tells us 'The action of the book is laid in the near future, when existing social tendencies have become more marked.' Unfortunately, even by the time of the novel's publication in 1930 the Bright Young People set was already old hat. Its members had been complaining

---

* 'Bogus' was another coterie word which was adopted by the BYPs — some sixty-five years before Bill and Ted.

since the mid-twenties of having been infiltrated by riffraff. They were probably alluding to people like Waugh, who was a middle-class publisher's son and had to endure the embarrassment of growing up in Hampstead rather than Belgravia.[*]

---

[*] Waugh actually lived between Hampstead and Golders Green. It is said that he always walked uphill to the Hampstead postbox, even though there was a nearer one downhill, so that his letters would bear the prestigious NW3 postmark.

28

The Warrior Feast

LOCATION: VALHALLA, ASGARD

HOST: ODIN

DATE: ALL ETERNITY (UNTIL RAGNARÖK)

From *The Prose Edda* (*c.* 1220) by Snorri Sturluson

The Host

Odin is the highest and the oldest of the Norse gods. The son of Bor and the giantess Bestla, his paternal grandfather Buri was uncovered in a block of hoar frost licked by the primeval cow Audhulma. Odin and his brothers killed the frost giant Ymir and created heaven and earth out of his corpse. 'From his blood they made the sea and the lakes. The earth was fashioned from the flesh, and mountain cliffs from the bones. They made stones and gravel from the teeth, the molars and those bones that were broken.' They also created Asgard, which was to be the dwelling place of the Æsir (gods). The first humans were whittled out of two pieces of driftwood found on the seashore and lived in a realm called Midgard.

Odin's brothers then seem to have conveniently vanished from the scene (though they occasionally return to provide holiday cover for him) leaving him to reign supreme over this new world. 'He rules in all matters, and, although the other gods are powerful, all serve him as children do their father.' He sired quite a few of the other deities, including Baldr, Vali and the thunder god Thor, better known today as Donald Blake's alter ego in Marvel comics.

Odin goes by over 150 names in total, including All-Father, Herjan (Lord), Hnikud (Thruster), Fjolnir (Wise One), Oski (Fulfiller of Desire), Omi (Resounding One), Biflindi (Spear Shaker), Vidrir (Ruler of Weather) and Val-Father (Father of the Slain).

The Invitation

Odin has an eight-legged horse, Sleipnir, on which he can travel between the worlds of the living and the dead. He invites all warriors who fall in battle to reside in Asgard, where he hosts a permanent party in their honour. The invitations to this post-humous revelry are handed out by maidens called Valkyries (Choosers of the Slain): 'They are sent by Odin to every battle, where they choose which men are to die and they determine who has the victory.'

The Venue

Valhalla, aka Valhöll (Hall of the Slain), is a vast building in Asgard with 540 doors. 'Golden shields covered its roof like shingles' and it is illuminated entirely by sword light. This is where the fallen warriors are welcomed. Unworthy men (i.e. anyone who was cowardly enough to die of old age or disease instead of gloriously in battle) had to go to Niflheim (Dark World) – a realm ruled over by Hel, daughter of the god of mischief, Loki. Sturluson tells us 'Mostly she is gloomy and cruel'.

The Guest List

These are the Einherjar (Lone Fighters), 'All men who have fallen in battle from the beginning of the world … A huge throng is already there, but many more are still to come.' Odin's only competition for the dead warriors is from the goddess Freyja, who will occasionally show up on a battlefield in her chariot drawn by two cats. 'Wherever she rides into battle, half of the slain belong to her. Odin takes the other half'.

An alternative place for those who perished in combat (perhaps those claimed by Freyja) was Vingolf (Friendly Quarters) – a hall which 'belonged to the goddesses, and it was exceptionally beautiful'. But being macho types the warriors probably preferred to go to Valhalla where, according to Norse chronicles, they could hang out with various real life celebrities such as Eirík Bloodaxe and Hákon the Good.

The Dress Code

The Prose Edda doesn't go into details of the dress code, but it was probably a 'come as you are' party (or perhaps that should be come as you were), so the late guests would have been in battle attire (but without those trademark horned helmets, as there is no archaeological evidence that Norsemen ever wore such things).

The Entertainment

The warriors are easily kept occupied. 'Every day, after they dress, they put on their war gear. Then they go out to the courtyard and battle, the one attacking the other. Such is their sport.' Any of them who have the bad luck to get slain a second time are resurrected at the end of the day.

The Food and Drink

'When it comes time to eat, they ride home to Valhalla and sit down to drink'. Feeding all these hungry warriors every day might have presented problems for mortal caterers, but luckily Odin has magical resources to hand. A boar named Sæhrimnir is cooked each day by the sooty-faced chef Andhrimnir in a large cauldron called Eldhrimnir. Every night Sæhrimnir is reborn whole, for the purpose of sandwiches for the next morning.

To fulfil the guests' drinking requirements a goat called Heidrun stands on the roof of Valhalla eating the leaves of the Yggdrasil, the ash tree at the centre of the world. 'From her udders streams the mead that daily fills a vat so large that from it all the Einherjar satisfy their thirst.' The fallen warriors are accorded the honour of being served their mead by the Valkyries who 'bring drink and see to the table and the ale cups'.

Odin is scornful of the possibility of teetotallers ('Would All-Father invite kings, jarls (earls) and other men of rank to his hall and give them water to drink?') but just in case there are any such people present the stag Eikthyrnir (Oak Antlers) is on hand. He also stands atop Valhalla and chews on the branches of the mystic tree and the moisture that drips from his horns forms the spring Hvergelmir, which gives rise to rivers called Sid, Vid and Vin (among others).

Odin spurns the daily rations of boiled pig flesh in favour of a liquid dinner: 'For him wine is both drink and food.' But his pet wolves Geri and Freki are on hand to ensure that his portions never go to waste.

The Conversation

No conversational details are provided, but presumably it involves tales of derring-do from the battlefield, which could be freshly updated every day.

The Outcome

If the warriors think that the idea of a permanent party with unlimited food and booze, divine waitresses, plus a good fight every day sounds too good to be true: it is. The reason they are being kept in Valhalla is so they can play their part in the final apocalyptic conflict of Ragnarök.

The Sibyl's Prophecy tells us that after six harsh years of winter, three of which are marked by world war, two wolves will swallow the sun and the moon, the stars will disappear from the heavens and an earthquake will cause the mountains to fall. In this upheaval the great wolf Fenrir, who is destined to slay Odin, will break free from his bonds.

'The sea will surge on to the land as the Midgard Serpent writhes in giant fury and advances up on the land. Then it also will happen that the ship Naglfar loosens from its moorings. It is made from the nails of dead men'.* This fateful ship is steered by the giant Hrym.

'Amid this din the sky splits apart and in ride the sons of Muspell.' These primordial beings from the southern realm of fire are joined by Loki and an army of frost giants, all of whom are soon drawn up on the battle plain called Vigrid, which 'lies a hundred leagues in each direction'.

The bad news for the Einherjar is that the prophecies fore-tell that they will all perish (again), but on the positive side so will everyone else in this battle to end all battles.

The Legacy

The world and language of *The Prose Edda* will already be familiar to anyone who has stayed awake during any of Richard Wagner's *Ring Cycle* operas or read the works of J. R. R. Tolkien. In fact the names of all thirteen of the dwarves who turn up unexpectedly for tea with Bilbo Baggins at the beginning of *The Hobbit* are lifted pretty much verbatim from the list of dwarf names handily provided in *The Prose Edda* (though Tolkien upgraded 'Gandalf' to a wizard).†

The Prose Edda and its accompanying *Poetic Edda* ('Edda' means 'great-grandmother' in Icelandic) is the source of much of our knowledge of Norse mythology. It is attributed to Snorri Sturluson — a thirteenth-century Icelandic chieftain, who twice held the position of speaker of the Althing (the equivalent of being prime minister). Iceland had formally adopted Christianity as

---

* Sturluson here dispenses some valuable manicure advice: 'for this reason it is worth considering the warning that if a person dies with untrimmed nails he contributes crucial material to Naglfar, a ship that both gods and men would prefer not to see built.'

† 'Gandalf' means 'magic wand' in Icelandic, which might explain his promotion.

its national religion two centuries previously, so Sturluson was careful to insert a few references to Adam and Eve and Jesus Christ into the text, which seem strangely incongruous amid all the elves, dwarfs and giants. There is even a namecheck for Attila the Hun (who we are told was the Valkyrie Brynhild's brother).

29
The Fifth Avenue Party

LOCATION: MANHATTAN, NEW YORK

HOSTS: LEON AND INEZ BAVARDAGE

DATE: 1980S

From *The Bonfire of the Vanities* (1987) by Tom Wolfe

The Invitation

An invitation to dinner from 'this year's host and hostess of the century' is not one that New York interior designer Judy McCoy is likely to turn down. On this matter she will brook no argument from her husband Sherman, Wall Street bond trader and self-styled Master of the Universe, even though he is rather keener on the idea of going to see his lawyer. That afternoon he has received a visit from the police investigating New York's cause célèbre of the moment – a hit and run accident in the Bronx, which has left a young black man in a coma. What Sherman has neglected to mention to his wife is that the Mercedes involved in the incident was his and that his mistress was at the wheel.

The Hosts

Leon and Inez Bavardage (their surname means 'chit-chat' in French) are 'the most busily and noisily arrived of the *arrivistes*' in 1980s Manhattan. A twentieth-century Trimalchio and Fortunata (see chapter 1), he is a New Orleans chicory salesman who made his fortune from real estate. She claims to be from an old

Louisiana family, the Belairs, and has become 'New York's reigning hostess'. She sports 'a teased blond pageboy bob and many tiny grinning teeth' and possesses the gift of being able to make every guest her 'closest, dearest, jolliest, most wittily conspiratorial friend . . . For at least forty-five seconds'.

The Venue

Despite living only six blocks away from the Bavardages' Fifth Avenue apartment the McCoys hire a car for the evening. Walking would not only be infra dig but physically impossible for Judy, whose dress has 'short puffed sleeves the size of Chinese lampshades ... A five-mile-an-hour head wind would have stopped her cold.' However, their rented chauffeur-driven Buick sedan is effortlessly eclipsed by the private limousines that the other guests roll up in.

The Bavardages' apartment has 'not so much as a hint of the twentieth century in the decor, not even in the lighting'. Mirrors have been deemed passé in Manhattan (soo 1970s); instead the room glints with light reflected from 'glazed tiles ... gilded English Regency furniture, silver candelabra, crystal bowls, School of Tiffany vases and sculpted silverware' and walls that have been painted with fourteen coats of burnt-apricot lacquer.

The living room is '*stuffed* ... with sofas, cushions, fat chairs, and hassocks, all of them braided, tasseled, banded, bordered and ... *stuffed*.' The walls are 'covered in some sort of padded fabric with stripes of red, purple and rose'.

Two tables are set for dinner. Each one has a handwoven basket of wildflowers as a faux naïf centrepiece, the trademark of New York's most in-demand florist, Huck Thigg, whose services will set the hosts back 3,300 dollars for the evening.

The Guest List

The twelve couples invited have been carefully selected to form the perfect Manhattan social balance of European aristocrats, literary and cultural figures, designers, business titans and VIFs ('very important fags'). All the guests are white. The minimum age for males is thirty-five to forty. The women come in two varieties: the 'social X-Rays' (the wives of the aforesaid men) – ladies of a certain age who are 'impeccably emaciated' and 'starved to near perfection'; and the 'Lemon Tarts' – the younger, shapelier and blonder versions who are slowly supplanting them.

Celebrity guests include:

BOBBY SHAFLETT (aka The Golden Hillbilly) – the leading tenor from the Metropolitan Opera.

NUNNALLY VOYD – the novelist.

BORIS KOROLEV – the ballet dancer.

LORD AUBREY BUFFING – the gay English poet.

THE SHADOW – the gossip columnist from society magazine 'The City Light'. She is 'A woman of a certain age with an outrageous mop of blond hair and false eyelashes so long and thick she could barely lift her upper lids', who is on hand for instant access to Manhattan's most desirable tittle-tattle.

The Conversation

At the pre-dinner drinks the guests naturally arrange themselves into 'clusters, conversational bouquets', entry to which is fiercely competitive. 'Not to be in one of them was to be an abject, incompetent social failure.' The only fate worse for a guest than not being part of a cluster was for them to be driven by isolation into conversing with their own spouse. Sherman manages to commit both crimes and finds himself 'a social light

of no wattage whatsoever in the Bavardage Celebrity Zoo', to the undying shame of his wife.

It's understandable that Sherman is not in a party mood. He's just blown a business deal that will probably cost him his job, his marriage is on the rocks, the police are closing in on him, and just when he thinks things can't get any worse he finds himself being snubbed by a real estate broker, the dreadfully named and dreadful Mrs Rawthrote. His mood of paranoia is not helped at dinner when he finds he has been – deliberately or otherwise – seated next to his mistress, Maria Ruskin.

The Dress Code

Suits (black or navy) with ties for the men. The women are attired in 'puffs, flounces, pleats, ruffles, bibs, bows, battings, scallops, laces, darts, or shirs on the bias'. All guests wear 'fire-proof grins' at all times.

The Food and Drink

Sparkling water for the ladies ('To say "Perrier" or any other brand name had become too trite'). The men, more cavalier in their calorie consumption, drink gin and tonic.

Eighties Manhattan culinary fashions were subject to such rapid fluctuations that the Bavardages have played it safe and opted for a menu which alternates between highly pretentious and down-to-earth dishes. The entrée, 'which looked like an Easter egg under a heavy white sauce on a plateau of red caviar resting on a bed of Bibb lettuce', is followed by a 'simple hearty American main course' consisting of 'slices of pink roast beef brought in on huge china platters, with ruffs of stewed onions, carrots and potatoes.'

'The dessert was apricot soufflé, prepared individually, for each diner, in a stout little crock of the Normandy sort, with borders *au rustaud* painted by hand near the rim.' This was a pudding which showed that you were counting the calories, but clearly not the cost, as 'to be able to serve twenty-four individual soufflés was a *tour de force*. It required quite a kitchen and a staff and a half.'

The Entertainment

Music or other formal entertainment is not provided. In any case the guests are far too busy networking with each other to have paid attention to it.

Instead the soundtrack to the Bavardages' 'hive' is provided by the loud expressions of mirth to which all present are required to give constant vent. The hostess's laugh of 'paroxysmal rapture' is like 'Vesuvius, Krakatoa and Mauna Loa' and takes the form of a strange 'hack hack hack' sound. Judy McCoy shows her delight and amusement at her fellow guests' bons mots with an 'automatic-weapon burst of laughter' which in sycophantic imitation of the hostess comes out as 'hock hock hock'. Opera singer Bobby Shaflett possesses a 'barnyard bray' into which he even manages to insert an extract from an aria from *Pagliacci* for effect.

The mood of self-satisfied rapture is only lowered after dinner when Lord Buffing delivers a rambling and embarrassingly serious speech of thanks in which he references Edgar Allan Poe's tale 'The Masque of the Red Death' (see chapter 23). The puzzled guests can see no relevance in his alluding to a parable of a deadly plague which kills off a bunch of rich, aloof, self-indulgent socialites.

The Outcome

Sherman is so haunted by the news coverage of his hit and run accident that he begins to believe that the other guests might be discussing the incident (highly unlikely as it involves poor and socially unconnected people who live on the wrong side of the Harlem river). His fatalism is further fuelled when Lord Buffing mentions that Edgar Allan Poe lived in the Bronx.

Sherman's mood of alienation causes him to take a deep dislike to the Bavardages and their guests, with their witless conversation, their affected laughs and their 'Faces full of grinning, glistening, boiling teeth', and he decides that the whole occasion is 'pretentious and vulgar'. Just when we find ourselves slightly warming to this arrogant, adulterous, and possibly homicidal yuppie he blows it all by opining that all these 'dancers, novelists and gigantic fairy opera singers' are 'nothing but court jesters, nothing but light entertainment for … The Masters of the Universe, those who push the levers that move the world.'

Ah. He means Wall Street bankers like him. It seems we were right about him first time.

The McCoys return home and their white-haired chauffeur presents them with a bill for $246.50 for his evening spent sitting reading 'The City Light' in the back of his Buick. Sherman is depressed and drunk, convinced that he has heard in Lord Buffing's witterings about Edgar Allan Poe 'the voice of an oracle' and a prophecy of 'the ruin of the dissolute' (i.e. him). Judy on the other hand goes to bed 'intoxicated, not by alcohol — alcohol was fattening — but by Society'.

The Legacy

Tom Wolfe took Thackeray's *Vanity Fair* as his model for *The Bonfire of the Vanities*, which originally appeared in twenty-seven bi-weekly instalments in *Rolling Stone* magazine from 1984. The novel hit the bookstores in October 1987, appropriately enough a week before the Wall Street Crash.

It was made into a movie in 1990 where its themes of hubris, ego and excess managed to manifest themselves behind the camera as much as in front of it. The film became such a monumental turkey that it regularly appears in the polls of the worst movies ever made and it even inspired a spin-off book, *The Devil's Candy* by critic Julie Salamon, which detailed all the backstage machinations of the production. To be fair on its director, Brian de Palma, he also made the movie version of another book described here, *Carrie*, which was really good (see chapter 36).

30

A Pooh Party

LOCATION: THE FOREST

HOST: CHRISTOPHER ROBIN

DATE: 'ONCE UPON A TIME, A VERY LONG
TIME AGO NOW, ABOUT LAST FRIDAY'

From *Winnie-the-Pooh* (1926) by A. A. Milne

The Venue

The Forest is home to the soft toys who make up the cast of *Winnie-the-Pooh*. Nature is just getting back to normal after a flood which left several of the animals stranded in their homes. Now 'the sun had come back over the Forest, bringing with it the scent of may, and all the streams of the Forest were tinkling happily to find themselves their own pretty shape again, and the little pools lay dreaming of the life they had seen and the big things they had done'.

The Host

Christopher Robin, aged five, who lives in a tree in the northeast of the Forest, has decided to throw a Pooh Party. 'And it's to be a special sort of party, because it's because of what Pooh did when he did what he did to save Piglet from the flood.'

Pooh, of course, is Winnie-the-Pooh (aka Edward Bear, who, confusingly, also lives 'under the name of Sanders'). Despite being 'a Bear of Very Little Brain' it was he who had the idea of using Christopher Robin's upturned umbrella as a boat in which the two of them could sail over the floodwaters to rescue their friend Piglet, who was trapped in his house. It turned out that Piglet was really only in danger of being bored to death by a long and dull story being told to him by Owl about 'an aunt who had once laid a seagull's egg by mistake', but all the same Pooh's feat is deemed worthy of a celebration.

The Invitation

Owl, despite being rather long-winded, has the advantage of being the only one of Christopher Robin's animals who can fly, so he is entrusted with the task of despatching the invitations to the guests who live in all four corners of the Forest and the Hundred Acre Wood.*

The Guest List

Owl flies first of all to the house of the party's guest of honour, Winnie-the-Pooh himself. Pooh, who tends to spend a good part of every day feeling it is 'time for a little something' is anxious to know whether there will be 'those little cake things with pink sugar icing' at the party. Owl feels it is beneath him to discuss the catering arrangements and flies off. Pooh then alternates between excitement about the forthcoming party and worry that the other guests will forget in whose honour the event has been organized. His dilemma inspires him to compose an 'Anxious Pooh Song'.

Next to be informed about the party is Eeyore, 'the old grey donkey', who is sunk in his habitual world of gloom and self-

---

* Owl and Rabbit were the only characters in the story who weren't based on toys owned by A. A. Milne's son, the real-life Christopher Robin, which is perhaps why they have boring names.

pity. He assumes that he is just to be offered the leftover food: 'I suppose they will be sending me down the odd bits which got trodden on. Kind and Thoughtful. Not at all, don't mention it.' When told that he is actually being asked to come to the party as a guest he can only imagine that the invitation must be intended for Piglet: the 'little fellow with the excited ears'.

We don't hear of Piglet's reaction to being invited, but it probably made him nervous, as most things do.

Christopher Robin has made a table out of some long pieces of wood and the other places at it are to be taken by the remaining inhabitants of the Forest: Kanga, baby Roo and Rabbit, with his ubiquitous ragtag of 'friends and relations'. Tigger is not on the guest list as he is yet to join Christopher Robin's menagerie (he doesn't arrive in the Forest until the second book, *The House at Pooh Corner*).

The Dress Code

A. A. Milne fails to mention the dress code, but E. H. Shepard's illustrations fill in the missing sartorial details. Christopher Robin wears a red romper suit and Piglet is attired in his customary green striped sleeveless bodice. The rest of the guests have come as they are, which, being animals, means naked.* Eeyore, in an unaccustomed outbreak of festive spirit, seems to have exchanged a red ribbon on his tail for a blue one for the party.

Perhaps in solidarity with Roo, all of the animals are depicted wearing bibs; with the exception of the lofty Owl of course, who would consider such a precaution unbecoming to his dignity.

---

* E. H. Shepard's illustrations of Winnie-the-Pooh were based on his son's teddy bear Growler, not Christopher Robin's. Pooh's trademark red shirt as seen in the Disney films didn't appear until 1932 on an RCA picture record.

The Conversation

It's Roo's first ever party and so he is understandably a little overexcited. He begins to talk as soon as everyone takes their places round the table. The dialogue is Beckettian, with Roo saying 'hallo' to each of the other guests, and them responding in turn by saying 'hallo' back. Christopher Robin is grateful for the diversion, as he has been buttonholed by Owl, who is recounting a story about 'an accident which had nearly happened to a friend of his whom Christopher Robin didn't know'.

Eeyore makes typically morose observations to anyone who will listen: 'It will rain soon, you see if it doesn't.' He probably secretly wants another flood, seeing in nature's callousness a pathetic fallacy that justifies his own glum world view.

Rabbit's friends and relations, hovering on the edge of the conversation, 'waited hopefully in case anybody spoke to them, or dropped anything, or asked them the time'.

The Food and Drink

Shepard's illustration of the party shows the after-dinner speech, where the guests' plates are already empty, so we never find out what was actually eaten. We know that Pooh is partial to 'hunny', that Piglet is fond of 'haycorns', and that Eeyore, masochistically, likes thistles. Owl might perhaps have been tempted to sample some of Rabbit's smaller rodent relations.

Roo drinks milk, but he fails to listen to his mother's advice to 'Drink up your milk first, dear, and talk afterwards', tries to do both at once and ends up with a case of the hiccups.

The Entertainment

'When they had all nearly eaten enough, Christopher Robin banged on the table with his spoon, and everybody stopped talking'. But his address is interrupted as he finds he has mislaid Pooh's present. Then Pooh's worst fears come true as Eeyore, who has taken it into his head that the party is being held in his honour, decides to deliver a speech of thanks.

All is soon put right and Pooh gets his present. 'It was a Special Pencil Case. There were pencils in it marked "B" for Bear, and pencils marked "HB" for Helping Bear, and pencils marked "BB" for Brave Bear.' This causes Eeyore (with perhaps a touch of authorial sarcasm) to comment: 'This writing business. Pencils and what-not. Over-rated, if you ask me. Silly stuff. Nothing in it.'

The Outcome

'Later on, when they had all said "Good-bye" and "Thank-you" to Christopher Robin, Pooh and Piglet walked home thoughtfully together in the golden evening.' This spells the end of the party, the end of the book and, for Christopher Robin, bath time.

The Legacy

Winnie-the-Pooh made his debut in the poem 'Teddy Bear', published in *Punch* magazine in February 1924. For 'a Bear with a Pleasing Manner but a Positively Startling Lack of Brain' he was to become a remarkable cash cow. His adventures have been translated into at least thirty-six languages including Frisian, Mongolian and Esperanto. The Latin translation, *Winnie ille Pu*, became the only Latin book ever to feature on the *New York Times* Best Seller list. The two Pooh collections, *Winnie-the-Pooh* and *The House at Pooh Corner*, total fewer than 70,000 words between them, which must make Milne one of the biggest grossing authors of all time on a money-per-word basis.

Despite the riches Pooh brought them, the three men responsible for creating him became Eeyore-like in their attitude to his fame and all came to resent him. Milne, who also wrote plays and detective stories, grumbled that thanks to Pooh they had all been forgotten (as indeed they have). Shepard, who lived to the age of ninety-six, wanted to be remembered as a political cartoonist and griped about 'that silly old bear'. He would have been furious (if he hadn't been dead) to find that a retrospective exhibition of his cartoons at The Political Cartoon Gallery in 2006 was titled 'The Man Who Hated Pooh'.

Christopher Robin, destined for ever to be remembered as a child of five or six, ground his axe for the rest of his life: 'It seemed to me almost that my father had got where he was by climbing on my infant shoulders, that he had filched from me my good name and left me nothing but empty fame,' he recounted bitterly in one of his two autobiographies.

31

The Manderley
Fancy Dress Ball

LOCATION: MANDERLEY, NR KERRITH, CORNWALL

HOSTS: MR AND MRS DE WINTER

DATE: 1930S

From *Rebecca* (1938) by Daphne du Maurier

The Hosts

Mr and Mrs Maximilian de Winter. The formal convention of referring to the wife by her husband's full name helps disguise the fact that the shy and gauche Mrs de Winter's first name is never revealed (even though she is the narrator of the novel). Her husband remarks tantalizingly that her name is 'very lovely and unusual' and he even knows how to spell it.

The couple had met and married a few months earlier in Monte Carlo. He is an enigmatic, recently widowed, aristocratic, older gentleman; she a young ingénue, employed as the paid companion to a wealthy American lady 'doing' Europe.

The snare in this fairy-tale romance is Maxim's late wife, the eponymous and seemingly perfect Rebecca, who possessed, according to Maxim's grandmother, 'the three things that matter in a wife ... breeding, brains and beauty'.

The Venue

' "Last night I dreamt I went to Manderley again" is the opening line of which novel?' is a hoary old pub-quiz question, the answer to which is known to men with beards and sweaters on Tuesday nights in public bars the length and breadth of the land. What they may not know is that Manderley is the ancestral seat of the de Winter family in Cornwall, with green lawns that slope down to the sea and an impressive collection of Van Dykes and Peter Lelys in the hallway. The imposing stately home which 'lived and breathed' is as daunting a presence as the spirit of its proud ex-mistress Rebecca, and both oppress the timid and socially inexperienced second Mrs de Winter.

The parties thrown at Manderley when Rebecca was alive were legendary 'with people sleeping in bathrooms and on sofas because of the squash'. The new Mrs de Winter soon finds herself pressurized by Lady Crowan – 'a tiresome gushing woman' who has a tendency to drop in uninvited – into reviving the annual fancy dress ball at the house.

The Invitation

'Life is too short to send out invitations' quips Maxim's sister, Beatrice. Of course the idle rich need not worry about such things, and Mrs de Winter doesn't have to lick a single stamp, all such clerical duties being delegated to Frank Crawley, the de Winters' estate agent.* Even the preparations of the house for the party are undertaken by an army of workmen marshalled

---

* Estate agent in the sense of the person who manages a gentleman's country property, not the shiny-suited spiv who flogs houses, though his name is appropriate for the latter role.

by Mrs Danvers, Manderley's sinister housekeeper and fanatical Rebecca acolyte.

The Guest List

'Everyone in the county came. A lot of people from London too' – a total of 500 guests. But for Mrs de Winter they are destined to be 'a sea of dim faces none of whom I knew' and not just because they are in fancy dress. Perhaps if she'd asserted her right to lick a few of those stamps after all, she might have registered some of the names on the envelopes.

The Dress Code

Despite the professed excitement of the local people over the revival of the Manderley fancy dress ball, which Lady Crowan says 'used to make the summer for all of us in this part of the world', they don't make much of an effort with their outfits. Her ladyship arrives 'monstrous in purple, disguised as I know not what romantic figure of the past, it might have been Marie Antoinette or Nell Gwynne'. Another woman 'wore a salmon-coloured gown hooped in crinoline form, a vague gesture to some past century but whether seventeenth, eighteenth or nineteenth I could not tell'. The men are no better: a motley assortment of home-made costume clichés: pirates, sailors, sheikhs and Chinamen.

It seems that only the hostess has gone to the trouble and expense of having her costume professionally made, but she ends up committing the biggest sartorial faux pas of the evening. Unenthused by suggestions that she dress up as little girl characters such as Alice in Wonderland or a Dresden shepherdess she vows to make her mark socially with her choice of outfit. Naively she follows the advice of the scheming Mrs Danvers – to copy a dress from one of the paintings hanging in the gallery, 'especially that one of the young lady in white, with her hat in her hand'. The Raeburn portrait is of Caroline de Winter, a sister of Maxim's great-great-grandfather. What Mrs Danvers omits to mention is that it is exactly the same outfit that Rebecca wore at the previous year's fancy dress ball.

The new Mrs de W's appearance at the head of the stairs is not the social triumph she expected and she is despatched back to the bedroom by her furious husband to change immediately.

Maxim, incidentally, like Mr Pickwick, refuses to don fancy dress. 'Why should I make myself hot and uncomfortable and a damn fool into the bargain?' he argues persuasively.

The Food and Drink

Sixteen select friends are invited to a private dinner beforehand, which the hostess manages to miss due to her costume debacle. For the rest of the guests there is a buffet, featuring cold salmon, cutlets in aspic, galantine of chicken, soufflé and of course the ubiquitous lobster mayonnaise. Champagne is served.

The Entertainment

The band in the minstrel gallery play a fairly standard set for the time including 'The Destiny Waltz', 'The Blue Danube' and *The Merry Widow*. Later their repertoire becomes a little odd (to the modern taste at any rate). Towards the end of the evening they strike up 'Auld Lang Syne' (despite the party taking place in August) and the guests link arms and join in with 'should auld acquaintance be forgot' with only Mrs de Winter fervently wishing they would all forget about their auld acquaintance- ship with a certain tall, elegant, raven-haired ex-mistress of the house. For its finale the band plays 'God Save the King' with the guests all standing stiffly to attention – not exactly the slow, smoochy number that a modern party would end on.

Alternative entertainment is available in the form of bridge in the library and the evening rounds off with a firework display in the garden.

The Conversation

The main subject of topical interest is what happened to the hostess's dress. To cover Mrs de Winter's embarrassment the official line is that the wrong dress was delivered by the shop where she had ordered it, which gives the guests the chance to grumble empathetically about the general unreliability of tradesmen.

The newlyweds don't exchange a word the whole evening. Confronted with a 'hotchpotch of humanity' Mrs de Winter becomes a 'dummy-stick of a person in my stead, a prop who wore a smile screwed to its face'. Maxim is 'the perfect host in his own inimitable way', but at the height of the ball his face is 'cold, expressionless' looking beyond 'to some place of pain and torture'. Perhaps some form of fancy dress would have been useful after all.

Daphne du Maurier's grim representation of upper-crust English society was probably influenced by the fact that she began writing *Rebecca* while she was an army wife in Egypt, where her husband, a lieutenant-colonel in the Grenadier Guards, was stationed. She abhorred the dreary duties of regimental social life and in her diary dismissed her fellow ex-pats as 'horrible Manchester folk'.

The Outcome

The ball at Manderley has always gone with a swing and this one proves no exception: everyone, except for the hosts, has a marvellous evening. By the time the final guests leave 'there was a grey light on the terrace ... the dawn of a tired day'. Mrs de Winter goes to bed alone, 'a niggling pain in the small of her back'. Her husband's bed remains unslept in.

Listlessly wandering the house the next morning she ends up in Rebecca's old bedroom in the west wing, where she is confronted by Mrs Danvers. Mrs Danvers points out Mrs de Winter's utter unworthiness to fill the shoes of Rebecca and pushes her in the general direction of a window overlooking the sea. 'What's the use of your staying here at Manderley? You're not happy. Mr de Winter doesn't love you. There's not much for you to live for, is there? Why don't you jump now and have done with it? Then you won't be unhappy any more,' she advises, rather overstepping the usual duties of a housekeeper to her mistress.

Maxim is saved from becoming a widow for the second time in barely a year by a sudden explosion of distress flares from a ship which has foundered on a reef, setting in motion events that will reveal the mystery of his first wife's death.

The Legacy

As a young woman on walks around Cornwall, Daphne du Maurier came across an abandoned estate called Menabilly, which she referred to as 'the House of Secrets'. The dilapidated stately home fired her imagination and inspired her to create Manderley. Following the commercial success of *Rebecca*, she was able to lease and restore Menabilly. She converted a garden shed in the grounds into a writer's studio and the house featured as a location in two further novels, *The King's General* and *My Cousin Rachel*. The original family took the house back in the 1960s and lost no time in capitalizing on its literary fame. Aspiring writers hoping to be inspired by du Maurier's muse can still take advantage of holiday lets there (if you book well in advance).

32
Mr Hosokawa's
53rd Birthday Party

LOCATION: AN UNIDENTIFIED
SOUTH AMERICAN COUNTRY
HOST: VICE-PRESIDENT RUBEN IGLESIAS
DATE: 22 OCTOBER 1996

From *Bel Canto* (2001) by Ann Patchett

The Invitation

The setting is a South American country – only ever referred to as 'the host country' (but bearing a strong resemblance to Peru) – whose principal exports are 'coca leaves and black-headed poppies'. In the interests of 'creating the illusion of a country moving away from the base matter of cocaine and heroin' its government is actively seeking foreign investment.

Mr Katsumi Hosokawa, 'the founder and chairman of Nansei, the largest electronics corporation in Japan', is just the sort of person the host country wants to suck up to. A renowned workaholic ('he worked harder than anyone in a country whose values are structured on hard work'), his only known hobby is opera.

In the hope of enticing Mr Hosokawa over from Tokyo a party has been organized to honour his 53rd birthday and lyric soprano Roxanne Coss has been laid on as bait. She is Mr Hosokawa's favourite singer (he has seen her perform eighteen times) and the news that she will be providing the entertainment is enough to cause him to accept the invitation to visit 'this godforsaken country' even though he has no intention of doing any business there.

The Host

The hosting duties are to be carried out by the country's vice-president, Ruben Iglesias. Of humble stock, he is an ex-janitor who put himself through law school and worked his way up the social ladder, getting where he is today via a combination of ambition, dedication and managing to impregnate the daughter of a senior partner at the Christmas party of the law firm where he worked.

He has risen to the second most powerful position in the land mainly due to the fact that he is shorter than the president, being 'a very small man, both in stature and girth, who had been chosen as a running mate as much for his size as for his political beliefs'.

The Venue

The vice-president's lavish official residence, a house in the capital city, which boasts Savonnerie carpets, a mantelpiece supported by marble caryatids and gold taps in the bathroom.

It has been specially kitted out for the party with a grand piano and paintings borrowed from the national museum. On 'every table sprays of yellow orchids, each flower no bigger than a thumbnail, all locally grown, trembled and balanced like mobiles, rearranging themselves with every exhalation of a guest'.

'The draperies and chandeliers, the soft, deep cushions of the sofas, the colors, gold and green and blue, every shade a jewel. Who would not want to be in this room?' Not bad for the diminutive son of a baggage handler.

The Guest List

'Representatives from more than a dozen countries who had been misled as to the nature of Mr Hosokawa's intentions were present at the party'. In total there are 191 guests, including 'ambassadors and various diplomats, cabinet members, bank presidents, corporation heads, a monseigneur and one opera star'.

The guest of honour, after Mr Hosokawa himself, was to have been the president of the host country, Eduardo Masuda. President Masuda is of Japanese parentage and stands almost a whole proud centimetre taller than his vice-president. However, the president 'had sent a note of regret saying that important matters beyond his control would prevent him from attending the evening's event'. The reality was that 'Mr Hosokawa's ill-timed birthday party' had fallen on a Tuesday, on which evening a bumper episode of the nation's favourite soap opera, *The Story of Maria*, was broadcast. 'The host country was mad for soap operas' and with the current storyline featuring Maria being held captive, the president, in solidarity with his people, decided to skip his official duties for the night to find out if she manages to escape.

Amid all the corporate drones the only other guest of any note is Roxane Coss herself. Born in Chicago and now in her mid-thirties, she possesses a voice of such magnificence that she only has to sing a few bars of Puccini to have every man in a room fall in love with her (her poor Scandinavian accompanist, Christopf, has overdosed heavily and is hopelessly besotted). 'Yellow hair, blue eyes, skin like white roses brushed in pink. Who would not be in love with Roxane Coss?'

Not on the guest list but hiding in the ventilation shafts of

the vice-president's house are eighteen freedom fighters from the Amazonian jungle. Just as Roxane finishes singing Mr Hokosawa's favourite aria* there is a change to the advertised programme and 'men burst into the party from every window and wall'.

The terrorist brigade comprises three generals ('Benjamin: raging shingles. Alfredo: mustache, first and second fingers missing on left hand. Hector: gold wire glasses that had lost one arm') and 'fifteen soldiers who ranged in age from twenty to fourteen.'

They have come to kidnap the president, but on finding that he has done a no-show they decide to hold the other guests hostage while they work out a Plan B. The building is quickly surrounded by government troops and an armed stand-off ensues. The Red Cross manages to secure the release of all

* 'The Song to the Moon' from Dvorak's *Rusalka*. This aria regularly appears in Classic FM's Hall of Fame, meaning no serious opera snob could possibly admit to liking it.

the female prisoners, with the exception of Roxane Coss. The generals hang on to her, not for anything as mercenary as her ransom value, but because they have been unable to help themselves from falling in love with her voice. This soppiness will be their undoing.

The Dress Code

The official guests are formally attired in dinner jackets and gowns, with the women sporting 'jewelry and jeweled hair combs and tiny satin evening bags fashioned to look like peonies'.

The interlopers are rather less well groomed: 'They wore faded clothing in dark colors, many in the dull green of shallow, sludgy ponds, a handful in denim or black' and 'some of the boots had fallen apart and were held together by silver electrical tape'.

The Food and Drink

At the official party a four-course dinner is served, which includes 'White asparagus in hollandaise, a fish course of turbot with crispy sweet onions, tiny chops, only three or four bites apiece, in a cranberry demiglaze', followed by lemon mousse and American bourbon. This is replaced, over the months to come, by supplies of gradually diminishing quality sent into the besieged house by the Red Cross.

The Entertainment

Originally contracted to sing six arias and be back in her hotel room by midnight, Roxane Coss ends up having to entertain her fellow hostages for several months.

Luckily these corporate guests are a remarkably cultured bunch. Tetsuya Kato, a senior vice-president and number cruncher at Nansei, proves to be a closet concert pianist, who is able to step into the breach after Roxane's regular accompanist pegs out. Viktor Fyodorov, Russian Secretary of Commerce, is revealed as a sensitive art connoisseur. And when the food deliveries from the outside world fall short of the guests' exacting culinary standards, the French ambassador, Simon Thibault, turns out, *naturellement*, to be a master chef.

The hostages are also all genuine opera lovers, who cry when they hear Roxane sing. No room here for the sort of guest you habitually find in corporate boxes at Covent Garden or the Met, who, attracted by the high prices and prestige, might be seen checking their BlackBerrys during Butterfly's death scene or skipping the third act of *Meistersinger* for the attractions of the crush bar.

Even the terrorists are noble savages who have deep reserves of spirituality. These teenage guerrillas have been brought up in the jungle and many of them have never seen a TV or a flushing lavatory before, but they all immediately fall in love with opera and specifically with Roxane ('Every boy there dreamed of crawling on top of her').

One of them, Cesar (who gets a stiffy whenever he hears La Coss sing), even turns out to possess an untutored operatic voice of great brilliance, causing Roxane to describe him as 'the boy who she was sure was meant to be the greatest singer of his time'.

The Conversation

After weeks of captivity some of the social chit-chat inevitably begins to dry up, especially as the guests don't speak each other's languages and rely on Mr Hosokawa's interpreter Gen Watanabe to be their go-between (he mainly has to translate declarations of love from male guests to Roxane).

Stockholm syndrome sets in as captors and captives fraternize. Luckily for the guests they have been taken prisoner by the rather feckless organization 'La Familia de Martin Suarez'. These 'cut-rate terrorists' are not very terrifying (the Red Cross negotiator confesses that 'He had never seen such an unprofessional group of terrorists. It was a complete and utter mystery to him how they had ever managed to overtake the house.'). Had it been the more macho 'La Dirección Auténtica' group the guests would have faced a more gruesome fate: 'LDA would have dragged one hostage up to the roof every day for the press to see, and then shot him in the head in an attempt to speed negotiations.'

As it is, Mr Hosokawa plays chess with General Benjamin, while Gen Watanabe has an affair with Carmen, one of the female freedom fighters. Regular soccer games are organized between guerrillas and guests. So imbued are the footballers with Roxane's singing that they punt the ball around to the rhythm of an aria from *The Barber of Seville*. Many of the dignitaries begin to appreciate the shallowness of their old corporate lifestyles and decide they are happier here in captivity than they ever were in their outside existence of stretch limousines, executive jets and five-star hotels.

The Outcome

All good things have to come to an end, and this party which has now dragged on for four and a half months is abruptly terminated by government troops storming the building. The terrorists are all shot, to set an example to political extremists and gatecrashers alike. The guests go reluctantly back to their limos and Gulfstream jets. Roxane ends up marrying the only man in the building who hadn't actually fallen in love with her.

The Legacy

The book was inspired by a real-life event, the Japanese Embassy Siege that occurred in Lima in 1996. Peruvian President Alberto Fujimori's tough line on the terrorists almost doubled his popularity rating in the country and allowed the electorate to turn a blind eye to him deciding to serve a third term in office (when the constitution restricted presidents to two). His aura soon wore off and he was later imprisoned for a litany of crimes that would have impressed even the LDA, including murder, kidnapping, bribery, corruption and actual bodily harm.

33
The Paris City Aldermen's Ball

LOCATION: THE HÔTEL DE VILLE, PARIS

HOST: THE PROVOST OF THE

MERCHANTS OF THE CITY OF PARIS

DATE: 3 OCTOBER 1625

From *The Three Musketeers* (1844) by Alexandre Dumas (père)

The Invitation

The sinister and scheming Cardinal Richelieu, the first minister of France and adviser to King Louis XIII, has got word that the Queen has given her prize diamonds as a love token to her foppish English admirer, the Duke of Buckingham. As part of Richelieu's plan to incriminate the Queen, whom he suspects of being a Spanish agent, he needs to arrange for her to appear at a public function without the diamonds.

  With no state occasion in the offing he commandeers a ball which is being organized by the Aldermen of the Paris City Council. In no time what would otherwise have been some forgettably dull civic function has been transformed. 'There was talk in Paris about nothing other than the ball that the Aldermen were to give for the King and Queen.'

The Host

The host of the occasion is the Provost of the Merchants of the City of Paris. The holder of this post – the equivalent of Lord Mayor – in 1625 was Nicolas de Bailleul. He distinguished himself later in his career as France's minister of finance, when he had to tackle the budget deficit, which he achieved by borrowing 12 million *livres*, raising the import duty on wine and selling honours. Plus ça change . . .

The Venue

The Hôtel de Ville of Paris. Not a hotel in that sense, but the French version of a town hall. The building was commissioned by King Francis I in 1533 and the construction work took the best part of a hundred years. It wasn't actually finished until 1628, three years after this ball was supposed to have taken place.

Eight days are spent in preparation for the event, with joiners called in to erect scaffolding for the *grandes dames* of Parisian society to sit on. The rooms are decorated with two hundred torches made from white wax ('which was an unheard-of luxury for those days').

Security is tight and at ten o'clock on the morning of the ball the Ensign of the King's Guards arrives to take possession of all the keys to the building. Fifty archers are stationed to cover the doors with additional protection provided by two companies of guards – one French and one Swiss.

The Guest List

Top of the revised guest list are their Majesties Louis XIII and Anne of Austria.

Louis XIII (1601–43), the second monarch of the Bourbon dynasty, was nicknamed Louis the Just on account of his enlightened political regime. He was also known as Louis the Chaste, because he didn't have any known mistresses. This has given rise to speculation that he might have been gay or bisexual.

The idea that he was just faithful to his wife is clearly considered too fanciful by the French. These days he is best known for his appearance in this novel and a brand of cognac named after him.

His Queen, the misleadingly named Anne of Austria, was actually Spanish and had been married off to Louis ten years previously when they were both fourteen. Pressure was immediately placed on them to produce an heir. Something modern fourteen-year-olds don't tend to get parental encouragement for. The Queen had still failed to perform this duty by the time of the ball, which might explain the somewhat frosty relations between the royal couple.

Also present are the King's various hangers-on: his younger brother (known simply as 'Monsieur'), the duc de Longueville, the duc d'Elbeuf, the comte d'Harcourt, the comte de La Roche-Guyon and various other real-life people of the era, who give writers the chance to add lots of authoritative historical footnotes.*

Missing from the guest list are the Three Musketeers themselves – Athos, Porthos and Aramis – who have all been recently wounded or detained on a secret mission to England to recover the Queen's jewels. The only member of the expedition to return safely was d'Artagnan (real name Charles de Batz-Castelmore) – an eighteen-year-old Gascon who epitomizes the spirit of the historical romance by falling in love with just about every woman he meets and challenging every man to a duel. He is present at the ball in his professional capacity as a member of the Company of the Guard under Monsieur des Essarts.

The guests begin to arrive at six o'clock and take their appointed places. The wife of the President of the Parliament of Paris (presumably a little miffed at being downgraded from guest

* But not this one.

of honour) arrives fashionably late at nine. But the King trumps her and doesn't show up until midnight; and the Queen not till half an hour later. One hopes the scaffold-style seating everyone else had been perched on for six hours was comfortable.

The Food and Drink

Before the ball the King is served 'a light meal of preserves'. If anyone else is permitted to eat it is not considered worthy of mention.

The Conversation

The main topic of discussion among the guests is how miserable the King and Queen are looking and the rather sharp exchanges between the royal couple are mainly on the subject of the whereabouts of the diamonds.

The Dress Code

The King and Queen arrive 'in full Court dress' and rooms have been provided for them to change into their fancy dress for the ball.

Louis, being a well-known devotee of country sports, emerges dressed in a 'hunting costume of a most elegant type ... it was the costume which became him best'. His brother and the other gentlemen are similarly attired. Earlier in the book the King professes himself 'the only man who takes any real interest in the art of hunting' and complains how his state duties get in the way of the important things in life, forcing him to devote his time to planning the slaughter of Protestants rather than the local wildlife.

The Queen also wears a hunting costume, with 'a felt hat with blue feathers, a coat of pearl-grey velvet with diamond clasps and a skirt of blue satin with a silver brocade', causing Dumas to enthuse 'if the King appeared to be the first gentleman of his Kingdom, the Queen was without doubt the most beautiful woman in France.'*

The Queen's outfit is seen to include her diamonds, but the question now is how many? Cardinal Richelieu (dressed this evening as a Spanish cavalier) had cunningly arranged for his agent in England, a bewitching beauty who goes under the name of Milady, to secretly snip off two of the diamonds while they were in the possession of the Duke of Buckingham.

The Entertainment

'Twenty violins had been engaged – at twice the standard rate – with the requirement that they are to play all night.' Clearly

---

* The Rubens portrait of Anne of Austria in the Louvre doesn't really bear out this claim. Dumas must have been wearing his most chivalric spectacles.

no expense has been spared, perhaps because the musical entertainment for the evening is to be the 'Ballet de la Merlaison',
which we are told is 'the King's favourite ballet'. This is a real
ballet, whose score still survives, and Louis's preference for it
might have something to do with the fact that he is believed to
have composed it. He also apparently wrote the text, designed
the costumes and danced the lead role. Unsurprisingly the work
depicts a blackbird hunt. 'The ballet lasted an hour and com-
prised sixteen entrées' – a further test for the guests' already
numb bottoms.

On this occasion the King's dance steps are hampered by his
furtive attempts to count the diamonds the Queen is wearing.

The Outcome

Even though the Queen has been rather indiscreet in handing
out jewels to flirtatious courtiers, the musketeers represent the
ideal of romantic chivalry, so their duty is to protect her dubious
honour rather than to observe their more formal oath to her
husband, poor old Louis the Chaste. As it turns out d'Artagnan
has ensured that the missing diamonds have been replaced
and the Queen is able to proudly sport the full complement of
twelve at the ball. Richelieu retires to lick his wounds and hatch
new dastardly plots, while d'Artagnan predictably falls in love
with Milady.

The Legacy

Alexandre Dumas published over 1,000 books in his lifetime
but still managed to end up living in poverty after squandering
his fortune. He based *The Three Musketeers* on a book called *The
Memoirs of Monsieur d'Artagnan*, which he borrowed from Marseilles

public library (and failed to return). Dumas's swashbuckling style proved to be a winning formula, drawing on the historical romantic tradition of Walter Scott, but missing out all the boring descriptions, and he succeeded in creating some of the most famous characters in literary history. A couple of less successful Musketeers sequels followed, but Hollywood took over where Dumas left off. There aren't many other authors whose works have been adapted with Mickey Mouse, Donald Duck and Goofy in the main roles.

34
Don Alejo's Election Party

LOCATION: EL BURDEL, ESTACIÓN EL OLIVO, CHILE
HOSTESS: LA JAPONESA
DATE: MID-1940S

From *El lugar sin límites* (*Hell Has No Limits*) (1966)
by José Donoso

The Invitation

Don Alejandro Cruz is 'like God' in Estación El Olivo. He owns the town and the surrounding vineyards and built the local train station. Ten days previously this patriarch with his china-blue eyes and pretty blonde wife had cemented his quasi divine status by winning a seat in the Chilean Chamber of Deputies. His political campaign, operating from the local post office shed, employed a range of slightly disreputable election tactics: the rich were bribed with discount barrels of wine and cheap land deals; the general electorate with complimentary wine and an all-day barbecue; and any reluctant voters were bundled into a truck, driven to the polling station and given a small cash disbursement for their trouble. This latter group 'were so happy with the whole thing that later on they went around asking when there were going to be more elections'.

The future of El Olivo depends on the advent of two modern innovations: the provision of electricity and the construction of 'El longitudinal', the Chilean section of the Pan-American

Highway, which, it is hoped, will pass through the town and bring much needed commerce. Don Alejo had secured his victory by pledging to deliver both.

Naturally a celebration party is planned for which 'invitations were sent to only the select few in the district'. There is only one place where it could be held.

The Hostess

'The real heart of the campaign had been the house of La Japonesa. Here the leaders gathered, from here were issued the orders, the projects, the assignments.'

The house in question is the town brothel and La Japonesa ('the Japanese Woman') is the madame. She is a local lady, now pushing forty, who 'owed her nickname to her myopic eyes, which were nothing more than two slanting slits under her high painted eyebrows'. She had once been Don Alejo's lover and still takes it upon herself to provide him with his own personal whores 'who no one else but him was allowed to touch'.

She is a staunch supporter of his political party for self-interested reasons ('the party of decent people who paid their debts and kept out of trouble, the people who went to her house for enjoyment') and she assisted his campaign by plying any of her clients who were floating voters with generous quantities of wine until their political position was 'as solid as a pear tree or could be said to be as indisputable as a knife'.

The Venue

Don Alejo returns La Japonesa's loyalty by charging her a peppercorn rent for the adobe house with rat-gnawed beams that her business operates from. 'Crude mud streets and cow dung' make up the byways of El Olivo, but the deputy and brothel keeper share a vision of a grand future for the town. Don Alejo plans to parcel out his land and sell model homes on easy credit terms, while La Japonesa envisages the new clients the expansion will bring. She dreams that one day her 'house will be more famous than that of the Wooden Breast'* (a brothel in the neighbouring city of Talca).

La Japonesa's premises are decorated for the occasion with portraits of the town's new political representative, adorned with yellow willow branches and green paper garlands, and covering the walls of the salon and patio.

The Guest List

La Japonesa doesn't open her doors to just anyone ('Only refined people. Only people with money in their pockets') so the guests are drawn from 'the most prestigious inhabitants of El Olivo', including the mayor, the police sergeant, the schoolmaster and the head of the post office. They instruct their wives to stay at home and these meek ladies instead of asking for divorces merely request their husbands to bring back some gossip and a doggy bag of any goodies.

The Dress Code

La Japonesa dons a low-cut black silk dress, her 'hair gathered in a discreet but coquettish bun', while her girls (she prides herself on them always being 'young and fresh') wear floral frocks.

---

* Wooden Breast ('El Pecho de Palo'). 'Pecho' means breast in both the literal and metaphorical sense, so we don't know if the proprietress of this establishment wears a falsie or if she is just hard-hearted.

The Food and Drink

'The wine began to flow as soon as the first guests arrived, while the aroma of the hogs starting to brown and oregano and garlic from the reheating sauces and onions and cucumbers marinating in the salad's juices drifted into the patio and salon.' The barbecue is served with local burgundy and strawberries.

The Conversation

The guests take the opportunity to buttonhole Don Alejo about his various campaign promises: getting the town put on the electricity grid, enlarging the sheds near the railway station and recruiting more police officers.*

The Entertainment

The primary entertainment of the night is supplied by the ladies of the establishment. Two extra whores have been requisitioned from the Wooden Breast to cater for the additional demand. One of them (Rosita) is reserved, according to house tradition, for the sole pleasure of the newly elected Deputy.

The musical fare comes courtesy of the Farías sisters, a guitar and harp ensemble of three stout siblings who play throughout the evening, seemingly 'immune to fatigue and heat'.

The star turn is Manuel González Astica (stage name: La Manuela), a drag queen flamenco dancer from Talca. 'Skinny as a broomstick with long hair', he is almost forty but still famed for his ability to 'dance until dawn and make a roomful of

---

* The rest of the novella takes place twenty years after the party, so we are able to ascertain that Don Alejo fails to keep any of his election pledges. This is naturally no impediment to his political career and he eventually rises to the rank of Senator.

drunks laugh and with laughter make them forget their snivelling wives'.

His appearance in a red flamenco dress provokes some outrage among the less than broadminded guests, who threaten to report him for being a 'degenerate' to the chief of police (who, conveniently, is 'sitting in the opposite corner with one of the whores on his lap').

However once La Manuela begins to dance he is not short of partners, with Don Alejo, the postmaster and the mayor fighting for his favours, while other guests, their previous homophobic outrage blunted by wine, take the opportunity to grope his 'skinny, hairy legs and bony backside'.

Afterwards the dignitaries improvise their own entertainment, which involves taking La Manuela out and chucking him in the local canal. He continues to sing and dance a paso doble ('El Relicario') while in the water and performs an impromptu striptease. The guests are impressed with the size of his manhood, though La Manuela protests, 'I don't use this thing for anything other than peeing.'

The Outcome

The revellers return to the party, shedding a few of their number on the way: 'their bodies heavy with wine, fell among the weeds on the bank of the street or in the station to sleep off their drunkenness'. Back at the whorehouse speculation now revolves around La Manuela's big willy and his claims to chastity. La Japonesa makes a bet with Don Alejo that she can bed him that night, which the deputy accepts on condition that he and the other guests can verify the outcome by watching through the window. If La Japonesa succeeds Don Alejo promises to sign over the lease on the building to her. However, La Manuela is unswayed by desire or the lure of cash to submit to the romp and only finally agrees when La Japonesa offers him a half share in her business.

Their commercial (if not romantic) partnership lasts almost two decades, though La Manuela never gets over the memory of sex with his business associate ('as if she were preparing a witches' brew in the fire that burned in the vegetation between her legs'). Following La Japonesa's death the running of the brothel is taken over by La Japonesita ('the Japanese girl') – the product of that one night stand.

The Legacy

José Donoso was part of the pioneering wave of writers (including Mario Vargas Llosa and Gabriel García Marquez) in the 1960s who put South American literature on the world map.

In his journals, which were posthumously released in 2008,

he admitted to his homosexuality. Many ordinary Chileans were apparently shocked at this revelation about one of their national literary icons. How, they must have asked themselves, could a man who could write a sentence like 'the mouth of that drunken woman searching for mine, like a pig rooting around in the mud, even though we'd agreed that we wouldn't kiss as it nauseated me' have been anything other than a 100 per cent red-blooded male?

35

The Society of Artists'
Fancy Dress Ball

LOCATION: THE GLOBE ROOMS,
AN UNIDENTIFIED CITY IN SWITZERLAND
HOSTS: THE SOCIETY OF ARTISTS
DATE: MID-1920S

From *Steppenwolf* (1927) by Hermann Hesse

The Invitation

Harry Haller is the last person who would normally accept an invitation to a lavish costume ball. He is 'a hermit in poor health' branded a 'genius of suffering', a loner who has reached the age of fifty without ever learning to dance. He lives on his own in a small attic flat in an unnamed Swiss city, spends his days reading and his nights roaming the streets, haunted by thoughts of suicide. After one of his nocturnal solitary rambles he is on the way home to his lodgings to cut his throat when he drops in at the Black Eagle tavern for a final glass of wine. Next to him at the bar is a 'pale and pretty girl' called Hermine. She quickly becomes his new best friend and introduces him to a life of jazz, dancing, sex and drugs.

She tells him that her aim is to make him fall in love with her so she can persuade him to kill her. 'You won't find it easy, but you will do it', she tells him earnestly. 'You will carry out my command and – kill me. There – ask no more.' This pair were clearly made for each other.

Before this ultimate request she invites him to put his new-found social skills to the test at a forthcoming fancy dress ball.

The Hosts

The fancy dress ball is hosted by the Society of Artists. Hermann Hesse doesn't provide us with any more details of this organization, but he was living in Zurich when he wrote *Der Steppenwolf*. During the First World War this city had played host to the Cabaret Voltaire, a nightclub that gave birth to Dadaism, a cultural movement which promoted an anti-art philosophy of art and shocked the public by displaying urinals in art galleries. But by the mid-1920s most of the cool artists had moved on to Paris and taken up the new fad for Surrealism.*

The Dress Code

Literary heroes have a habit of eschewing the dress code at fancy dress balls. Harry Haller, like Maxim de Winter and Mr Pickwick, refuses to join 'the crowd of grotesquely masked figures' and turns up in evening dress. Perhaps this is because Harry feels he is already wearing a disguise. He believes that his outward appearance is just a 'thin covering' beneath which lurks a wolf of the steppes, 'a shy, beautiful, dazed wolf with frightened eyes that smoldered now with anger, now with sadness'. His two natures, human and lupine, are in constant conflict, 'one existed simply and solely to harm the other'.

* The Dadaists believed that art should be participated in, rather than simply observed and they elevated parties to a form of artistic expression as opposed to a mere celebration. In 1926 Hermann Hesse attended a fancy dress ball organized by Jean Arp, the Dadaist artist who had a fixation for moustaches. The Alsatian-born Arp, like Harry Haller, had two identities. He called himself Jean when speaking French and Hans when speaking German.

The Venue

Wolves are pack animals, so they would probably quite enjoy a big get-together of their species. Harry, though, prefers 'to trot alone' and the Globe Rooms where the party is held – large, crowded and noisy – confirm all his worse fears. He has 'a schoolboy's shyness of the strange atmosphere and the world of pleasure and dancing'. The entire building, including its bars, buffets, champagne parlours and a brilliantly lit principal room, is devoted to the festivities. The walls are decorated with 'wild and cheerful paintings by the latest artists' and the basement has been transformed into a representation of Hell, with pitch-black walls and 'wicked garish lights'.

The Guest List

As an introvert and social misfit who doesn't have any friends Harry is not best placed to give us an insight into the who's who of the guest list. We are told that 'all the world was there, artists, journalists, professors, businessmen, and of course every adherent of pleasure in the town', but, apart from Hermine, who he can't find in the masked throng, the only people Harry knows at the party are two of her friends. One is Maria, a beautiful hooker 'richly endowed in the little arts of making love' whose professional services Hermine has engaged for Harry. The other is Pablo, a 'handsome, saxophone player' and drug-dealer, who is playing in one of the bands.

The Food and Drink

Wine is the Steppenwolf's comforter which helps him 'spend one more night in my lonely bed and to endure life for one more day'. The couple of glasses he has at the ball fail to have the required mollifying effect and he sits glaring and growling at women who try to sit coquettishly on his lap, finding the proceedings 'forced and stupid.'

The Conversation

Harry is not a great one for conversation at the best of times, considering it to be an insincere obligation carried out by 'the majority of men day by day and hour by hour in their daily lives and affairs'. It's no surprise then that by 1 a.m. he has failed to pull or make any friends, and so he heads for the coat check. Here a stranger in a demon costume hands him a mysterious card that reads: 'TONIGHT AT THE MAGIC THEATRE, FOR MADMEN ONLY, PRICE OF ADMITTANCE YOUR MIND. NOT FOR EVERYBODY. HERMINE IS IN HELL.'

'Never did sinner show more haste to get to hell' but when Harry arrives in the basement (after dallying for a brief kiss and dance with Maria) he is unable to find Hermine. He seats himself next to a 'pretty young fellow without a mask and in evening dress' at the bar who scrutinizes him 'with a cursory and mocking glance'. There is something naggingly familiar about the boy and Harry finally decides it must be his old school friend Herman. It takes a while before he realizes that it is Hermine in drag.

They swill champagne and discuss 'those years of childhood when the capacity for love, in its first youth, embraces not only both sexes, but all and everything, sensuous and spiritual, and endows all things with a spell of love and a fairylike ease of transformation such as in later years comes again only to a chosen few and to poets, and to them rarely.'

Hermine had failed to make Harry fall in love with her as a woman, but now under 'the spell of hermaphrodite' he is smitten.

The Entertainment

A black jazz band, a peasant ensemble and an orchestra of devils in the basement provide the evening's musical entertainment. Their repertoire proves a big success and every part of the great building including the 'Corridors and stairs were filled to overflowing with masks and dancing and music and laughter and tumult'. The hit tune of the evening is a foxtrot called 'Yearning' which 'had swept the world that winter'.[*]

Because Hermine is dressed as a man Harry is unable to dance with her. (Interwar Berlin was a well-documented hotbed of decadence, but the Swiss were seemingly coy in comparison.) Instead Harry and 'Herman' compete for the attention of the women on the dance floor. Hermine disappears with one girl

[*] The Benny Davis and Joe Burke number 'Yearning (Just for You)' (published in 1925).Recorded by Frank Sinatra and Nat King Cole.

and makes 'a conquest of her not as a man but as a woman, with the spell of Lesbos'.

Harry loses track of her again, until he belatedly realizes that a black Pierrette with white-painted face is in fact Hermine after a swift costume change.

Not even a character out of an opera written by Harry's beloved Mozart would be stupid enough not to recognize their loved one in disguise twice, so this is the point in the book where we begin to suspect that maybe Hermine isn't real but is just a facet of Harry's own persona. Perhaps it's not a coincidence that her name is the female version of Hesse's first name and that Harry Haller shares the same initials as him.

The Outcome

Now that Hermine is finally dressed as a woman Harry can put his newly acquired skills in the foxtrot into practice and they dance until dawn. This man who formerly abhorred parties now feels his personality dissolve 'in the intoxication of the festivity like salt in water' and contemplates 'the mysterious merging of the personality in the mass, the mystic union of joy'.

Even after the last guests have departed, there is still the second invitation: the one temptingly offered as 'for madmen only' to the Magic Theatre. Pablo the saxophonist, now dressed in a gorgeous silk dressing gown, turns out to be the host of this after-party. He is a 'master in the mixing and prescribing' of drugs and he produces a nameless elixir in 'a quaint little bottle' and some 'long thin yellow cigarettes', which the three of them partake of.

Harry heads off to the theatre, accompanied by Hermine, and under the influence of Pablo's pharmaceutical concoction he meets Mozart, takes part in a war against machines and has various other surreal adventures.

The Legacy

Der Steppenwolf was censured on its original publication in the 1920s for its open depiction of drug usage. It was adopted as a cult book in the 1960s for exactly the same reason. Cafes and bars across America named themselves 'Steppenwolf' and 'the Magic Theatre' in tribute. But the novel's greatest counter-cultural resonance was inspiring the name of the rock group Steppenwolf, whose song 'Born to Be Wild' was used as the opening credits music to the biker movie *Easy Rider* in 1969. Its lyrics coined the term 'heavy metal'.

Hermann Hesse felt that *Der Steppenwolf* was the most misunderstood of his books. Its depressing tone and bleak Weltanschauung were clearly autobiographical, but all the stuff about suicide was probably just romantic posturing in the hope of snapping up a few teenage readers: Hesse lived to the ripe old age of eighty-five.

36

The Thomas Ewen High School Prom

LOCATION: THOMAS EWEN HIGH SCHOOL,
CHAMBERLAIN, MAINE, USA
HOSTS: THOMAS EVERETT ROSS
AND CARIETTA WHITE
DATE: 27 MAY 1979

From *Carrie* (1974) by Stephen King

The Invitation

Carietta White, a 'chunky girl with pimples', a weirdo, only child loner with a psychotic born-again Christian for a mother, hardly fits the bill as the dream prom date for the boys at Thomas Ewen High School. So Carrie is disbelieving when Tommy Ross, the archetypal high school hunk (straight As, athletic, good-looking) asks her to accompany him to that quintessential American high-school rite-of-passage event, the night to remember and look back fondly on in later years.

What Carrie doesn't know is that Tommy's sorority sweetheart, Sue Snell, has put him up to it: 'it'll bring her out of her shell'. Sue also feels guilty over her participation in an incident in which Carrie experienced her first period in the school showers and was mocked and humiliated by the other girls. Most girls on reaching puberty get PMT, but Carrie gets TK (telekinetic powers) and finds herself with the ability not only to move objects with her mind but also destroy them.

The Hosts

The Spring Ball is presided over by the King and Queen of the Prom who are voted for by the attendees at the end of the evening. Couples on the shortlist for this honour are George & Frieda, Peter & Myra, Frank & Jessica, Don & Helen and Tommy & Carrie.

'There was a gaining student move afoot to do away with the King and Queen business all together — some of the girls claimed it was sexist, the boys thought it was just plain stupid and a little embarrassing. Chances were good that this would be the last year the dance would be so formal or traditional.' This is to be a prom that proves to be neither formal nor traditional.

The Venue

The fifteen students who sit on the Spring Ball Decoration Committee of Thomas Ewen High School have chosen 'Spring Time in Venice' as 1979's theme. By monumental use of crêpe paper the transformation of the school gymnasium into the City of Canals is achieved. A large Venetian mural painted by the students featuring gondolas at sunset ('a gorgeous panoply of pinks and reds and oranges stained both sky and water') hangs behind twin bandstands. Waiting in the wings are the King and Queen's thrones 'strewn with real flowers'.

The Guest List

'Those who were not in attendance were largely the unpopular members of the Junior and Senior classes.' But within a few hours these geeks, nerds and losers sitting at home on prom night reading their Marvel comics would find themselves deeply thankful for the acne, bad haircuts and lack of dress sense which had led to them being excluded from the event. Of the popular students at the school Sue Snell is one of the very few who lives to tell the tale of what comes to be dubbed 'the Black Prom' (which she does in her cash-in book 'My Name is Susan Snell'). As her boyfriend is squiring Carrie, Sue chooses to stay at home rather than go to the party without a date: and so avoids social death . . . and of course the real thing.

The Dress Code

With no friends or social life Carrie has spent a lot of time sitting at home sewing, which means she is able to run up her own prom dress: a red crushed-velvet gown with a 'princess waistline, juliet sleeves and simple straight skirt'. In prom tradition she pins to this a corsage (a small nosegay of flowers) given to her by her date. For most mothers the sight of their teenage daughter dressed for the prom ranks among their proudest memories. Carrie's mother, however, compares her to Jezebel, the biblical harlot, and suggests they burn the gown in the incinerator together and pray for forgiveness. 'I can see your dirtypillows' (her euphemism for breasts), she says in disgust.

It is left to Carrie's date, Tommy, 'nearly blinding in white dinner jacket and dark dress pants', to pay her the more traditional compliment: 'You're beautiful' he says and 'She was.'

Arriving at the prom Carrie finds it a pageant of forbidden glamour and carnality: 'Beautiful shadows rustled about in chiffon, lace, silk, satin ... Girls in dresses with low backs, with scooped bodices showing actual cleavage, with Empire waists. Long skirts, pumps. Blinding white dinner jackets, cummerbunds, black shoes that had been spit-shined.'

The Conversation

Carrie has zero social skills, but after being paid a couple of compliments on her dress she starts to come out of her shell, as Sue had hoped. She even makes a few jokes and finds herself 'amazed by her own wit—and audacity'.

The main topic on everyone's lips is the impending vote for King and Queen of the Prom. Hot favourites are Frank Grier & Jessica MacLean and, surprisingly, Thomas Ross & Carrie White.

The Food and Drink

The Refreshment Committee prove to be a complete waste of space. As far as we can ascertain, the only party fare they organize is punch served in Dixie paper cups and gondolas filled with Planters' mixed nuts. The guests would have got a better last meal on Death Row.

The Entertainment

The Entertainment Committee turn out to have been more zealous and there is a full musical programme, including a display of baton twirling, a folk duo, and 'Two bands: one rock, one mellow'. The musical repertoire is mainly drawn from the 1960s (even though this is supposedly 1979). It is left to the Thomas Ewen High School Chorus to perform the most contemporary number on the programme – 'Bridge Over Troubled Waters' [*sic*].*

But the main entertainment is to be the vote for the King and Queen of the prom. The first poll results in a dead heat

---

* Stephen King wrote *Carrie* in 1973 but set it in 1979. He obviously presumed that musical tastes wouldn't change over the decade. Perhaps they didn't in Maine.

between Tommy & Carrie and Frank & Jessica. So it goes to a run-off.

Carrie thinks she and Tommy shouldn't vote for themselves, but he overrules her – a decision he won't live to regret. As Josie and the Moonglows treat the audience to a rock version of 'Pomp and Circumstance' the result of the second ballot is announced. Tommy and Carrie have won by that solitary self-cast vote. A 'sceptre wrapped in aluminium foil was thrust into Tommy's hand, a robe with a lush dog-fur collar was thrown over Carrie's shoulders'. As the King and Queen take their thrones the assembled guests start to sing the school song: 'All rise for Thomas Ewen High, We'll raise your banners to the sky'. Ironic, considering Thomas Ewen High is shortly to be razed to the ground.

The Outcome

Outside the building lurk the bitchy Christine Hargensen and her 'white-soxer' boyfriend Billy Nolan. Christine was barred from the prom after the shower bullying incident and has hatched a plan to get her revenge on Carrie. Billy has suspended two buckets of pigs' blood from the rafters above the thrones on the stage. As the school song is sung Christine pulls a string and the gore cascades down over the King and Queen, drenching them from head to foot. There is a scream, a moment of shocked silence, and then the guests begin to laugh. What they don't know is Carrie comes a close second to Dr Bruce Banner as a person you don't want to make angry.

'There were only twelve survivors from what has become known in the popular press as Prom Night.' Carrie's telekinetic fury is unleashed and the result is a holocaust: those students who aren't electrocuted by the short-circuiting sound equipment after Carrie sets off the sprinklers are burned alive when the resulting fire causes the school's fuel-oil tanks to explode. Carrie then goes on to destroy most of the rest of Chamberlain for good measure and finally returns home to kill her mother (who to be fair was about to kill her) before herself expiring.

The body count as a result of this outburst of teenage angst is second only to 'The Masque of the Red Death' (see chapter 23). Stephen King is vague over the exact death toll ('409 with 49 still listed as missing' we are told at one point) but math clearly wasn't his strong subject at whatever prototype for Ewen High he attended. Carrie's birthday is given as 21 September 1963, which would make her fifteen at the time of the prom, though King tells us that she has reached 'the age of nearly seventeen'.

The Legacy

Tabitha King was another of those writers' wives (like Yelena Bulgakova) who salvaged her husband's work for posterity. Stephen King was teaching English at a high school in Maine and had binned his first draft of *Carrie*, but was persuaded by Tabitha to persevere with the book. He did so 'mostly to please her'. The novel was published by Doubleday in 1974 and sold a million copies in paperback. The proceeds enabled King to give up his day job (after describing the gruesome destruction of such an establishment it might have been a bit difficult to continue) and move their young family out of the trailer they were living in.

37
Finnegan's Wake

LOCATION: MULLINGAR HOUSE,
CHAPELIZOD, DUBLIN
HOSTS: H.C.E. & A.L.P.
DATE: A 'THUNDERSDAY' ('THIRSTAY')
AT 'CHRISSORMISS'

From *Finnegans Wake* (1939) by James Joyce

The Invitation

Tim Finnegan, aka 'Bygmester Finnegan, of the Stuttering Hand' is a 'dacent gaylabouring youth' who plies his trade as a 'man of hod, cement and edi-fices'. He had worked in New York, as a 'wallstrait oldparr', where he was involved in the construction of the Woolworth Building: 'a skyerscape of most eyeful hoyth entowerly'.

Unfortunately the 'Oftwhile balbulous' Finnegan had a weakness for the tipple. Back in Dublin one 'thirstay' just before 'chrissormiss' he was up his ladder with his hod, somewhat the worse for wear. No one can be sure what was to blame for his subsequent accident ('a missfired brick' or a 'collupsus of his back promises') but 'his howd feeled heavy, his hoddit did shake. (There was a wall of course in erection) Dimb! He stot-tered from the latter. Damb! he was dud.'

News of Finnegan's fatal fall '(bababadalgharaghtakam-minarronnkonnbronntonnerronntuonnthunntrovarr-

262

hounawnskawntoohoohoordenenthur — nuk!)' soon spreads and, in traditional Irish fashion, his friends gather for a wake.*

The Venue

Finnegan's body is carried off to a local pub, the 'Mullingcan Inn', where 'they laid him brawdawn alanglast bed'.†

Humphrey Chimpden Earwicker is the inn's publican 'in the licensed boosiness primises of his del-hightful bazar'. He is also one of Finnegan's various alter egos in the book.

The Hosts

This dual identity means that Finnegan doubles up as both the guest of honour and the host at his wake (try to keep up, it gets

---

* The story is taken from a nineteenth-century Irish-American ballad 'Finnegan's Wake'. Joyce missed out the apostrophe in the title supposedly to make Finnegan more universal, but probably just to annoy pedants.

† Mullingar House is a real pub that still exists in Chapelizod, a picturesque village on the banks of the Liffey. These days it offers regular live entertainment in the lounge and a quiz evening on Thursdays. Finnegan's association with the establishment is commemorated by a plaque on the wall and a James Joyce burger on the menu (reviews of the restaurant don't mention whether it tastes of fish).

more confusing). Mr Earwicker is a 'Great Sommboddy within the Omniboss' who is usually referred to by his initials H.C.E. He spends a lot of his time out philandering ('the roughty old rappe! Minxing marrage and making loof.') leaving his wife Anna Livia Plurabelle (commonly known as A.L.P.) to run the pub: 'she'll do all a turfwoman can to piff the business on'.

The Guest List

In a book where the characters have multiple identities and regularly change the spelling of their names, pinning down the exact guest list (or as Joyce puts it 'idendifine the individuone') at the wake is tricky.

The people we are fairly certain are present include the Finnegan family (aka the Earwicker family): wife Annie/Anna; sons Kevin, 'a doat with his cherub cheek' (aka Shaun, Mutt or Chef); his twin brother Jerry, a 'tarandtan plaidboy, making encostive inkum out of the last of his lavings' (aka Shem, Jute, Dolph, or Glugg); and their sister Isabel (aka Iseult la Belle, Nuvoletta, Margareena or Miss Butys Pott), an ex-convent girl who is now 'making her rep at Lanner's twicenightly. With the tabarine tamtammers of the whirligigmagees.' It is rumoured that she has been having an 'ensectuous' relationship with her father/s.

Also there is Kate, the Earwickers' gossipy charlady, 'kook-and-dishdrudge', 'homeswab homely' and 'refined souprette'.

The other friends and acquaintances of the deceased come from all walks of Dublin life. 'There was plumbs and grumes and cheriffs and citherers and raiders and cinemen too.' Isabel has brought along a bunch of school friends (twenty-eight dancing girls to be precise).

There are twelve official mourners, regulars at the pub,

who later pop up in the book as twelve members of the jury, the twelve signs of the zodiac, the twelve tribes of Israel and, for all we know, the Twelve Days of Christmas.

The Dress Code

The guests are all in their best clobber with 'heegills and collines, sitton aroont, scentbreeched and somepotreek, in their swishawish satins and their taffetaffe tights'. Kate has made a particularly special effort and is dressed in burlesque style 'with my bust alla brooche and the padbun under my matelote, showing my jigotty sleeves and all my new toulong touloosies'. The late Mr Finnegan is resplendent for the occasion in his 'blood-eagle waistcoat and all'.

The Food and Drink

The deceased is well provisioned for his voyage to the afterlife with alcoholic refreshment laid out alongside him on the bed: 'With a bockalips of finisky fore his feet. And a barrowload of guenesis hoer his head.'

Despite the short notice the landlady Anna manages to ensure the mourners are well fed, 'And even if Humpty shell fall frumpty times as awkward again in the beardsboosoloom of all our grand remonstrancers there'll be iggs for the brekkers come to mourn-him, sunny side up with care.'

But even her hospitality isn't enough for the hungry guests and they soon fall to eating Finnegan himself, 'quaffoff his fraud-stuff and sink teeth through that pyth of a flowerwhite bodey'. His flesh apparently tastes of fish so they re-christen him 'Fin-foefom the Fush' ('that meal's dead off for summan, schlook, schlice and goodridhirring').

The Conversation

Traditionally one is not supposed to speak ill of the dead, but Kate can't resist spreading some tittle-tattle. It turns out that the deceased (who is now known as 'Tim Timmycan') was a peeping tom who once spied on two girls relieving themselves in Phoenix Park. Kate refers to the fact that there is a statue of the Duke of Wellington in the park and gilds the whole story in an allegory of 'Willingdone' and his adversary 'Lipoleum' at the appropriately named Battle of Waterloo. It seems the sight of the girls peeing caused the deceased to become sexually aroused and he chased the 'rinnaway jinnies' brandishing his 'marmorial tallowscoop'. Unfortunately his antics were observed by three soldiers, 'Touchole Fitz Tuo-mush. Dirty Mac Dyke. And Hairy O'Hurry' and this is one Waterloo which Willingdone ended up losing.

The twins Mutt and Jute engage in conversation, but with one being 'jeffmute' and the other hardly 'haudibble' the result is mutual incomprehension with Jute becoming exasperated at his inability to understand all the 'rutterdamrotter' (the reader can empathize with him at this point, and we've only got to page 12).

The Entertainment

Naturally there is much sadness at Tim's unexpected passing: 'Sobs they sighdid at Fillagain's chrissormis wake, all the hoolivans of the nation, prostrated in their consternation, and their duodisimally profusive plethora of ululation.' The late builder's soul is piped into the afterlife in time-honoured fashion, 'oboboes shall wail him rockbound' and the guests fall into a mixture of traditional Irish mourning and some Parisian vaudeville dancing: 'Some in kinkin corass, more, kankan keening'.

But wakes are meant to be celebrations too and before long the mood at this 'funferall' lightens and 'there's leps of flam in Funnycoon's Wick'. The chorus girls dance ('And all his morties calisenic, tripping a trepas, neniatwantyng') and the guests sing: 'Tee the tootal of the fluid hang the twoddle of the fuddled, O!'

The Outcome

All is going swimmingly until someone mentions the word whisky ('Usgueadbaugham!'), which causes Finnegan (despite having been previously eaten) to wake up. He curses his friends and scolds them for believing that he was dead: 'Anam muck an dhoul ! Did ye drink me doornail?'

But the mourners are having a good time and don't want the unexpected revival of the deceased to spoil the occasion. So they try to persuade him to remain in the 'land of souls' in the company of such illustrious dead potentates as 'Nobucketnozzler and the Guinnghis Khan'.

They needn't have worried. This is destined to be a party that never ends. Any intrepid reader who makes it through to page 628 of *Finnegans Wake* finds that the last sentence is unfinished and turns out to be the missing first half of the opening sentence of the book. Which means we (like the deceased's namesake Michael) have to begin again.

The Legacy

Written in a mixture of languages, ancient and modern, with liberal doses of gobbledegook, *Finnegans Wake* has now provided careers for several generations of academics trying to figure out what on earth Joyce was going on about.

When physicist Murray Gell-Mann postulated the existence of a new subatomic particle in 1964 he named it the 'quark' in honour of one of Joyce's neologisms from *Finnegans Wake* ('Three quarks for Muster Mark' being a drinks order from the regulars at the Mullingar House). Clearly the scientist recognized the similarities between particle physics and literary criticism of the *Wake*: both disciplines relying much on wild guesswork and random theorizing.

Finnegans Wake was James Joyce's final novel. It took him seventeen years to write. Many people have spent longer attempting to read it.

38
The Flying Party

LOCATION: SOMEWHERE ABOVE A NAMELESS
PLANET IN AN UNIDENTIFIED GALAXY
HOST: UNKNOWN
DATE: AN UNSPECIFIED TIME IN THE FUTURE/PAST

From *Life, the Universe and Everything* (1982)
by Douglas Adams

The Host

The host or hostess of the 'longest and most destructive party ever held' is unknown, but as the party is 'now into its fourth generation and still no one shows any signs of leaving' we can presume that the original party-giver is long dead and, considering the huge quantities of alcohol consumed by the guests, that his or her name has already been forgotten by all present.

The Venue

The other unusual aspect of this party is that, though it started in a conventional building on an alien planet, many years ago 'a band of drunken astro-engineers of the first generation' decided to rig up the building so it was capable of flight, and the party is now to be found 'floating like a young and uncertain bird over the treetops'.

The Invitation

This doesn't seem to be the sort of do that one needs to be invited to and 'People had been dropping in on the party now for some years, fashionable gatecrashers from other worlds'. In view of the fact that the party is airborne and due to the 'erratic and unpredictable way in which it lurches round the sky' the most practical way to get there is by teleport.

The Guest List

The original guest list is lost in the mists of time as 'all the people at the party are either the children or the grandchildren or the great-grandchildren of the people who wouldn't leave in the first place'. This necessary inbreeding among the diehards has created a diminished gene pool from which the current guests are drawn and 'it means that all the people now at the party are either absolutely fanatical partygoers, or gibbering idiots, or, more and more frequently, both.'

Recent arrivals include:

ARTHUR DENT, itinerant Earthman and hero of the *Hitchhiker's Guide to the Galaxy* series of novels, who is hit in the small of the back by the party building while flying around a planet to which he had been lured by a vindictive reincarnated rabbit named Agrajag. Finding himself clinging to the building Arthur manages to infiltrate the party, despite not having brought a bottle.

TRILLIAN (aka Tricia McMillan), an Earthwoman, who is on the rebound after having a row with her flamboyant boyfriend, Zaphod Beeblebrox, the ex-president of the galaxy, recently voted 'the worst-dressed sentient being in the known universe for the seventh time'.* Trillian has ended up at the flying party by the happy chance of setting the teleport of *The Heart of Gold* starship (which Zaphod had stolen) to random. When Arthur arrives he finds to his annoyance that Trillian is being chatted up by the Thunder God Thor whom she once met (several billion years in the future) in the Restaurant at the End of the Universe.

SLARTIBARTFAST – a designer of planetary coastlines, specializing in fjords. He is searching for the Silver Bail. This is one of the five elements that will form the key that can unlock the Slo-Time envelope which has been placed around the planet Krikkit by the galactic court as punishment for its people's relentless warmongering. Evil white Krikkiter robots are also trying to locate the Silver Bail and have already stolen several of the other components of the key, including the Ashes from Lord's cricket ground. Rumour has it that the Silver Bail is to be found somewhere at this very party.

FORD PREFECT – a roving reporter for *The Hitchhiker's Guide to the Galaxy* (who told Arthur he was from Guildford but, it turns out, was actually born on a small planet in the vicinity of Betelgeuse). His reasons for wanting to go to the party are not to save the galaxy, but the rather more mundane in order 'to drink a lot and dance with girls'.

The Dress Code

As guests frequently spend their entire lives at the party there is presumably little opportunity for buying special outfits. Arthur Dent arrives in his dressing gown, which he has now been wearing throughout several billion years of galactic history, as it

---

*. Due to the uncertain chronology maybe this honour is yet to come in the future.

was all he had time to throw on before his house (and then the Earth) was destroyed. 'I didn't realize I'd be coming to a party,' he explains self-consciously to the other guests.

At a social occasion where so many aliens are present it can be hard to tell what is part of their outfit from what is part of their anatomy, and social gaffes can result. Ford Prefect compliments the female creature he is dancing with on her hat, which is shaped like Sydney Opera House, only to find out that it is a series of ridges in the bone structure of her head.

The Conversation

Most of the conversation is lost in a 'heaving throng of happy, noisy creatures, cheerfully yelling things that nobody could hear at each other and occasionally having crises'. This is fine because we are reminded that 'you shouldn't believe anything you hear at parties, and particularly not anything you hear at this one.'

The party gives Arthur Dent a rare respite from being blown up, shot at and abused by various alien creatures and he has the chance to bore another guest with his life story and about how things have gone downhill since his home planet the Earth was demolished by a Vogon Constructor Fleet to make way for a hyperspace bypass.

The Food and Drink

This 'large and extremely disreputable cocktail party' requires a steady supply of 'cheese crackers, avocado dip, spare ribs and wine and spirits' which all have to be sourced from the planet below. This is done in a series of raiding and looting expeditions by the party building, which the drunken astro-engineers had the foresight to arm rather heavily. Over the decades the demands for cheese and wine from the merrymakers has gradually devastated the economy and ecology of the world below, which makes the happy partygoers realize that the 'problem of when the drink is going to run out is, however, going to have to be faced one day'.

We are not told whether the universe's most notorious cocktail – the Pan Galactic Gargle Blaster, 'the drink which has been described as the alcoholic equivalent of a mugging' – is part of the fare.

The Entertainment

The musicians (who must presumably be the descendants of the original players) are beginning to flag in popularity due to 'the enormous number of times that the band had already played all the numbers it knew over the years.'

We are not told what instruments they play (possibly the

octaventral heebiephone?) and the only item from their repertoire that we know is performed (several thousand times) is 'I
Left My Leg in Jaglan Beta'. The 'band playing it were very tired,
and some members of it were playing in three-four time, some
in four-four, and some in a kind of pie-eyed πr^2.'

The Outcome

The evil Krikkiter robots arrive and unceremoniously steal the
Silver Bail, which turns out to be masquerading as a Rory, an
award presented at the 'Annual Ursa Minor Alpha Recreational
Illusions Institute Awards Ceremony'. This is being clutched in
the hand of a grumpy writer who has recently won it for 'The
Most Gratuitous Use of the Word "Fuck" in a Serious Screenplay'.

Despite being immortal and therefore liable to outstay any
of the other guests, Thor is keen to take Trillian on to an even
better permanent party he knows of, in Valhalla (see chapter
28). Forgetting about the danger posed to the entire known
universe by the Krikkiter robots, Arthur decides to increase his
own personal peril by picking a fight with the Thunder God.
Of course as this is only the third book in the numerically chal-
lenged Hitchhiker 'trilogy' (which runs to five volumes in total)
we know that both he and the whole of creation are going to be
fine in the end.

The Legacy

Douglas Adams clearly had a great insight into parties. But he
also liked going to them rather more than he did sitting down
on his own and writing about them. To finish the subsequent
book in this 'increasingly inaccurately named trilogy' his pub-

lisher had to lock him in a hotel room until the manuscript was completed. Adams famously said of his inability to write to order: 'I love deadlines. I like the whooshing sound they make as they fly by.'

39
McMurphy's Ward Party

LOCATION: A MENTAL INSTITUTION
NEAR PORTLAND, OREGON, USA
HOST: RANDLE MCMURPHY
DATE: LATE 1950S

From *One Flew Over the Cuckoo's Nest* (1962)
by Ken Kesey

The Host

Randle Patrick McMurphy is a thirty-five-year-old, red-headed, Irish American drinker, gambler, brawler and womanizer. Like Dmitri Karamazov his '*repeated* outbreaks of passion' end up landing him in trouble with the law (see chapter 4). He had a chequered military career during the Korean War, winning a Distinguished Service Cross for 'leading an escape from a Communist prison camp', followed by a dishonourable discharge for insubordination. Civilian life back in his home state of Oregon was 'a history of street brawls and barroom fights', culminating in arrest for 'gambling and battery', which resulted in a six-month sentence at the Pendleton Work Farm.

After two months of weeding peas, he got himself transferred to a mental hospital to be assessed for possible psychosis. In his words 'If it gets me outta those damned pea fields I'll be whatever their little heart desires, be it psychopath or mad dog or werewolf'.

The Venue

American psychiatric institutions have 'come a long way' by the 1960s, according to the 'fat-faced Public Relation' – a spokesman for the 'Combine', the symbolic all-pervading oppressive establishment authority whose aim is to stamp out any expression of individuality. 'They've made life look very pleasant with paint and decorations and chrome bathroom fixtures' we are told. Powerful sedatives have replaced 'confinement jackets it took you hours of hard work to get out of' and patients can now watch TV, exercise in the swimming pool and eat chicken twice a month.

The reality is rather less wholesome. McMurphy finds himself in a ward with the 'smell of piss and sour old-man manure', which is ruled over by Miss Ratched, aka the 'Big Nurse' and 'old frozen face'. Her aim is to have her outfit 'running like a smooth, accurate, precision-made machine'. Any miscreants are dealt with by her orderlies, Williams, Washington, Warren and Geever, collectively known as 'the black boys'. For persistent troublemakers she employs more persuasive methods: electric shock therapy and prefrontal lobotomies.

Nurse Ratched is 'a high-ranking official' in the Combine and every patient on her ward is expected to 'knuckle under to that smiling flower-faced old mother with the too-red lipstick and the too big boobs'.

The Invitation

McMurphy's first act on arrival is to appoint himself 'bull goose loony' of the ward and set himself up as a direct challenger to the authority of the Big Nurse.

He manages to get official permission to re-open the disused tub room across the hall from the day room where the patients eke out their drab lives. He converts this into a poker den where he can relieve the other inmates of their money and cigarettes. But his biggest coup comes when he arranges for a group of patients to be allowed a day pass to go on a fishing trip. He tells the authorities that they will be chaperoned by 'two sweet old aunts from a little place outside of Oregon City' (though he later admits to his fellow residents that the ladies in question are in fact 'workin' shimmy dancers and hustlers I know from Portland').

In the event only one of McMurphy's 'aunts' shows up: Candy Starr, blonde, green-eyed and so pretty that her appearance in the ward causes the bed-ridden patients' catheters to pop off. During the fishing trip Billy Bibbit, a thirty-one-year-old virgin and self-harmer with a severe speech impediment, develops a huge crush on her. McMurphy arranges to throw a party on the ward two weeks later, to which Candy is invited, to give Billy the opportunity to 'cash in his cherry'.

The Guest List

The forty patients on the Big Nurse's ward are split by psychiatric diagnosis into two types: Acutes and Chronics. The Acutes are so-called 'because the doctors figure them still sick enough to be fixed'. The Chronics on the other hand (subdivided into Walkers, Wheelers and Vegetables) are 'Not in the hospital, these, to get fixed, but just to keep them from walking around the streets giving the product a bad name'.

Six Acutes and one Chronic make it on to McMurphy's guest list: Billy Bibbit, in whose honour the party is being held; Dale Harding, an educated and articulate closet gay; Scanlon, a pyromaniac obsessed with explosives; Martini, a psychotic suffering from persistent hallucinations; and two epileptics, Sefelt and Fredrickson. Representing the Chronics is Chief Bromden, the novel's narrator, a six-foot-eight half-Native American, whose way of defying the Combine is to pretend to be deaf and dumb and spend his day sweeping the floor.

Candy shows up with her friend, Sandra Gilfillian (McMurphy's other 'aunt'), a big girl with 'long hard-working legs' who looks 'like a cowgirl trying to pass herself off as a society lady'.

The final guest is Mr Turkle, the night porter who works the 'long lonely shift from 11 to 7' and is bribed with the promise of alcohol and sexual favours to open the window and allow the hookers in.

The Dress Code

It's a pyjama party by virtue of the fact that all the inmates are tucked up in bed and medicated when it begins. Mr Turkle wears his white staff livery and the girls are attired in the uniforms of their trade: tight skirts, sweaters and nylons and both 'red-cheeked and giggling'. McMurphy sports his signature outfit: a 'primer-black motorcycle cap' and coal-black shorts 'covered with big white whales with red eyes'. He plans to make a bid for freedom under cover of darkness, so the party is doubling up as his leaving do.

The Food and Drink

Alcohol is off limits on the ward but fortunately Candy and Sandy have brought a gallon of red port wine and a bottle of vodka. A raid on the medicine cabinet yields mixers for the vodka in the form of a bottle of cough syrup ('twenty percent alcohol ... and ten percent codeine'). The resulting cocktail, according to Chief Bromden, had 'a taste like a kid's drink but a punch like the cactus apple wine we used to get in The Dalles, cold and soothing on the throat and hot and furious once it got down.'*

Nibbles are also lacking, so the patients neck vitamin 'pills the size of birds' eggs'.

The Conversation

Despite the presence of a couple of obliging ladies of the night, the object of the patients' sexual fantasies (like Oskar Mazerath in *The Tin Drum* – see chapter 10) is nurses and they discuss 'how it would be to lay that little nurse with the birthmark who went off at midnight', speculating on the use of thermometers as sexual aids, which causes them to laugh till they 'were rolling about the couches and chairs, choking and teary-eyed'.

The ward's house philosopher, Harding, delivers a soliloquy on how the party 'is our last fling. We are doomed henceforth ... We shall all of us be shot at dawn.' The Big Nurse will load her gun with Miltowns, Thorazines, Libriums and Stelazines, he imagines, and 'tranquilize all of us completely out of existence'.

The Entertainment

The programme of events begins with juvenile mischief as the patients amuse themselves in the nurses' station, perusing their medical files. They then improvise a flashlight-illuminated game of 'tag up and down the hall with wheelchairs from storage'.

Sefelt is the first to take advantage of the alternative enter-

* The rapper DJ Screw popularized 'Purple Drank' – a cough medicine cocktail – in the 1990s. He showcased its potency by dying at the age of twenty-nine. The coroner's report listed evidence of a codeine overdose in addition to mixed drug intoxication.

tainment on offer, courtesy of McMurphy's 'aunts'. Inconveniently he has an epileptic seizure in mid-coitus with Sandy. On regaining consciousness his immediate plea is: 'Medicate me and turn me loose again.'

The paranoid Chief Bromden finds it hard to believe that he and his fellow patients are 'Drunk and running and laughing and carrying on with women square in the center of the Combine's most powerful stronghold!' He even starts to entertain the seditious thought that 'Maybe the Combine wasn't all-powerful.'

The highlight of the night is to be the loss of Billy Bibbit's virginity. Some time after 4 a.m. Billy asks Turkle to unlock the aptly named Seclusion Room ('a fine honeymoon shack for the lovers') for his tryst with Candy and 'they went off under an arch of flashlight beams'.

McMurphy, under the unwise influence of a spliff he earlier shared with Mr Turkle, decides to grab 'a little shut-eye' before his big getaway and settles down for an hour's nap with Sandy.

The Outcome

'And that's the way the black boys found them when they came to turn on the dorm lights at six-thirty': McMurphy in bed with a whore, Billy Bibbit in the Seclusion Room with another, the night porter asleep in the linen cupboard, the nurse's station trashed and a 'fleet of wheelchairs parked at the end of the hall like empty rides in an amusement park'.

The Combine's retribution is swift and brutal and the fall-out is high: Billy ends up dead and McMurphy joins the Vegetables after a trans-orbital lobotomy following an attempt to strangle Nurse Ratched.

Harding's prediction proves correct and the ward soon disintegrates, with the voluntary patients discharging themselves, while others transfer to a different ward. Chief Bromden denies the Combine its victory and smothers the brain-dead McMurphy with a pillow before hopping out of the window to freedom.

It's not clear whether the Chief escapes for good. The 'police never press too hard to pick up AWOLs from the hospital because ninety per cent of them always show back up in a few days, broke and drunk and looking for that free bed and board.' He seems to be back in the Big Nurse's custody when he begins relating the story. 'But it's the truth even if it didn't happen', he tells us confusingly at the outset. Well, what do you expect with a delusional paranoid schizophrenic for a narrator?

The Legacy

Over 40,000 lobotomies were performed in the Land of the Free throughout the mid-twentieth century (its ideological enemy, the Soviet Union, had made the procedure illegal in 1950), sometimes on patients as young as twelve. Its most famous recipient was Rose Kennedy, JFK's mentally retarded sister, who was given the treatment at the age of twenty-three out of the Kennedy family's fears that she might inadvertently do something to disgrace the clan. Pyschosurgery was on the wane by the 1960s when modern neuroleptic medications came in and Ken Kesey's book, and the subsequent Broadway play and feature film, helped further discredit the practice.

The 1975 movie adaptation of *One Flew Over the Cuckoo's Nest* is one of only three films ever to have scooped all of the Big Five Academy Awards (Best Picture, Best Actor, Best Actress, Best Director and Best Screenplay). The only other modern-day movie to have achieved this feat is *The Silence of the Lambs* (1991). Note to aspiring directors: to help your chances of achieving a clean sweep at the Oscars be sure to put an animal name in your title.

40

The Wonderland Banquet

LOCATION: TEMPELHOF AIRPORT,
BERLIN, GERMANY
HOST: DIDIER LAXALT
DATE: FRIDAY 24 OCTOBER 2008

From *Lights Out in Wonderland* (2010) by DBC Pierre

The Invitation

After losing his job and his girlfriend, Gabriel Brockwell, a
twenty-five-year-old 'microwave chef' and anti-capitalist pamphleteer, discharges himself from rehab with the intention
of committing suicide. Checking out of life is, he believes, an
occasion that needs to be finessed: 'attend to your death like a
banquet of gods, pay more attention to it than your wedding'.
So, like Raphaël de Valentin,* Gabriel wishes for one last bacchanal before putting an end to himself, an 'evening more
splendid than any since the fall of Rome'. With no magic skin to
hand, he appropriates £5,000 from the bank account of the mili-
tant action group he belongs to and flies himself business class to
Tokyo to visit his childhood friend, Nelson Smuts, 'a man never
far from wine and debauch.'

Laden with drugs and the maxim 'all happiness not derived
from intoxicants is false', Gabriel heads for Shinjuku, 'a bustling,
money-infested district of Tokyo', and the San Toropez restau-

---

* See chapter 19. There are various parallels with *The Wild Ass's Skin*. Both Gabriel and
Raphaël are named after angels, aged twenty-five, penniless, try to drown themselves
and end up going to a big decadent party instead.

rant where Smuts is employed. It is rarely advisable to consume a cocktail of rum, cocaine, whisky and MDMA during working hours, but especially not when you're a chef at a restaurant whose signature dish is Fugu – a poisonous blowfish which has to be expertly prepared to avoid delivering a lethal dose of toxins to the diner. Under Gabriel's bad influence Smuts manages to poison his boss's favourite client (who inconveniently is also a gangster) and ends up in prison on a murder rap.

The only way for Gabriel to save his friend (you'll have to trust me on this one) is for him to help organize the ultimate party.

The Host

Didier 'Le Basque' Laxalt is 'the godfather of high-octane catering' who can 'fill a stadium with Michelin stars and still find somewhere better to eat.' An ex-Foreign Legionnaire, his culinary forte is the sourcing of rare produce (like the wild Fugu sold at the San Toropez) with which he 'supplies the suppliers who supply the world with special things.'

He also hosts legendary banquets for the super-rich and is on the lookout for a suitably sublime venue for his upcoming event. If Gabriel can find one then Didier might be persuadable to use his influence to get Smuts out of jail.

The Venue

Gabriel comes across just such a place in Berlin: Tempelhof Airport, which is due to be mothballed in a week's time. This vast building had been commissioned by Hitler's architect Albert Speer as part of his vision for transforming Berlin into a fitting capital city for the Thousand Year Reich. It is 'an underground

Alhambra' with 'more than five kilometres of bunkers and tunnels'.

Under the pretext of shooting a movie, Didier's crew moves in and transforms the airport into a 'Mythical underworld decadence, a Gothic palazzo, empty, soundless, windowless ... A wonderland.' 'The concourse of arches overflows with rugs, cushions, plants and entertainments, with a long table running under dazzling chandeliers.'

The venue's most attractive feature is its two runways, which allow guests to fly their jets right into the party.

The Guest List

This highly exclusive one-off event has a guest list of just seven people (of whom only two are apparently not billionaires). They are 'extreme high-flyers from those quarters of banking and commerce responsible for the global recession'. This night is to be their heroic last stand 'before vanishing in advance of government investigations'.

The entry fee is payable in diamonds – small change to such types.

The Dress Code

The bankers 'descend in tailcoats and human masks' while their host wears a shiny tailcoat and 'the half-mask of a cat'.

Gabriel, not being rich enough to be invited to the event he facilitated, is appointed the pursuivant (a glorified usher) for the evening. Dressed in a black cape, tricorn hat and a white half mask, his role is to signal the start of the party with a pistol shot and the end by turning the lights out.

The Conversation

These bankers didn't get to be billionaires by having hobbies or personalities and they talk shop, relentlessly spouting buzzwords about stochastic theory, the Black–Scholes model and low value FMCGs.

The Food and Drink

According to Didier Laxalt, 'What we put into the body isn't just calories. It's medication, spirit, symbol. It's divinity.' So he provides a fountain filled with Marius, a red wine made from 'a grape with the answer to life inside it', which is grown in soil rich with 'prehistoric minerals, passion and virgin's cum.'

But it is in the food that Didier really lives up to his culinary reputation, outdoing Trimalchio with a menu comprising twelve punishing courses, many of which feature endangered species.

THE MENU

First course — Platters of 'oysters, fruits, snails, cocaine, cheese, raw ham and truffle' accompanied by crystal glasses of infants' tears.

Second course — 'Boys and girls wait with trays of abalone, cheese of human breast-milk, pomegranates and honeycomb, while maidens bear a beluga sturgeon on a bed of sea snails, scooping caviar from its gut with their hands.'

Third course — Steaming Kiwi and Hummingbird Broth with Porcini Agnoletti and Leeks 'attended by maidens whirling and naked beneath frocks'.

Fourth course — Western Fanshell Mussel Soufflé with Black Rhino Horn.

Fifth course — Olive Ridley Turtle Necks in Parmesan and Brioche Crumbs with Celeriac Remoulade.

Sixth course — An anaconda — 'the most precise tenderiser of meats the world has ever known' — is sliced open at table by the chef to reveal its last meal: 'a perfect human baby'. Happily cannibalism is the last taboo (even for the 'shadowy forces' of capitalism) and the 'baby' turns out to be made from pork and veal with lobster eyes.

Seventh course — Golden Lion Tamarin Brain and Blue Cheese Ravioli.

Eighth course — Giant Panda Paw with Borlotti Beans and Baby Root Vegetables.

Ninth course — Confit of Koala Leg with Lemon Saffron Chutney followed by a Digestive Elixir of Infant's tears.

Tenth course — Sea horse tails and oyster mussels.

Eleventh course — Caramelized Milk-Fed White Tiger Cub.

Twelfth course — hundred-year-old Giant Tortoise (purportedly Lonesome George from the Galapagos Islands).

Just in case any readers are interested in replicating the Wonderland banquet in their own homes, DBC Pierre helpfully provides us with seven of the recipes in full.

The Entertainment

Didier believes that 'hormones should simmer to a lusty boil during the course of a meal' so his guests enter a chamber where a 'voluptuary's roundabout' awaits them. The 'man-sized carousel' consists 'of seven wedge-like cabinets' each filled with a naked person bent 'head-down inside, trunks and limbs tucked away, sexes straining up through cushioned holes, a jamboree of vulvas and loins as diverse as faces, each with its nature and charm'.

The erotic entertainment continues at the dinner table when an 'organ-grinder emerges with a monkey in a uniform of blue and gold'. The monkey hands out cards, each printed with the pattern of a dress worn by one of the attendant 'maidens'. 'Quaffing wine,' the bankers look for their appointed girl 'and hold up the card to call her over'. Boys are available by special request. There are no lap-dancing style rules about no touching here: maidens hand-feed honey to their hosts 'in various ways' and 'certain boys or maidens go down on their host with tongues'.

For any guests with flagging spirits, narcotic stimulants are also provided. Cocaine is served as a side dish and opium and fine cigars are dispensed by 'the tiniest, most delicate and translucent oriental woman the world can have ever seen' reclining on cushions in a miniature litter borne by 'sturdy dwarves'.

The Outcome

A central plank of the host's philosophy is: 'The greatest event will be damaged if at the end the guests are allowed to drift away – so a perfect event starts and ends precisely. It must end slightly earlier than the guests would like – in this way it stays freshly pickled in their memory, keeps the excitement of unused potential, as well as a necessary drop of regret. These elements together make the heart of what we look for in pleasure.' Accordingly Gabriel is scheduled to sound the closing alarum at 11.55 pm precisely.

But by 10.45 things have got out of hand. With Didier having departed in search of a curry, 'the banquet has collapsed to the floor, Wonderland has become a writhing mass of cloth and flesh' with guests 'squirming like maggots, grunting and rasping'. One of the bankers is relieving himself in the fountain of wine.

Just in case we hadn't spotted the symbolism, Gabriel's friend Gottfried explains to him 'it's a scene from a nightmare, the animals on plates are only symbols, in life these people are devouring everything. Devouring me, Anna, you, your friends and all the world around.' This prompts Gabriel to decide that there is still time to impress Anna, the girl he fancies, by rescuing Lonesome George from being served up as the *pièce de résistance.* *
He lets off a firecracker and the bankers scatter, like a flock of pigeons startled by a car backfiring, leaving 'the salon as empty as the scene of a bombing, the floor sparking with diamonds'.

We are left to contemplate the book's fundamental insight into the principles of hedonism: 'that human pleasure comes from opening a door, not from walking through it'. In other words the value of an aesthetic experience is in its anticipation rather than its realization. For example, the reader's expectation

---

* Lonesome George did indeed survive becoming a dish at a bankers' banquet. He died on 24 June 2012 in his corral on the Galapagos, making his subspecies – the Pinta Island tortoise – extinct.

that the novel will have a proper ending is more important than the novel necessarily having any such thing.

The Legacy

DBC Pierre would have been writing *Lights Out in Wonderland* while the credit crunch of 2007–2008 was raging and he could be forgiven for thinking that the bankers who had brought about the global financial crisis were about to get their comeuppance. By the time his novel was published, DBC probably reasoned, this would be a matter of known historical fact. Maybe the evil money men would have been strung up from lamp posts by raging mobs, or handed long prison sentences by angry governments, or at least told in no uncertain terms that they really mustn't ever be so greedy and reckless again. At the time that I am writing this (summer 2012) none of the above had happened.

Bibliography

Introduction

Samuel Pepys, *The Diary of Samuel Pepys: A Selection*, London: Penguin Books, 2003

Stuart Flexner, *Wise Words and Wives' Tales: The Origins, Meanings, and Time-Honoured Wisdom of Proverbs and Folk Sayings, Olde and New*, New York: Avon Books, 1993

1 Trimalchio's Dinner Party

Petronius Arbiter, *The Satyricon*, translation by P. G. Walsh, Oxford: Oxford University Press, 1997

Petronius Arbiter, *The Satyricon*, translation by W. C. Firebaugh, New York: Boni and Liveright, 1922

Jesse Browner, *The Uncertain Hour*, New York: Bloomsbury USA, 2007

2 Gatsby's Saturday Night Parties

F. Scott Fitzgerald, *The Great Gatsby*, London: Collector's Library, 2005

André Le Vot, *F. Scott Fitzgerald*, London: Allen Lane, 1984

3 Queen Alice's Feast

Michael Bakewell, *Lewis Carroll − A Biography*, London: Heinemann, 1996

Lewis Carroll, *The Annotated Alice*, edited by Martin Gardner, London: Penguin, 1965

4 *Dmitri Karamazov's Revel at Mokroye*

Федор Достоевский, Братья Карамазовы, Москва: ЕКСМО, 2011

Fyodor Dostoevsky, *The Brothers Karamazov*, translation by Constance Garnett, London: William Heinemann, 1959

Sigmund Freud, *Die Urgestalt der Brüder Karamasoff*, München : R. Piper, 1928

Richard Peace, *Dostoyevsky — An Examination of the Major Novels*, Cambridge: Cambridge University Press, 1971

5 *A Little Ball at Roxana's House*

Daniel Defoe, *Roxana — The Fortunate Mistress*, edited with an introduction and notes by John Mullan, New York: Oxford University Press, 2008

Maximillian E. Novak, *Daniel Defoe: Master of Fictions*, Oxford: Oxford University Press, 2001

6 *The Strange Fête*

Alain-Fournier, *Le Grand Meaulnes*, Paris: Éditions Gallimard, 2009

Alain-Fournier, *The Lost Estate*, London: Penguin Classics, 2007

7 *The Ball at Mansfield Park*

Jane Austen, *Mansfield Park*, Hertfordshire: Wordsworth Editions, 2000

Andrew Norman, *Jane Austen: An Unrequited Love*, Stroud: The History Press, 2009

8 *Belshazzar's Feast*

The Bible — Authorized King James Version with Apocrypha, Oxford: Oxford University Press, 2003

Stephen Bertman, *Handbook to Life in Ancient Mesopotamia*, Oxford: Oxford University Press, 2003

Irving Finkel and Michael Seymour, *Babylon — City of Wonders*, London: The British Museum Press, 2008

Joan Oates, *Babylon*, London: Thames & Hudson, 1979

André Parrot, *Babylon and the Old Testament*, London: SCM Press Ltd, 1958

Norman W. Porteus, *Daniel — A Commentary* from *The Old Testament Library*, London: SCM Press, 1965

Svend Aage Pallis, *The Babylonian Akitu Festival*, København: A.F. Høst, 1926

9 *The Duchess of Richmond's Ball*

Nick Foulkes, *Dancing into Battle*, London: Weidenfeld and Nicolson, 2006

David Miller, *The Duchess of Richmond's Ball 15 June 1815*, Staplehurst: Spellmount, 2005

William Makepeace Thackeray, *Vanity Fair*, Oxford: Wordsworth Editions, 1992

10 *The Onion Cellar*

Günter Grass, *The Tin Drum*, translation by Ralph Manheim, London: Vintage, 2005

11 *The Chief of Police's Reception*

Николай Гоголь, Миргород. Пьесы, Москва: ЕКСМО, 2010

Nikolai Gogol, *The Collected Tales of Nikolai Gogol*, translated and annotated by Richard Pevear and Larissa Volokhonsky, London: Granta Books, 2003

Vladimir Vladimirovich Nabokov, *Nikolai Gogol*, London: Editions Poetry, 1947

James B. Woodward, *The Symbolic Art of Gogol: Essays on his Short Fiction*, Columbus, Ohio: Slavica, 1982

12 *The Beverly Hills Party*

Jackie Collins, *Hollywood Wives*, London: Pan Books, 2008

13 *Bilbo Baggins's Eleventy-First Birthday Party*

Mark Horne, *J. R. R. Tolkien*, Tennessee: Thomas Nelson, 1982

J. R. R. Tolkien, *The Fellowship of the Ring*, London: George Allen & Unwin, 1978

J. R. R. Tolkien, *The Hobbit, or, There and Back Again*, London: George Allen & Unwin, 1975

14 *The Ponteleone Ball*

Giuseppe Tomasi di Lampedusa, *The Leopard*, translation by Archibald Colquhoun, London: Vintage, 2007

15 *The Symposium*

Plato, *The Symposium*, translation by Christopher Gill, London: Penguin, 1999

Plato, *The Symposium*, translation by Tom Griffith, London: Everyman, 2000

R. B. Rutherford, *The Art of Plato: Ten Essays in Platonic Interpretation*, London: Duckworth, 1995

16 *The Marquise de Saint-Euverte's Musical Soirée*

Patrick Alexander, *Marcel Proust's Search for Lost Time — A Reader's Guide to the Remembrance of Things Past*, New York: Vintage, 2007

Richard Davenport-Hines, *A Night at the Majestic: Proust and the Great Modernist Dinner Party*, London: Faber, 2006

Eric Karpeles (ed.), *Paintings in Proust: A Visual Companion to In Search of Lost Time*, London: Thames & Hudson, 2008

Marcel Proust, *Du côté de chez Swann*, Paris: Éditions Gallimard, 1988

Marcel Proust, *The Way By Swann's*, translated and with an introduction by Lydia Davis, London: Penguin Books, 2003

Roger Shattuck, *Proust's Way — A Field Guide to In Search of Lost Time*, London: Allen Lane, The Penguin Press, 2000

17 *Satan's Rout*

Михаил Булгаков, Сочинения, Москва: Книжная Палата, 2011

Mikhail Bulgakov, *The Master and Margarita*, translated by Michael Glenny, London: Vintage Digital, 2010

18 *The Lord Mayor's Ball*

George and Weedon Grossmith, *The Diary of a Nobody*, London: Collins, 1955

Sally Jeffery, *The Official Guide to the Mansion House*, London: Corporation of London, 1993

19 *The Bacchanal of the Century*

Honoré de Balzac, *La Peau de chagrin*, Paris: Éditions Gallimard, 1974

Honoré de Balzac, *The Wild Ass's Skin*, translated and with an introduction by Herbert J. Hunt, London: Penguin Books, 1977

20 *Dick Hawk-Monitor's 21st Birthday Party*

Stella Gibbons, *Cold Comfort Farm*, London: Penguin Classics, 2006

21 *The Blossom Viewing Party*

Ivan Morris, *The World of the Shining Prince — Court Life in Ancient Japan*, Oxford: Oxford University Press, 1964

William J. Puette, *The Tale of Genji — A Reader's Guide*, Vermont: Tuttle Publishing, 1983

Bibliography

Murasaki Shikibu, *The Tale of Genji*, translation by Edward G. Seidensticker, London: Secker and Warburg, 1976

Murasaki Shikibu, *The Tale of Genji*, translation by Royall Tyler, London: Penguin, 2001

22 *Mrs Leo Hunter's Costume Breakfast*

Jane R. Cohen, *Charles Dickens and His Original Illustrators*, Columbus: Ohio State University Press, 1980

Bradley Deane, *The Making of the Victorian Novelist: Anxieties of Authorship in the Mass Market*, New York: Taylor and Francis, 2003

Charles Dickens, *The Pickwick Papers*, London: Penguin Popular Classics, 1994

23 *The Masque of the Red Death*

Scott Peeples, *The Afterlife of Edgar Allan Poe*, New York: Camden House, 2004

Edgar Allan Poe, *The Masque of the Red Death and Other Stories*, London: Penguin Books, 2008

Peter Richardson, *Herod: King of the Jews and Friend of the Romans*, Edinburgh: T&T Clark, 1999

24 *The Feddens' 25th Wedding Anniversary Party*

Alan Hollinghurst, *The Line of Beauty*, London: Picador, 2005

25 *The College Summer Ball*

Kingsley Amis, *Lucky Jim*, London: Victor Gollancz, 1965

26 *The* Anubis *Orgy*

Charles Clerc (ed.), *Approaches to Gravity's Rainbow*, Columbus: Ohio State University Press, 1983

Thomas Pynchon, *Gravity's Rainbow*, London: Picador, 2005

Steven C. Weisenberger, *A Gravity's Rainbow Companion*, Georgia: Georgia University Press, 2006

27 *Lady Metroland's Party*

D. J. Taylor, *Bright Young People: The Rise and Fall of a Generation 1918–1940*, London: Chatto and Windus, 2007
Evelyn Waugh, *Decline and Fall*, London: Penguin Classics, 2011
Evelyn Waugh, *Vile Bodies*, London: Penguin Classics, 2011

28 *The Warrior Feast*

John Lindow, *Norse Mythology – A Guide to the Gods, Heroes, Rituals and Beliefs*, Oxford: Oxford University Press, 2001
Snorri Sturluson, *The Prose Edda*, translation by Jesse L. Byock, London: Penguin, 2005

29 *The Fifth Avenue Party*

Tom Wolfe, *The Bonfire of the Vanities*, London: Cape, 1988

30 *A Pooh Party*

A. A. Milne, *Winnie-the-Pooh*, London: Metheun, 1982
Christopher Milne, *The Enchanted Places*, London: Eyre Methuen, 1974
Ernest H. Shepard, *The Pooh Sketchbook*, London: Egmont, 2004

31 *The Manderley Fancy Dress Ball*

Daphne du Maurier, *Rebecca*, London: Virago Press, 2010

32 *Mr Hosokawa's 53rd Birthday Party*

Ann Patchett, *Bel Canto*, London: Fourth Estate, 2002
Profile: Alberto Fujimori, BBC website, 8 December 2011

33 *The Paris City Aldermen's Ball*

Alexandre Dumas (père), *Les Trois Mousquetaires*, Paris: Éditions Gallimard, 2001

Alexandre Dumas (père), *The Three Musketeers*, translated and with an introduction by Lord Sudley, London: Penguin Classics, 1982

Cécile Hugon, *Social France in the XVII century*, London: Methuen, 1911

34 *Don Alejo's Election Party*

José Donoso, *El Lugar sin Limites* (quotations translated by Suzette Field), Barcelona: Plaza & Janés, 1994

35 *The Society of Artists' Fancy Dress Ball*

Herman Hesse, *Steppenwolf*, translation by Basil Creighton (revised by Walter Sorell), London: Penguin, 1965

36 *The Thomas Ewen High School Prom*

Stephen King, *Carrie*, London: Hodder, 2007

37 *Finnegan's Wake*

Joseph Campbell, *A Skeleton Key to Finnegans Wake*, Novato, California: New World Library, 2005

Finn Fordham, *Lots of Fun at Finnegans Wake: Unravelling Universals*, Oxford: Oxford University Press, 2007

James Joyce, *Finnegans Wake*, London: Faber, 1950

Roland McHugh, *Annotations to Finnegans Wake*, Maryland: The Johns Hopkins University Press, 2006

William York Tindall, *A Reader's Guide to Finnegans Wake*, New York: Syracuse University Press, 1996

38 *The Flying Party*

Douglas Adams, *Life, the Universe and Everything*, London: Pan Books, 1982

39 *McMurphy's Ward Party*

Ken Kesey, *One Flew Over the Cuckoo's Nest*, London: Marion Boyars, 1979

Jennie Weiss Block, *Copious Hosting: A Theology of Access for People With Disabilities*, Illinois: Charles C. Thomas, 2006

G. Neil Martin, Neil R. Carlson, William Buskist, *Psychology*, Harlow, New York: Allyn and Bacon 2006

Jesse Serwer, 'DJ Screw: from cough syrup to full-blown fever', *Guardian*, Thursday 11 November 2010

40 *The Wonderland Banquet*

DBC Pierre, *Lights Out in Wonderland*, London: Faber and Faber, 2010

'Last Pinta giant tortoise Lonesome George dies', BBC, 24 June 2012

Acknowledgements

I'd like to say thank you to the following well-read people who suggested parties that I'd never have thought of: Catherine Boyle, Dickon Edwards, Jeni Giambona, Emma Heath, Jonathan Iliffe, Jessica Katz, Patrick Knill, Louise Levene, Ivan Mulcahy, Frances Taylor, Russell Taylor and Viktor Wynd. And my thanks go to the academics and specialists who offered their expertise on the texts I might have been too daunted to cover without their help: Catherine Boyle on Donoso, Finn Fordham on Joyce, Natalie Haynes on Petronius, Raphael Woolf on Plato, Patrick ffrench on Proust, Alan Marshall on Pynchon, Patrick Knill on Shikibu and Helga Hlaðgerður Lúthersdóttir on Sturluson.

Also many thanks to the people who enabled me to keep two businesses going while I was ensconced in the London Library: Viktor Wynd for ensuring our curios shop was always well stocked with dead things, Patrick Knill and Vadim Kosmos for persuading customers to buy them, Sasha Olshanetsky for running the parties, Leonie Morris for handling the design work and Sarah Archer for curating a wonderful exhibition on parties in art.

My especial gratitude goes to my agent, Ivan Mucalhy, for believing in the book from the onset, and editor Kris Doyle at Picador for all of his encouragement and help. Thanks also to my mom, Nina Field (she was heading to a party the night I was born — it's in the blood), and brother, Patrick (who regularly flies in from California to attend my parties). And not forgetting

Acknowledgements

the Taylor family (Hal, Iona, Frances and Karen) for providing emergency babysitting services while I was proofreading my text.

But the biggest thank you of all goes to my boyfriend, Russell Taylor. Not only did he turn down countless party invitations to spend his evenings at home helping me wade through weighty tomes in search of fictional fetes, but he also provided the French and Russian translations, acted as my in-house proofreader and editor and suggested many of the jokes.